# THE EMERGENCE OF

# THE MOUNDBUILDERS

# THE EMERGENCE OF
# THE MOUNDBUILDERS

## THE ARCHAEOLOGY OF TRIBAL SOCIETIES
## IN SOUTHEASTERN OHIO

Edited by Elliot M. Abrams and AnnCorinne Freter

OHIO UNIVERSITY PRESS   ATHENS

Ohio University Press, Athens, Ohio 45701

www.ohio.edu/press

© 2005 by Ohio University Press

Printed in the United States of America

All rights reserved

Ohio University Press books are printed on acid-free paper ⊚ ™

13  12  11  10  09  08  07  06  05      5  4  3  2  1

Library of Congress Cataloging-in-Publication Data

The emergence of the moundbuilders : the archaeology of tribal societies in
Southeastern Ohio / edited by Elliot M. Abrams and AnnCorinne Freter.
  p. cm.
   Includes bibliographical references and index.
   ISBN 0-8214-1609-X (cloth : alk. paper) — ISBN 0-8214-1610-3 (pbk. :
alk. paper) 1. Mound-builders—Ohio—Hocking River Valley. 2. Indians of
North America—Ohio—Hocking River Valley—Antiquities. 3. Indians of
North America—Ohio—Hocking River Valley—Social life and customs. 4.
Excavations (Archaeology)—Ohio—Hocking River Valley. 5. Hocking River
Valley (Ohio)—Antiquities. I. Abrams, Elliot Marc, 1954– II. Freter,
AnnCorinne, 1957–
   E78.O3E64 2004
   977.1'9701—dc22
                              2004018890

THIS BOOK IS DEDICATED TO THE MEMORY OF

DAVID L. HUDNELL (1945–96)

# CONTENTS

# PREFACE

THE VAST MAJORITY of societies that have existed did so in the absence of writing, precluding self-description or documentation by anthropologists, historians, folklorists, or other social scientists. For these people who lived before the written record or the curious eye of outside observers, archaeology remains the only means through which they may be included in the broad spectrum of the human experience. To bring these cultures to light is the challenge of archaeology. From research design to fieldwork, from analysis to results, archaeology remains an ambitious undertaking, yet it is unmatched in furthering our understanding of the people who lived during these early eras in human social history.

The indigenous societies of the Ohio Valley were part of an ancestry that extended back at least ten thousand years. The description and understanding of these societies, largely known through archaeology, is relevant to living descendants and others interested in how these unique societies lived, grew, and changed in the millennia prior to the modern industrial world. This book is about the indigenous societies of one such valley in southeastern Ohio—the Hocking River Valley. We present archaeological data collected over the past two decades, in conjunction with earlier research. We begin this sequence of societal change at the Late Archaic period, about 3000 B.C., when people lived in nomadic hunting and gathering communities and end at the Late Prehistoric period, about A.D. 1450, as communities of settled maize agriculturalists developed. Each chapter details this process based on time-specific data, and accordingly, the book chapters are arranged chronologically, moving the reader through time to facilitate the analysis of culture change.

Scholarship from various arenas in archaeology is assembled to produce this nearly five-thousand-year narrative in the Hocking Valley. A diverse assemblage of archaeologists from academia, government, and the private sector brings to this volume expertise in anthropology, geography, material science, and botany. Accordingly, chapters variously describe and analyze the spatial modeling of settlement patterns, the foods hunted, collected, or grown by varying groups through time, and the physical attributes of tools manufactured by distinct communities. However, the overarching theme of each chapter is drawn from anthropology, linking societies from each time period to a broad model considering the emergence and expansion of *tribal* institutions; that is, each chapter contributes more data and analysis to document the *process* through which the descendants of nomadic hunting and gathering societies eventually became sedentary agriculturalists. This process occurred in many regions of the world, particularly the Near East, Mesoamerica, Africa, and South America, and this volume ultimately aligns indigenous Hocking Valley societies with them, illuminating the importance of the valley's rich archaeological heritage.

To accomplish this goal we employ an array of modern methods. This volume contains the first Geographic Information System (GIS) analysis of sites throughout the valley and offers the first demographic reconstruction of communities. Through the use of radiocarbon accelerator mass spectroscopy (AMS) dating, we present the earliest direct evidence for maize agriculture in the Hocking Valley, and suites of regular radiocarbon dates confirm the earliest use of pottery. Detailed archaeobotanical analyses serve as the basis for dietary and economic reconstruction, while x-ray diffraction and x-ray fluorescence are used to identify pottery clay sources. These and other contemporary scientific techniques collectively make possible the identification of behaviors and institutions as they were modified through the generations.

One of the primary goals of contemporary archaeology is to disseminate research findings to as broad an audience as possible, especially the interested and informed public, since the preservation of the archaeological heritage left to us by this country's first inhabitants lies in the public's appreciation of its irreplaceable worth. Therefore, although professional jargon is sometimes unavoidable, all authors have tried to produce chapters that are readable by the interested layperson yet retain the rigor of the professional archaeologist.

# ACKNOWLEDGMENTS

THIS BOOK IS the result of the effort and consideration of many individuals and institutions. Ohio University has steadily supported the Field School in Ohio Archaeology conducted by Abrams since 1986, providing financial support in 1986, 1988, and 1990. We specifically thank the dean's office of the College of Arts and Sciences in this regard. The David L. Hudnell Fund for Archaeological Research and Field School has contributed funds for equipment used in the field school at Ohio University since 1998. Funding for radiocarbon dating of samples from the Boudinot 4 site, the County Home site, and the Allen site was generously provided by the John Baker Foundation of Ohio University in three separate grants to Abrams. Partial funding of the radiocarbon dating from site 33AT441 came from the David L. Hudnell Fund, and funding for dating from the County Home site was supplemented by the Jeanette Grasselli Brown Teaching Award to Abrams.

Logistical support for the Allen site lithic analysis was provided by BHE Environmental, Inc., and equipment for the survey and mapping of the Swinehart Village site was provided by Ohio Valley Archaeological Consultants, Inc. The Ohio Historic Preservation Office, and especially Kyle Smith and Brian Kleinhenz, kindly provided settlement data used in the volume, and the staff of the Archaeology Department at the Ohio Historical Society and Dr. Martha Otto made the Robert M. Goslin Collections available to John Schweikart. Further support came from the Cartography Lab at Ohio University and the Department of Sociology and Anthropology, Ohio University.

The data in this volume could not have been obtained without the very generous permission offered by landowners. The landowners we have known over the years truly have assumed the role of caretakers of the archaeological record in this region. On behalf of ourselves and the contributors in the volume, we thank Tom and Ann Walker, the Athens County Commissioner's Office, Jack Frech and the staff of the Athens County

Department of Job and Family Services, Allen Boudinot and the Boudinot family of Millfield, Joyce Miller, Emery Allen and family, Daryl Meyers and family, Thomas Kranik, Mary and Roscoe Wise, Dr. Richard Conard, Lantz Repp, Pete and Linda Clark, Ann Cramer and the staff from the Wayne National Forest, as well as other landowners who wish to remain anonymous. Others who assisted in various aspects of our research were Richard and Sandy Elliott, Meghan Pelot, Allan Clark, Darrin Rubino, Eric Cruciotti, Ralph Moran, Dr. Patricia Heiser, Elizabeth Pitts, the late Dr. Jeff Smith, Jon Walker, Dr. Katherine Jellison, Eric Brooks, Dr. David Kidder, and our son, Zach Abrams.

We also thank each of the contributors to the volume and their families and friends who supported their work. We set some pretty tough deadlines and each of them came through with great cheer and true professionalism.

Many archaeologists over the years have contributed thoughts that have influenced this research. The editors thank Martha Otto, William Dancey, Ann Cramer, and Mark Seeman. Most significantly, we express our thanks to Richard Yerkes of the Ohio State University, whose painstaking critique of an earlier draft of the manuscript can only be described as herculean in effort and quality. Brian Redmond kindly offered further constructive comments which improved the manuscript. Despite the collective input of other scholars, however, all the authors accept responsibility for empirical flaws contained in their chapters, and we as editors assume responsibility for structural flaws within each chapter.

We further thank all those who assisted in the book's production, including David Sanders, director of Ohio University Press, Sharon Rose, our project editor, and Bob Furnish, our copyeditor. Kim Johnson kindly compiled the index, while Chiquita Babb served as the volume's designer. Many of the drawings and photographs were provided or processed by Peggy Sattler, Lars Lutton, and the staff at Instructional Media and Technology Services at Ohio University.

The unsung heroes in the recovery of much of the data in this book are the students from Ohio University who participated in the field schools. We cannot say enough about how hard these students worked, often under trying conditions. Without their diligence and energy, none of this would be possible. We thank and recognize them all.

*1986: The Boudinot 4 site*

Robert Ball, Pam Britton, James Dye, Terri Gooch, Mike Renard, Pam Schooley, John Snyder, Kristen Stuckey, Thomas Wartinger, and Shawn Wilson.

### 1987: The Armitage Mound

Harley Baker, Patricia Bresnan, Diane Houdek, David Hudnell, Stephen Lowe, Carrie Pepiot, Tom Remaley, Tom Schwarm, Andrew Scovoda, Lisa Sheets, Suzanne Stephens, Shelley Stevens, Ronald Webb, Marishka Wile, and Larry Zoloty.

### 1988: The Boudinot survey

Norma Dennis, Darla Evans, Craig Goldstein, Pamela Kelly, Rizvana Macchiwalla, Suzanne Perdan, and Mark Shelly.

### 1990: The Allen site

Warren Brooks, Rachel Evans, Gina Fedash, Jeannine Finney, Kelee Garrison, Valerie Grimes, Mike Hanning, Kathryn Henkels, David Hudnell, Erin Hughes, Lowell Jacobs, Kathryn Klingaman, William Lasater, Jay Moore, Kevin Schwarz, Elizabeth Sturges, Thomas Thacker, and Robert (Vince) Whitlatch.

### 1992: The Allen site

Gary Brownstein, Bill Ciesielczyk, Ron Clark, Brian Dayton, Jennifer Demuria, Aimee Eden, Gary Frost, Sal Giordano, Dean Gray, John Hamilton, Mike Hanning, Amy Holt, Julie Longstreth, Katherine Lower, Dale McClure, Mark Richardson, Kristen Risch, Carlotta Roberts, Michael Savage, Ralph Scarmack, Duane Simpson, Alissa Smitha, Bram Tucker, Miguel Valenzuela, and John Waldron.

### 1994: The Allen site

Jennifer Bailey, Julie Christensen, Linda Cone, Wendi Dotson, Mark Gillespie, Russ Hartley, Christina Hill, Carleen Hudnell, Todd Jasin, Caroline (Carrie) Lanza, Jennifer McGann, Angela Okada, Andrew Peacock, Erin Peavler, Thomas Riley, Chado Rogers, Erik, Seebohm, Paul Shovlin, Edward Smith, Ted Stearns, Sandra Wade, Kristin Wagner, Michael (Ian) Whan, and Douglas Whitlatch.

### 1996: The Allen site

Nathan Anderson, Jamie Beals, Brenda Bodo, Sally Brown, Stephen Emmerich, Julia Farver, Brenna Gamble, Adam Herrold, Julia Honnold, Bradley Huth, Jennifer Jacobberger, Niles Love, Echo Mayberry, Christopher Morehart, Vanessa Nagle, Kelli O'Leary, Mary O'Malley, Daphne Rozen, John Thompson, Jeremy Thornberg, Tonya Weaver, and Ernest (Quent) Winterhoff.

*1998: The Wise, Walker, and County Home sites*

Jeremy Blazier, Jason Crabill, David Crowell, Eric Cruciotti, Sara DeAloia, Tessa Drake, Michael Ensor, Marjorie Heyman, Patti Keniray, Jacqueline Lincoln, Jackie Middleton, Jamie Miller, Meghan Moran, Jesse Paschke, Jennifer Patrick, Sommer Peters, Chad Poniewasz, Katherine Rose, Kyle Smith, and Benjamin Stewart.

*2000: The Clark and Taber Well sites*

Sam Biehl, Jamie Davis, Jodie Ericson, Nadia Fortman, Angelo Giallombardo, Benjamin Heinlen, Mandy Reese, Amy Jones, Megan Jukich, Jennifer Kelley, Zach Lee, Michael Masters, Patrick Mingus, Aric Patterson, Darissa Phipps, Aaron Pulcifer, Krista Spratlin, Nicole Stump, Jonathon Vaffis, and Shannon Wilson.

*2002: The Conard and Taber Well sites*

Travis Andres, Vicki Campbell, Kelly Cassandra, Russell Claus, Melissa Dalton, Christopher Diekhans, Bryan Eppert, Kristina Gjorgjeva, Mike Gulley, Aidan McCarty, Holly Noland, Alan Nungesser, Nicole Peoples, Justin Preston, Zachary Schultheis, Katy Tribuzzo, Lindsey Wolfe, James Wynn, and Justin Zink.

Finally, we express our thanks to Carla, Carleen, and the late Dave Hudnell for their unending support of the OU field school and our work in the Athens area. Dave's contribution began with the very first field school. He was a natural archaeologist with an uncanny knack for doing just the right things. The field schools would not have been nearly as successful without Dave's participation, humor, insight, and camaraderie, all of which emanated from his great love for people, archaeology, and Native American culture. He was a great friend and a great person. His premature passing was a loss to all who knew him. In memory of Dave, we respectfully dedicate this volume.

# THE EMERGENCE OF
# THE MOUNDBUILDERS

# THE ARCHAEOLOGICAL RESEARCH HISTORY AND ENVIRONMENTAL SETTING OF THE HOCKING VALLEY

Elliot M. Abrams and AnnCorinne Freter

BY THE NINTH MILLENNIUM B.C., descendants of the original prehistoric immigrants to North America migrated into what is today the Hocking River Valley of southeastern Ohio (fig. 1.1). In the wake of postglacial warming some twelve thousand years ago, these first familial communities moved within and between river valleys for economic and social reasons. Food acquisition was centered on hunting and gathering wild resources widely dispersed across the landscape. Over time a greater permanence of place within specific river valleys was established and basic economic, social, and political lifeways began to change, predicated on a growing dependence on gardening. During the first millennium B.C., burial mounds and circular earthworks were built as part of religious ritual and social ceremonialism. By the end of the first millennium A.D., gardening of local species yielded to larger-scale agriculture involving the introduced crops maize and beans. These more sedentary villages could have eventually expanded into chiefdoms or small kingdoms had the devastating impact of the Euro-American conquest not irreversibly altered the lives, history, and cultural-evolutionary trajectory of the indigenous population.

This brief general outline of preconquest culture change within the Hocking Valley applies to hundreds of riverine societies in the Mississippi River

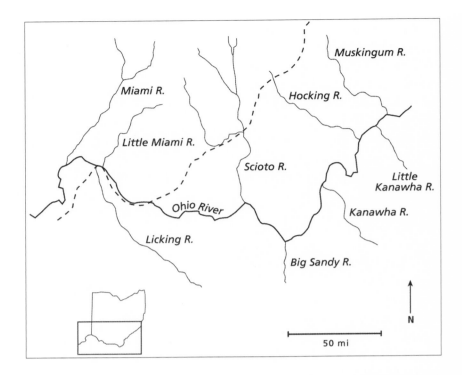

FIG. 1.1. The Hocking River Valley. Dotted line represents southern extent of Wisconsin glacial advance, ca. 10,000 B.C. (Modified from Seeman and Dancey 2000.)

watershed. The ethnohistoric record, describing Ohio Valley societies at the time of contact, offers insights into the lives and specific cultures of the Shawnee (Callender 1978; Howard 1981), the Delaware (Wallace 1990; Olmstead 1991), and other groups anthropologists classify as tribes. This general trajectory of tribal origins and growth can be written for societies in nearly all regions of the world since the complex pattern of change from small nomadic bands to more sedentary tribes represents one of the most significant transitions in the cultural evolutionary experience of humankind.

Each of the indigenous riverine societies of the central United States was historically unique. Although influenced to varying degrees by groups external to their society, each riverine community met the demands of the dynamic opportunities and challenges presented by its immediate natural and social ecological setting. Since all archaeology is ultimately local, it is incumbent on archaeologists to materially document and attempt to explain this cultural variability within a common general evolutionary schema.

This book moves us closer to a definition of the cultures and patterns of change affecting those indigenous societies of the Hocking Valley from ca. 2500 B.C. to A.D. 1450. Those four millennia witnessed the establishment and expansion of tribal communities, and the overarching goal of this book is to better discern this process of tribal formation. This involves the reconstruction of the demographic, economic, and sociopolitical cultural systems specific to each time period so that a description of sequential change or an archaeological culture history of the valley is possible. Based on this culture history, our final goal is to offer explanations for such instituted tribal cultural changes within the framework of ecological anthropology. The result is the most current anthropological and comparative presentation of prehistoric tribal formation for this tributary of the Ohio River.

## Past Research

The earliest archaeological research in the Hocking Valley was conducted with little if any interest in the indigenous population; in fact, the earliest efforts were often intended to deny native groups their rightful heritage as occupants of the midcontinent (Patterson 1995). Instead, the building of the ancient earthworks was credited to "the moundbuilders," a society of varied origins who, to some, were replaced by the Native American population (Silverberg 1986). "The idea that Indians themselves drove off or killed the glorious moundbuilders made it easier to rationalize their inevitable demise as a form of historic justice" (Meltzer 1998, 2).

Support for the "moundbuilder race" most notably came from the early, antiquarian archaeological effort of Squier and Davis in their classic *Ancient Monuments of the Mississippi Valley* (1848). In this volume, earthworks throughout the midcontinent are defined in terms of form, location, and in many cases interior contents from trenching excavations. The authors note that, relative to other areas of Ohio, "[t]here are very few enclosures, so far as known, in the Hocking river valley; there are, however, numerous mounds upon the narrow terraces and on the hills bordering them. In the vicinity of Athens are a number of the largest size, and also several enclosures" (100). This latter reference alluded to those earthworks centered in The Plains, as mapped by S. P. Hildreth in 1836 and published in Squier and Davis's volume (plate 23, no. 2). The only other earthwork from the Hocking Valley published in their volume is the Rock Mill earthworks near Lancaster.

Their publication popularized the presence of earthworks, which in the Hocking Valley led to extensive trenching excavations and further mapping of mounds both in The Plains and throughout the valley (Andrews 1877). This focus on burial mounds in quest of artifacts for museum display or personal gain typified these years of antiquarian archaeology in this and many other regions of the Midwest. Regrettably, none of the artifacts or skeletal data retrieved by E. B. Andrews, the primary excavator, have been relocated and are lost to museum researchers.

A research focus on Hocking Valley mound locations continued, achieving its grandest expression in William Mills's *Archaeological Atlas of Ohio* (1914), which describes the results of Mills's travels through Ohio "verifying wherever possible those monuments already known and at the same time adding new records to the map" (iii). He notes the presence of numerous mounds and circular and square enclosures throughout Athens, Fairfield, and, to a lesser degree, Hocking Counties. Mills adds that The Plains "is dotted with mounds and enclosures so abundant that from almost any one of them it is possible to see another" (5).

Archaeology conducted by professionals in the first half of the twentieth century was oriented toward artifact description, the goal being to generate archaeological cultures based on the cataloging of traits (Willey and Sabloff 1980). This was exemplified by Emerson Greenman's (1932) excavation of the Coon Mound in The Plains, reflecting the early fascination with "the monumental" at the expense of more domestic or utilitarian sites, a pattern evidenced in many parts of the world (Abrams 1989a). By carefully excavating the contents of a single mound and responsibly publishing those results, Greenman helped define the concept of the "Adena" culture (see chapter 12 for a discussion of this term). The interest in mounds in the Hocking Valley persisted with the publication of additional earthwork locations by William Peters (1947).

Epitomizing the classificatory stage in American archaeology, Griffin (1966 [1943]) described and seriated potsherds from a range of sites in southern Ohio to create a formal ceramic typology and chronology for the Fort Ancient culture within the Late Prehistoric period. His work included ceramics from the Baldwin site (see fig. 1.2), a small Late Woodland village near Lancaster. The data from this site were opportunistically collected between 1919 and 1939 by a local collector (Griffin 1966, 54). Griffin's research is significant on many levels but certainly is noteworthy as the first serious research focused on nonmound materials.

Following the wave of changes within the "new" processual archaeology, the 1960s initiated a more anthropologically focused body of research in the valley. The Ohio Woodland Project was designed to move research from building ceramic typologies toward reconstructing a "socio-cultural reality" (Prufer and Shane 1970). This approach led to the excavation of two important nonmound sites in the Hocking region—Chesser rockshelter (Prufer 1967) and the Graham site (McKenzie 1967)—and introduced settlement

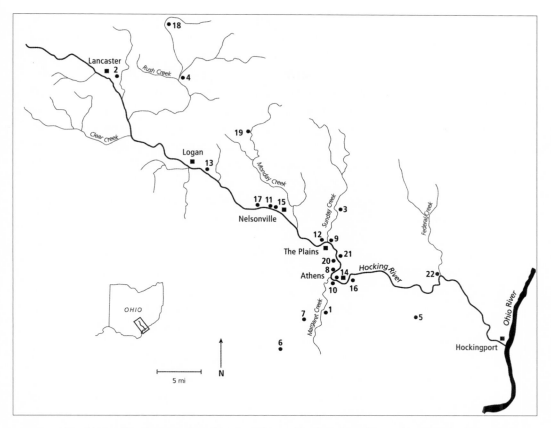

FIG. 1.2. Hocking Valley Sites mentioned in the volume. (1) Allen, (2) Baldwin, (3) Boudinot 4, (4) Bremen, (5) Bruce Chapman Mound, (6) Chesser rockshelter, (7) Clark, (8) Conard, (9) County Home, (10) Daines Mound 1, (11) Diamond, (12) Gabriel, (13) Graham, (14) McCune, (15) Parks, (16) Rock Riffle Run Mound, (17) Sims, (18) Swinehart Village, (19) Taber Well, (20) 33AT467/468, (21) Walker, (22) Wise. (Modified from Skinner and Norris 1981.)

survey and the systematic cataloging of all sites in the Hocking, including the smaller habitation sites lacking mounds (Shane and Murphy 1967). The Graham site research represents the first habitation site professionally excavated in the entire valley. A major contributor to defining the culture history of the Hocking Valley is James Murphy. In addition to the brief survey work cited above, Murphy conducted the excavation of two Late Prehistoric habitation sites—McCune and Gabriel—and his collective observations were synthesized in *An Archaeological History of the Hocking Valley* (1989).

Beyond two regional settlement studies involving Early Woodland (Black 1979) and Fort Ancient (Essenpreis 1978) communities, significant contributions beginning in the 1970s came from Cultural Resource Management (CRM) projects. The construction of highways in this rural portion of Ohio generated the majority of reports (e.g., Skinner and Norris 1981; DeWert, Kime, and Gardner 1981; H. Murphy 1986), although housing developments have also prompted significant archaeological research (e.g., Skinner and Norris 1984; Striker et al. 2001). While this research led to the collection of a wide range of data and a fuller reconstruction of the culture historic patterns (especially by Shaune Skinner and her colleagues), the full potential of these data remains unrealized, as is typical of CRM-obtained data (Green and Doershuk 1998).

This hundred-year research record has left sizeable gaps in our reconstruction of the past cultures of the Hocking Valley for all time periods. Murphy states, "Much heat and little light has been generated by the apparent dearth of Middle Woodland remains in the Hocking Valley" (1989, 348). Little progress has been made beyond the fact that we know that people existed in the valley during the Middle Woodland period, a logical inference derivable from the Coon Mound excavation (Greenman 1932). Murphy further states (1989, 351) that there is little understanding and considerable confusion surrounding even the basic description of Late Woodland and Fort Ancient (or Late Prehistoric) community life, chronology, and overall cultural systematics. A review of the very well detailed but ultimately limited data in Murphy's volume reminds us that we have yet to achieve the scale of sociopolitical reality aspired to by Prufer and Shane for the Hocking Valley.

Our understanding of societies in the Hocking is limited largely by the overall scarcity of residential site excavation, the lack of integrated settlement data, and the absence of a holistic, long-term research design. While mounds provide important data concerning religion, ritual, and regional participation, they yield little relating to the daily framework of community life. With this in mind, a field school in archaeology at Ohio University was established by Elliot Abrams in 1986 with the goal of better understanding the cultural evolution of tribal institutions by excavating habitation and other nonmound sites from various time periods. To date, the Ohio University field school has excavated nonmound sites spanning from the Late Archaic to the Late Prehistoric periods, including the Boudinot 4 (33AT521), Taber Well (33HO611), County Home (33AT40), Conard (33AT947), Allen (33AT653), Wise (33AT654), Walker (33AT960), and Clark (33AT961) sites. One mound site in The Plains, the Armitage mound (33AT434; Abrams 1992a), was excavated in response to its imminent destruction for a development project. Additionally, the CRM work previously cited has furthered our knowledge of the region's settlement. Consequently, the field school focus on extensive excavation of residential sites from a variety of time periods, combined with the CRM regional settlement data, has yielded a balanced and complementary data set from which to infer Hocking Valley tribal formation.

This volume updates our current understanding of indigenous Hocking Valley societies by presenting the analysis of nearly two decades of new data. By targeting the issue of tribal formation, this volume complements other recent and similarly designed archaeological research (Dancey and Pacheco 1997; Emerson, McElrath, and Fortier 2000; Farnsworth and Emerson 1986; Genheimer 2000; Muller 1986; Pacheco 1996b; Prufer, Pedde, and Meindl 2001; Seeman 1992b; Yerkes 1988). Our focus on a single river valley in no way is meant to encourage a provincial perspective; rather the analyses from the Hocking Valley are designed to enrich our understanding of the processes of tribal formation in this one locale for ultimate consideration in a broader comparative perspective (Parkinson 2002a).

## Tribal Society

Since the research focus of the last two decades in Hocking Valley archaeology has been on better understanding the processual history of tribal emergence and expansion, a brief definition of tribal society is in order. Although the term *tribe* was used by social scholars as early as the nineteenth century (see Fried 1975), the concept and definition of tribe as an ethnological construct was formalized in anthropology by Elman Service (1962) and Marshall Sahlins (1961, 1968). Both Service and Sahlins sought to create a category of human organization more complex than nomadic bands yet less complex than chiefdoms or states. Service notes, "A tribe is of the order of a large collection of bands, but it is not *simply* a collection of bands" (1962, 100; italics in original). What distinguished the tribal community was its expanded set of social identities which established solidarity through alliances with *other* tribal communities. It is the set of "social inventions that had latent integrating effects" (102) that define tribal membership.

Sahlins best articulated the specific organizational principle guiding the varied forms of community integration. He described the "segmentary system" (1968, 15) as the appropriate structure for best understanding tribal behavior and identity. In its simplest form, Sahlins viewed a tribal community as linked to similar communities in an ever-growing sphere of political and social inclusiveness. The household, the foundational organization in social life, was part of a lineage, one or more of which comprised a village.

Unified villages formed a subtribe and two or more subtribes formed a single, regional tribe (16). According to Sahlins, the brilliance of the segmentary system was its flexibility: any demographic scale of inclusiveness could be harnessed if necessary, made possible by those various integrating mechanisms of shared identities, such as descent or sodalities (Parkinson 2002b). Critical in Sahlins's conception of tribes is the notion that decision making ultimately rests at the local level; that the broader sociopolitical units are ephemeral and temporary. This theme is echoed by Morton Fried (1967, 1975) who noted that, while indigenous tribal society emerged in archaeological settings, contemporary tribes observed by ethnographers were often "secondary," the result of contact with powerful states.

There has been much written concerning tribes since the early works of these pioneering ethnologists, including refinements to the limitations of the concept of tribes as defined by Service and Sahlins (see chapter 12). Despite the variability that scholars recognize in defining the tribe, the essential common elements are flexible horizontal inclusiveness, integrating social identities, and mechanisms for alliances. In the Hocking Valley these core elements correspond in general with increased sedentism and involvement in horticulture.

## Chronology

Any reconstruction of cultural change over millennia requires a clear statement of temporal categories (table 1.1). The chronological taxonomy employed throughout this book follows the standard divisions and terminology in Midwest archaeology (Fagan 2000). As with all terminologies, these temporal categories are heuristic—simplifications meant to guide conceptualization of time rather than serve as analytic bases from which interpretation of the past is inferred. Further, the data described in this book indicate that changes were neither wholesale nor sudden steplike progressions, as the time period categories might subtly suggest. Instead, all changes were continuous and gradual, indicating a conservativeness to the historical process of tribal formation. Fortunately, we are not seeking categoric purity. Rather, the value of these temporal categories is that they communicate a general definition of the distinct structural elements of society, including demographics (local and regional population size), settlement patterns, economy, and sociopolitical relations.

Researchers in the Midwest before 1950 could establish only a relative chronology based on stratigraphy, seriation, and cross-dating through the

Table 1.1. General Chronology of the Hocking River Valley

| Period | Duration |
| --- | --- |
| Early Paleoindian | 15,000(?)–9500 B.C. |
| Late Paleoindian | 9500–8000 B.C. |
| Early Archaic | 8000–5500 B.C. |
| Middle Archaic | 5500–3000 B.C. |
| Late Archaic | 3000–1500 B.C. |
| Early Woodland | 1500 B.C.–A.D. 1 |
| Middle Woodland | A.D. 1–400 |
| Late Woodland | A.D. 400–700 |
| Late Prehistoric | A.D. 700–1450 |
| Protohistoric | A.D. 1450–1600 |
| Historic | A.D. 1600–present |

Source: Based on J. Murphy 1989.

analysis of artifact form and frequency. Cross-dating was most commonly applied in the Hocking Valley, involving the acceptance of a temporal placement for a local site based on the similarity in artifact form (usually point types or the presence of earthworks) from sites outside the area. Although this technique establishes a general chronology, logic dictates that the beginning and ending dates of any particular point type which diffused into the Hocking Valley may differ from those dates for the place of origin. Today, relative dating techniques are supplemented by traditional radiocarbon and more recently atomic mass spectroscopy dating, which yield a statistically based calendar date. These techniques are just beginning to refine the generalized chronology of culture change within the Hocking. All the radiocarbon dates cited in the present volume were uniformly calibrated using INTCAL 98 (Stuiver et al. 1998) by Jarrod Burks and are presented in table 1.2 and figure 1.3.

## Theoretical Foundation

Scholarship is the product of a specific cultural and historic setting, and this volume is no exception. The educational experiences of the writers, the cultural environment of area-specific archaeological research, and even the scholarly language that we use influence the direction and presentation of all research (e.g., Appadurai 1986; Joyce 2002). As such, varied dimensions

## Table 1.2. Radiocarbon Dates Cited in Text

| Lab Number [a] | RCYBP [b] | Calibrated Calendar Date [c] |
|---|---|---|
| Beta 66178 | 5330 ± 90 | B.C. 4346 (4221, 4192, 4163, 4118, 4112, 4056, 4055) 3963 |
| Beta 146168 | 3980 ± 60 | B.C. 2826 (2472) 2302 |
| Beta 169751 | 3970 ± 90 | B.C. 2859 (2470) 2201 |
| Beta 169747 | 3340 ± 70 | B.C. 1861 (1677, 1673, 1622) 1449 |
| Beta 146167 | 3290 ± 120 | B.C. 1881 (1596, 1592, 1525) 1315 |
| Beta 178823 | 3250 ± 40 | B.C. 1676 (1519) 1430 |
| Beta 141235 | 3220 ± 70 | B.C. 1682 (1500) 1320 |
| Beta 141234 | 3080 ± 80 | B.C. 1518 (1381, 1334, 1321) 1126 |
| Beta 136254 | 3070 ± 60 | B.C. 1488 (1374, 1338, 1319) 1130 |
| Beta 143697 | 2960 ± 40 | B.C. 1368 (1209, 1200, 1191, 1177, 1163, 1140, 1131) 1019 |
| Beta 27478 | 2900 ± 60 | B.C. 1291 (1106, 1104, 1050) 916 |
| Beta 139636 | 2820 ± 70 | B.C. 1210 (973, 956, 941) 826 |
| Beta 26743 | 2610 ± 80 | B.C. 911 (799) 519 |
| Beta 27479 | 2370 ± 90 | B.C. 787 (403) 204 |
| DIC 2955 | 2180 ± 55 | B.C. 388 (342, 324, 202) 53 |
| Beta 26752 | 2070 ± 60 | B.C. 348 (87, 81, 54) A.D. 65 |
| Beta 160109 | 2040 ± 40 | B.C. 168 (43, 6, 4) A.D. 54 |
| DIC 2860 | 1930 ± 45 | B.C. 39 (A.D. 75) A.D. 213 |
| DIC 2873 | 1920 ± 310–320 | B.C. 789 (A.D. 78) A.D. 764 |
| Beta 27705 | 1880 ± 90 | B.C. 50 (A.D. 128) A.D. 380 |
| Beta 169749 | 1810 ± 80 | A.D. 28 (236) 414 |
| SMU 2161 | 1810 ± 45 | A.D. 83 (236) 340 |
| DIC 2859B | 1790 ± 50 | A.D. 88 (240) 384 |
| Beta 66177 | 1490 ± 90 | A.D. 395 (598) 687 |
| Beta 75193 | 1300 ± 100 | A.D. 561 (689) 977 |
| Beta 75192 | 1300 ± 60 | A.D. 642 (689) 886 |
| DIC 2861 | 1200 ± 145 | A.D. 597 (782, 815, 842, 859) 1158 |
| Beta 75190 | 1140 ± 80 | A.D. 688 (894, 925, 935) 1025 |
| Beta 75189 | 1100 ± 80 | A.D. 723 (904, 910, 976) 1152 |
| Beta 77729 | 1090 ± 60 | A.D. 780 (979) 1030 |
| Beta 75191 | 1000 ± 80 | A.D. 889 (1021) 1216 |
| Beta 75187 | 880 ± 70 | A.D. 1018 (1163, 1173, 1180) 1281 |
| Beta 75188 | 790 ± 70 | A.D. 1042 (1259) 1379 |
| Beta 75194 | 650 ± 80 | A.D. 1223 (1301, 1372, 1378) 1431 |
| Beta 77730 | 330 ± 70 | A.D. 1436 (1522, 1573, 1627) 1945 |
| Beta 66179 | 90 ± 60 | A.D. 1665 (1890, 1908, 1950) 1955 |

*Source:* Compiled by Jarrod Burks.

[a] Beta = Beta Analytic, Inc.; DIC = Dicarb Radioisotope Co.; SMU = Southern Methodist University.

[b] Radiocarbon years before present.

[c] Calibration based on Stuiver et al. 1998.

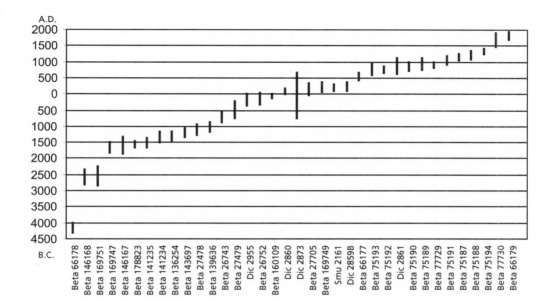

FIG. 1.3. Chart of all radiocarbon dates cited in the text. (Compiled by Jarrod Burks; based on Stuiver et al. 1998.)

of research can be scrutinized from a range of theoretical perspectives, necessitating an explicit statement of theoretical influence.

First and foremost, we fully subscribe to the philosophy that technical and analogical scrutiny of the material record allows us to infer normative behaviors performed by past people. To accept an alternative is to lead us into what Patty Jo Watson termed "the terminal skeptical crisis" (1986, 450), or a lack of faith in the validity of archaeological data and subsequent analysis (contra Shanks and Tilley 1992). On the other hand, the often sparse archaeological record—a consequence of the limited preservable material inventory of nomadic communities and the high rate of destruction of the record owing to natural and cultural processes—cautions against too narrow an empirical expectation of the data to confirm models. That our deductive models outstrip our data typifies archaeology, and it is certainly the case in the Hocking Valley.

Second, we recognize that theory is informed by the depth of available data, the nature of the specific societies from the archaeological past, and the history of research itself. In effect, there are various "archaeologies" applicable to distinct regions and time frames. For example, archaeologists conducting research of a past society who created a durable epigraphic record may employ social psychological models to better approach their emic (or insider's) meaning. The eschewing of such models in considering nonliterate hunter-gatherer societies is often less a theoretical stance than a positivistic statement of the researcher's sense of the appropriate theoretical applicability to the available data.

In this context, we know little of the historical specifics of the Hocking populations. We lack historic texts from which to glean political and social history. We lack the names of people, the language and dialect spoken, and the historic events that shaped the lives of any one individual. Even the ethnohistoric record specific to the Hocking is extremely limited (Grumet 1995). As noted above, natural and cultural transforms have destroyed the once rich organic inventory of artifacts used by the past population. Wooden artifacts, for example, may have constituted the vast majority of raw material types. Further, we lack a history of research focused on households or domestic sites where everyday activities were conducted. Collectively, this research context informs theory by encouraging if not requiring a focus on the general macrolevel of the *institutional framework* of social behavior as it changed or remained stable through time. This same artifactual context encourages a sweeping view of time rather than a more detailed historicity of change.

This macroscale of change and stability of institutions aligns our research with the theoretical concept of cultural process. By that we mean that the institutional changes evidenced from the archaeological data are probabilistically nonrandom; that there are contingent but not inevitable patterns of change on a societal scale with sufficient longevity to be evidenced archaeologically that were mediated through the psychology of people but were influenced by factors external in origin to one's psychology. Further, the research in this volume is subsumed within the perspective of *ecological anthropology* in its broadest sense (Moran 2000). This acceptance of systemic and dynamic interaction between social institutions and the natural environment is the most inclusive theoretical perspective in anthropology and is the appropriate focal scale for our current archaeological research questions. However, it is also anticipated that this macroscale ecological research will serve as the foundation for more detailed research as our understanding of the Hocking Valley continues to be refined.

## The Environmental Variability of the Hocking Valley

A significant contribution of archaeological research over the last several decades has been the empirical demonstration that natural and social environments are neither static nor monolithic entities but rather are interconnected within a profoundly dynamic set of synergistic relationships (Dincauze 2000). In order to understand human cultural reactions to various possible choices, a detailed consideration of human environments is required.

Human societies mediate environmental effects through their technology, their subsistence techniques, and their cognition and worldview; in other words, they respond to environmental challenges via their culture—that uniquely human means of adaptation. Thus, while the environment does not determine the path a human society will take (and no environmental determinism will be found in this book), it does provide an active, changing context under which culture synergistically evolves and within which cultural decisions are made. Consequently, a detailed discussion of the relevant environmental characteristics of the Hocking Valley is required.

## Geological Background

The Hocking River flows southeasterly to the Ohio River for roughly 78 mi (126 km). Its headwaters flow through the flat, glaciated till plain in the vicinity of Lancaster (fig. 1.2), through a short section of the glaciated Allegheny Plateau and finally through the unglaciated Allegheny Plateau which contains the majority of the valley. Given the relative softness of the sedimentary bedrock, the river has created a highly dissected valley with relatively rugged hills and steep slopes (Sturgeon et al. 1958; Murphy 1989). The major glacial advances of the Pleistocene epoch extended only to the upper portion of the Hocking River (fig. 1.1). However, the impact of repeated recessions of both the Illinoian and Wisconsin glaciers were considerable. Collectively, these glacial episodes widened and deepened the river channel, redirected the flow of the Hocking River to its current southeastern direction, and left a series of outwash soil deposits which formed the terrace of the valley. The Plains, upon which were built relatively extensive Adena mounds, is one such remnant terrace (Sturgeon et al. 1958). The geologic formation of the Hocking Valley created six distinct watersheds, or hydrologic segments separated by high ridges (fig. 1.4). The hydrology is graded (Schumm 1977, 10) and dendritic in that a wide variety of scales of waterways exists, ranging from the main stem of the Hocking to small seasonal rills.

This geological history produced distinct physiographic zones (fig. 1.5) of the valley: (1) a dendritic hydrology consisting of the main river, creeks, and streams; (2) the floodplains, including the river bank; (3) the relatively flat terrace zones above the floodplains; (4) the slopes or taluses of the ridges; and (5) the ridgetops. Each section of the river and each tributary display

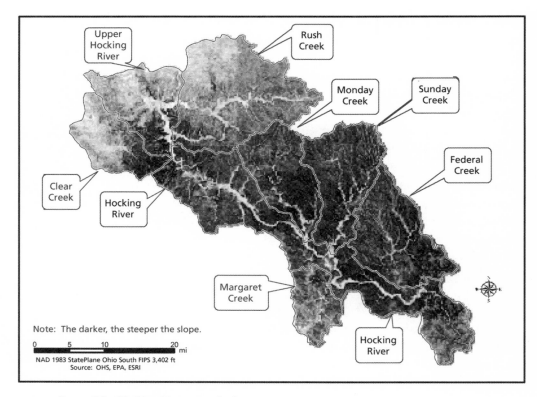

FIG. 1.4. Slope of the Hocking River watershed

FIG. 1.5. Physiographic zonation and reconstructed vegetation zonation

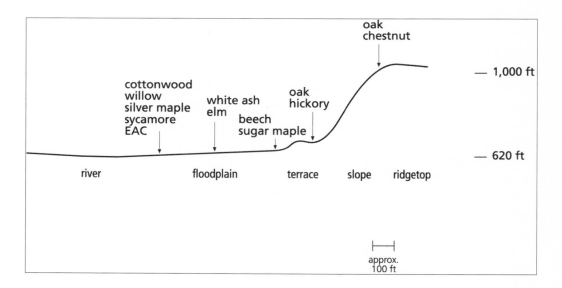

specific variations on this general structure, creating distinctive micro-environments. Additionally, each physiographic zone is internally variable; for example, the floodplain along the Hocking narrows in some sections of the valley yet is ample in others, primarily at river confluences.

Maslowski and Seeman (1992) refined this ecological segmenting of river valleys by discerning the percentages of each physiographic zone for the Ohio, the Scioto, and the Hocking Rivers. For the Hocking Valley, they based their calculations within an 8 km radius centered in The Plains, observing that the Hocking river channel constituted 2% of the environment, the floodplain and low terraces 16%, the higher Wisconsin terraces 6%, the Illinoian terraces 8%, and the uplands 68% (12). They also observed that the terrace zones were limited and discontinuous in the Hocking Valley, a key attribute of this particular riverine system (fig. 1.5).

By excluding the relatively wide Illinoian terrace of The Plains, percentages better reflect the more typical structure of the majority of Hocking Valley. Consequently, following Maslowski and Seeman (1992), a square of 10.5 km on each side was drawn within the Stewart quadrangle map, creating a 110.25 sq km area that included all physiographic valley zones. This exercise yielded the following results: 1% river channel, 7% floodplain, 3% terrace, and 89% slope and uplands. The 3% terrace zone is augmented by 2%–3% of the lower terraces that occupy the upper margins of the floodplain. Accordingly, only roughly 5% of the valley provides a protected, level land surface free from floods and suitable for relatively large residential communities. In addition, this exercise revealed that terraces and floodplain zones were predominantly located along the main stem of the Hocking River. It was determined that about 94% of these physiographic zones abut the main river in contrast to Federal Creek, the main tributary of the Hocking River on the Stewart quadrangle. This indicates that flat land elevated above the level of annual flooding was a limited resource within the central and lower valley.

The absence of natural lakes in the Hocking Valley is also notable. Although lakes exist in the watershed today, all are the result of modern water management projects. This absence of ancient lakes would have limited the number of lacustrine species such as beaver, muskrat, and otter, as well as lake-related flora. An unknown dimension of lakes or ponds is the creation of such natural features through the dam-building activities of beavers (or the indigenous human population) along the main river and especially tributaries. The creating of ponds or small lakes would have enhanced the biotic diversity of the region at relatively little, if any, cost to the past society.

The valley in general has abundant clays for the manufacture of pottery, cherts, or flints of varying quality for lithic tool manufacture and soils for the growing of crops. Although there is variability in the distribution and quality of clay, chert, and productive soil, all the geological requisites for supporting human occupation were present. The dispersed, heterogeneous pattern of resources, however, would have required seasonal travel to areas of more localized resources such as lithics or exchange with groups who resided in closer proximity to these resources (or both).

A final natural resource that affected past societies in the Hocking Valley is salt. Salt is used as a dietary requirement as well as a food preservative and a draw for animals. Even preservation techniques based on drying involve the salting of foods (Kurlansky 2002), and some of the easiest travel during the seventeenth and eighteenth centuries was along "roads" produced by large animals such as buffalo traveling between salt licks. Brine, or salty water from underground deposits, is often exposed to the land surface along waterways of all sizes in the mid-Ohio valley. Once the water evaporates the remaining salty land is termed a salt lick. Large outcrops such as the Scioto Saline and the Great Kanawha salt licks were the basis for the growth of eighteenth-century cities and industry (Jakle 1969; Stealey 1993), but smaller salt licks dot the central Hocking Valley. No comprehensive locational study of salt licks has been conducted, but the presence of (1) the community of Salinas, just north of The Plains, identified by a salt well on Hildreth's 1838 map of The Plains; (2) salt licks near the Boudinot 4 site and the County Home site; and (3) Salt Creek and other geographic references to salt intimate that salt was a significant resource for the past populations.

## Floral and Faunal Resources

Prior botanical research in the Athens area by Boetticher (1929), Rypma (1961), and Wymer (1984, 1990) provides the basis on which the botanical setting for each physiographic zone can be offered (fig. 1.5). The original vegetation of the floodplain is what Rypma termed "swamp succession." This includes a set of mesic species that change rapidly with microlevel alterations in moisture and drainage. The "river's edge" species constitute willow (*Salix* spp.; the dominant species), silver maple (*Acer saccharinum*), sycamore (*Platanus occidentalis*), and cottonwood (*Populus deltoides*). On slightly better drained soils are established elm (*Ulmus* spp.), sycamore, silver maple, white ash (*Fraxinus americana*), and boxelder (*Acer negundo*). Less common species in slightly better drained floodplain microenvironments are bitternut hickory (*Carya cordiformis*), pignut hickory (*C. glabra*), pin oak (*Quer-*

*cus palustris*), and swamp white oak (*Q. bicolor*). Understory species in the floodplain include cattails (*Typha* spp.), buttonbush (*Cephalanthus occidentalis*), and various willows, sedges, grasses, and alders. Significantly, this floodplain zone is the natural home to those seed-bearing species that were eventually domesticated and collectively are known as the Eastern Agricultural Complex, including marsh elder (*Iva* spp.), sunflower (*Helianthus* spp.), erect knotweed (*Polygonum erectum*), maygrass (*Phalaris caroliniana*), and various chenopods (*Chenopodium* spp.).

An upper-floodplain, or transitional, zone between the floodplain and the terrace zones developed in some sections of the valley. Rypma (1961) suggests this microenvironment would have been characterized by the beech–sugar maple mesic association. These two species constitute between 40% and 60% of this forest (Boetticher 1929, 15). The tree taxon most associated with the sugar maple and beech is the white ash, followed in frequency by various hickories, oaks, black walnut, butternut (*Juglan cinerea*), basswood, buckeye, elm, black cherry, black gum, and tulip tree. The understory species in this zone consist of blue beech, pawpaw, witch hazel, spicebush, and hop hornbeam (Rypma 1961).

In addition to this upper floodplain habitat, the beech–sugar maple association is prominent on well-drained, lacustrine, and alluvial terraces (Rypma 1961). In areas such as The Plains and the flats at Millfield and Chauncey, beech forests were found (e.g., Wymer 1984). The northern portion of the old Albany drainage near the mouth of Margaret Creek was also a beech–sugar maple flat. The dominant arboreal association in the terrace zone was the oak-hickory forest. White oak (*Quercus alba*), black oak (*Q. velutina*), red oak (*Q. rubra*), and shagbark hickory (*C. ovata*) were the dominant tree species (Wymer 1990). Associated species included pignut and mockernut hickories (*C. tomentosa*), black gum, red maple (*A. rubrum*), sassafras (*Sassafras albidum*), sourwood (*Oxydendrum arboreum*), and white ash. The understory species within this forest were most frequently dogwood, sassafras, redbud, arrowwood, slippery elm, dwarf sumac, wild grape, greenbrier, black huckleberry, and foxglove.

Finally, the sandy ridgetops—and particularly the upper south and west-facing slopes—were characterized by the chestnut oak–chestnut association (Wymer 1990). The dominant species were the chestnut (*Castanea dentata*) and black and chestnut oak (*Q. prinus*). The Mixed Oak Association was transitional to this forest structure, similar to the chestnut oak–chestnut forest but with an increase in the variety of oak species and an absence of chestnut trees. Included in this oak forest were black oak, chestnut oak, and white oak, with sporadic occurrence of scarlet oak (*Q. coccinea*), post oak

(*Q. stellata*), and chinquapin oak (*Q. muehlenbergii*). Understory species were relatively sparse, dominated by ericaceous (heath-related) taxa (e.g., blueberry [*Vaccinium* spp.]) interspersed with the occasional dogwood or serviceberry (*Amelanchier canadensis;* Wymer 1990).

The Hocking Valley was populated by a wide range of faunal species, although these too have fluctuated through time. In general, the riverine zones supported a diversity of species including fish (e.g., perch, gar, drum, and catfish), shellfish, amphibians (e.g., frogs), reptiles (e.g., turtles and snakes), migratory fowl (ducks and geese), and small riverine mammals (otters and beavers). The forests of the terraces and hills were populated by large mammals, of which white-tailed deer, bear, elk, and bobcat were most

Table 1.3. Distribution of Major Food Resources in the Hocking Valley

| Species | Primary Locations | Seasonality |
| --- | --- | --- |
| **Nuts** | | |
| Hickory | Floodplain, terrace, uplands | Late summer, fall |
| Acorn | Floodplain, terrace, uplands | Late summer, fall |
| Black walnut | Floodplain, terrace, uplands | Late summer, fall |
| Chestnut | Uplands | Fall |
| **Seed-Bearing Plants** | | |
| Chenopods | Floodplain | Late summer, fall |
| Marsh elder | Floodplain | Fall |
| Erect knotweed | Floodplain | Late summer, fall |
| Maygrass | Floodplain | Spring |
| **Aquatic** | | |
| Fish | River | Spring, summer |
| Mussel | River | Spring, summer, fall |
| Beaver | River, riverbank | Fall, winter, spring |
| Snapping turtle | River, riverbank | Fall, winter, spring |
| **Game** | | |
| White-tailed deer | All | All, esp. winter |
| Elk | All | All, esp. winter |
| Black bear | All | Fall, winter |
| Turkey | Uplands | All |
| Raccoon | Floodplain | Fall, winter |
| Woodchuck | Floodplain | Fall, spring |

*Source:* Compiled from Reidhead 1984; Sutton and Sutton 1985; Keene 1981.

useful to the human population. Smaller mammals—including groundhog, squirrel, opossum, and fox—were also important resources (J. Murphy 1989, 28–29). The most significant plant and animal species for human consumption are summarized in table 1.3 according to physiographic zone and primary season of availability.

Table 1.3 conveys several key ecological attributes of the Hocking Valley. First, all physiographic zones harbored plants or animals of use to the human population; consequently archaeological sites should be found in all zones. Second, more permanent settlement should be located on the terraces and floodplain zones, given the greater abundance and seasonal diversity of food resources. Third, fall is the season of greatest abundance, balanced by the least productive season, winter. Fourth, resources within these different zones were not uniform; the three major tree species, for example, while naturally found in all physiographic zones, are unevenly distributed among them, and similar variations in faunal resource distributions are equally probable (table 1.4).

## Climatic Variability

The Hocking Valley provided a wide array of natural resources that indigenous societies could utilize. However, these resources were not available uniformly over time or space; accordingly, native populations had to develop adaptive strategies to cope with these ecological vicissitudes produced by exogenous factors as well as cultural practices. Thus resource exploitation was part of a dynamic feedback between the human population and the environment.

Any single year within the Hocking Valley is marked by significant climatic variability characterized most dramatically by fluctuations in temperature and precipitation. In the Athens area, for example, the average temperature is 51.8° F, but the July temperature averages 74.7° and the January temperature 31.4° (Maslowski and Seeman 1992, 13). Precipitation

Table 1.4. Trees per Square Mile by Physiographic Zone in the Ohio Valley

| Species | River Zone | % | Floodplain | % | Terrace-Talus Slope | % | Upland | % |
|---------|-----------|------|-----------|------|--------------------|------|--------|------|
| Hickory | 4,161 | 12.2% | 7,008 | 20.6% | 12,784 | 37.6% | 10,080 | 29.6% |
| Black walnut | 1,679 | 15.4% | 5,402 | 49.6% | 3,060 | 28.1% | 756 | 6.9% |
| White oak | 5,402 | 17.8% | 3,796 | 12.5% | 5,100 | 16.8% | 16,128 | 53.0% |

Source: Reidhead 1984.
Note: Due to rounding, not all percentages total 100.0.

variation for the area is less striking. Of the yearly rainfall average of 38.1 in (96.8 cm), 11.3 in (28.7 cm) falls in the summer (June, July, August), 10.6 in (26.9 cm) in the spring (March, April, May), and 8.3 in (21.1 cm) in the fall (September, October, November). The combination of these two variables, as well as associated factors such as sunlight and frost, account for the abundance of food resources in the late summer and fall relative to those available in the winter (table 1.3).

Although the rainfall distribution is relatively even across any single year, the added 2–3 in during the spring account for annual flooding in areas at or below 623 fasl (feet above sea level) (189.9 masl [meters above sea level]) (Maslowski and Seeman 1992, 13). Flooding represents a significant ecological condition which had to be considered by the human population, particularly in terms of habitation location and food access. Often, flooding had a positive resource impact, expanding backwater areas for spring fishing and other riverine resource access, and depositing rich alluvial soils along river floodplains.

## Mesoterm Ecological Variability

Variability in precipitation and temperature between years significantly influenced the populations of the Hocking Valley. The 107-year trend of spring variability in temperature and precipitation for Ohio is reflected in the Hocking Valley (fig. 1.6). These figures clearly reflect the heterogeneity that existed, which in turn affected the *predictability* of resource availability. Environmental research indicates that even slight variations in temperature and rainfall can severely affect productivity. For example, "[i]n a mature mesic forest area of southeastern Ohio, a nine-year study showed an average annual production of hickory nuts (all species) of 21.2 kg per hectare, *with a yearly average ranging from 3.4 to 49.2 kg*" (Talalay, Keller, and Munson 1984, 341; italics added). Similarly, studies of individual trees have shown that productivity fluctuates considerably across years, not only in terms of external factors such as drought and predation but also in terms of the genetic makeup of each tree (McCarthy and Quinn 1989, 1992).

Variations in rainfall, especially during the late winter and spring, have a profound impact on flooding. This is particularly acute in the Hocking Valley. Maslowski and Seeman (1992, 13) state that the 5-year flood is evidenced at 624 fasl (190.2 masl), only one foot higher than the annual flood. The 10-year flood is evidenced at 625.4 fasl (190.6 masl), the 50-year flood at 627 fasl (191.1 masl), and the 100-year flood at 627.5 fasl (191.3 masl). These data indicate that with only slightly heightened rainfall, severe floods can

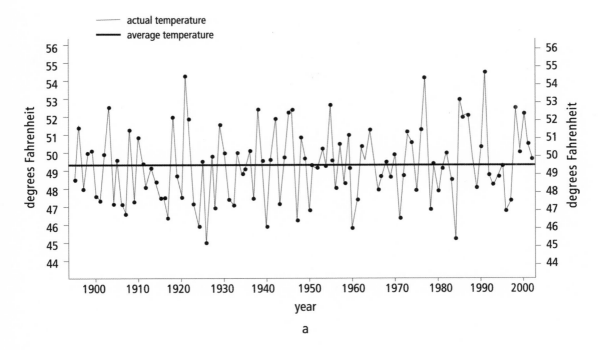

a

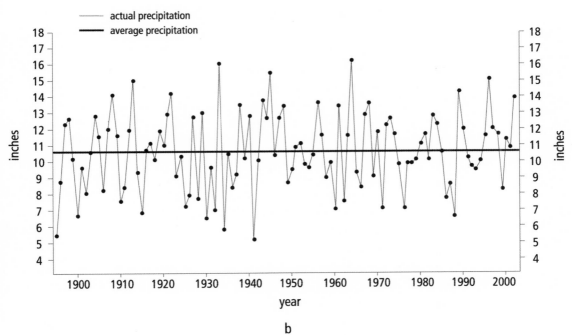

b

FIG. 1.6. Trends in spring (a) temperature and (b) precipitation, 1895–2003 (from NOAA)

Table 1.5. Timing of Killing Frosts in the Athens Area

| Year | Earliest Frost (Fall) | Latest Frost (Spring) |
|------|----------------------|----------------------|
| 1929 | October 15 | May 8 |
| 1930 | — | May 30 |
| 1931 | October 18 | May 4 |
| 1932 | October 7 | April 28 |
| 1933 | October 14 | April 27 |
| 1934 | October 13 | April 28 |
| 1935 | October 4 | April 18 |
| 1936 | October 28 | April 23 |
| 1937 | October 8 | April 12 |
| 1938 | October 8 | May 12 |
| 1939 | October 15 | May 1 |
| 1940 | October 17 | April 22 |
| 1941 | October 29 | May 11 |
| 1942 | September 29 | April 22 |
| 1943 | October 19 | May 2 |
| 1944 | October 16 | April 30 |

Source: NOAA.

result. Finally, the frost variability (table 1.5), coupled with a relatively short growing season of 158 days (Maslowski and Seeman 1992, 13), may have compounded the difficulties of ensuring horticultural and agricultural productivity.

## Macroecological Variability: Paleoclimatic Reconstructions over Centuries

Paleoclimatic reconstructions in the Hocking Valley are based on pollen extracted from natural lakebeds. These macroscale trends are best viewed in concert with the meso-microscale variability discussed above. For example, as temperatures gradually increase through time, any single summer could have temperatures three or four degrees above that increasing norm, exacerbating the general trend.

There are no pollen profiles from the Hocking Valley, given the absence of natural lakes within this unglaciated portion of the Allegheny Plateau. However, pollen data from lake bottom soil profiles in Ohio are a source of proxy data for general climatic trends. Specifically, the pollen data that best

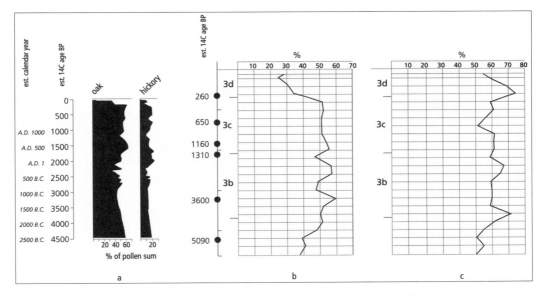

FIG. 1.7. Pollen profile sections from (a) Stages Pond, oak and hickory profile; (b) Silver Lake, core SL-1, oak relative to all pollen; and (c) Silver Lake, core SL-1, oak relative to arboreal pollen. (Modified from Shane, Snyder, and Anderson 2001; Ogden 1966.)

reflect patterns in the Hocking Valley come from Stages Pond, in south-central Ohio (the Scioto Valley), at approximately the same latitude and elevation as Athens (Shane, Snyder, and Anderson 2001, 50). The most relevant aspects of the Stages Pond core are presented in figure 1.7, as are those from Silver Lake in Logan County.

These pollen data collectively indicate that the Late Archaic period in the Hocking Valley was characterized by relatively warm temperatures and high rainfall, reflected especially by the oak and hickory profiles. The major factors, temperature and precipitation, from roughly 2500 B.C. to 1500 B.C. would have been conducive to high productivity of food resources. During this time oak, hickory, elm, sycamore, ash, and beech reached their maximal abundance in the valley. This general climatological condition is supported by the pollen data from the Silver Lake profile, which indicates that from ca. 3000 B.C. to 1500 B.C. there was an abundance of oak, hickory, chestnut, and ash, with some species (such as oak) reaching their maximum. Walnut, on the other hand, declined during the Late Archaic (Ogden 1966).

The ensuing millennium, from ca. 1500 B.C. to 500 B.C., was characterized by a severe warming and drying period known as the "Xerothermic interval" (Ogden 1966, 387). During this phase of higher annual temperatures and lower rainfall, arboreal species declined significantly. According to the Silver Lake profile, oak declined roughly by 20% and hickory by 50%. The Stages Pond data indicate nearly the same trend, with oak declining by 30% and hickory by 50%. Beech, a good indicator of moisture, declined in all portions of Ohio (Shane, Snyder, and Anderson 2001) during this Early Woodland period. At the same time, nonarboreal species (grasses, herbs, shrubs) increased rapidly (44), which is significant since this is the period when horticulture, based on some of these grass species, emerged. People, through their altering of the vegetative landscape, may have contributed to some climatic changes. Further, the profile from Stages Pond indicates continued warming from roughly 700 B.C. to 300 B.C., or during the last centuries of the Early Woodland period. A similar warming trend occurred later in the profile, from roughly A.D. 200 to 700. Again, grass species expanded considerably during this later span, which witnessed a reduction in oak by roughly 20% and hickory by nearly 50%.

In sum, the Hocking River Valley presented the past human population with diverse resources necessary to sustain generations for at least 11 millennia. Although the natural resources are plentiful, the Hocking Valley offered fewer resources than the adjacent Scioto Valley. Further, there was a marked resource unpredictability. These obstacles to accessing resources were a permanent part of the temporal landscape—spring's floods and frost, winter's debilitating cold and snow, summer's heat and torrential rain. Whatever foods could be amassed in the abundance of the fall could be eliminated during the winter, that season serving as the great equalizer to differential resource access by distinct communities. These conditions challenged the population, which over time modified both the physical environment and their own ways of life. The following chapters document these changes.

# 2

# A PRELIMINARY GIS ANALYSIS OF HOCKING VALLEY ARCHAIC AND WOODLAND SETTLEMENT TRENDS

Nicole I. Stump, James Lein, Elliot M. Abrams, and AnnCorinne Freter

IN MIDWEST ARCHAEOLOGY, THE ARCHAIC PERIOD represents those millennia (8000–1500 B.C.) during which a variety of forms of hunting and gathering economies were created to support small bands of generally nomadic people. The great length of this period is often taken to reflect a conservatism of culture change. Recent research, however, argues that hunting and gathering economies and the lifeways of nomadic populations were complex, transforming adaptations (Price and Brown 1985; Price and Feinman 1995; Price and Gebauer 1995; Hayden 2001). Most of the data on Archaic society relate to the Late Archaic Period (3000–1500 B.C.), or to those centuries during which the hunting and gathering economy was intensified in various ways, involving in some cases the cultivation of weedy plants (Dunne and Green 1998).

## The Application of Geographical Information Systems to Archaeological Inquiry

A Geographical Information System (GIS) is a powerful set of tools for collecting, storing, retrieving, transforming, and displaying spatial data from the real world for a particular set of purposes (Burrough and McDonnell

1998). GIS can be useful in understanding complex spatial patterns. Analysts can simultaneously observe how various layers of spatial information relate to one another and can make useful decisions based on those observations. There are two types of GIS: vector GIS employs points, lines, and polygons to represent spatial phenomena, while raster GIS utilizes a series of grid cells. Each method has its advantages and limitations for data analysis and graphical representation, and often both must be employed to most effectively approach some research questions.

The spatial and temporal dimensions that characterize prehistoric sites make archaeology an ideal field of study for analysis within a GIS. Archaeology documents changes over long time periods to identify broad trends in human landscape usage and examines transitions and changes in those trends, such as the change from hunting and gathering to agricultural subsistence economies. Archaeological sites are spatial; a site is any geographic place where there is evidence of past human activity. The site boundaries are reached when there is no longer a physical presence of human activity. Sites are also composed of spatial clusters of artifacts, features, and ecofacts divided into various periods of occupation.

Settlement archaeologists study the spatial distribution of prehistoric human activities and occupation, focusing on the arrangement of sites within a regional landscape. Archaeological settlement analyses at a regional scale increasingly employ GIS to investigate more comprehensive and complex research questions. Unfortunately, the current application of GIS to archaeology has been limited and it remains underused as an analytical tool to explore human interaction within a prehistoric landscape (Westcott and Brandon 2000, xiii). Accordingly, one of the goals of this study is to advance GIS applications in Ohio archaeology, elucidating its utility in spatial data analysis through its application to the archaeological landscape of the Hocking Valley in southeastern Ohio.

## Establishment of the Hocking Valley Computerized GIS Database

### Database Collection

The settlement universe for this study was defined as the Hocking River drainage basin (fig. 2.1), and the points of interest were all recorded archaeological sites assigned to the Middle Archaic, Late Archaic, Early Woodland, and Middle Woodland periods. Several data sets were integrated into this GIS analysis. A GIS database of all archaeological sites from Ohio has been

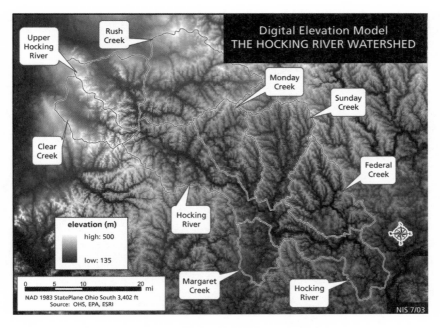

Digital Elevation Model
THE HOCKING RIVER WATERSHED

Upper Hocking River

Rush Creek

Monday Creek

Sunday Creek

Clear Creek

Federal Creek

elevation (m)
high: 500
low: 135

Hocking River

Margaret Creek

Hocking River

0  5  10  20  mi
NAD 1983 StatePlane Ohio South 3,402 ft
Source: OHS, EPA, ESRI

NIS 7/03

FIG. 2.1. Digital elevation model of the Hocking River watershed

created based on the OAI forms submitted by diverse researchers. Data from these site forms were provided by the Ohio Preservation Office of the Ohio Historical Society in the form of Environmental Systems Research Institute (ESRI) shapefiles as point features.

To establish topography, the National Elevation Datasets (NED) for northern Ohio (no. 12) and southern Ohio (no. 13) were obtained from the Ohio University Cartographic Center's collection of geospatial data. Stream networks and ridges were highlighted by applying various color ramps for elevation. Since the survey universe is the Hocking River drainage basin, a shapefile for the watershed was required. The U.S. Environmental Protection Agency provides coverage of all major watersheds in the country. Each watershed has a code, and that of the Hocking River watershed is 05030204. The subbasins within this watershed were digitized in ArcMap by analyzing the stream networks and ridges clearly visible from the NED. The hydrology of the Hocking watershed was obtained from the Census TIGER Internet files. The streams included in the TIGER files represent modern streams. The hydrologic modeling extension in ArcView was used to determine stream networks from the NED. The shapefiles of soils were obtained online from the Ohio Department of Natural Resources on a per county basis. These shapefiles had been digitized from original soil maps, and soil characteristics, especially relating to crop productivity, were included.

## Database Integration

Several technical steps were necessary to make these data manageable within the GIS. First, the OAI data, which are coded by county, had to be combined into a continuous layer of archaeological sites. This was done using the Geoprocessing wizard in ArcMap with the operation "merge." Second, those sites that fell outside the Hocking watershed were "clipped" from the OAI site layer, again with the Geoprocessing wizard. Third, soil layers by county were merged to create a continuous layer, and those soils outside the survey universe were similarly clipped. Finally, to compare time periods, sites from each period were saved as their own shapefile. Given the inadequacies of chronological site control, the Early and Middle Woodland sites were bundled into a single category; accordingly, employing the Query Builder in ArcMap, three temporal settlement categories—Middle Archaic, Late Archaic, and Early/Middle Woodland—were created for spatial comparison. One of the values of this categorization is that each of the three periods is roughly of equal length—about two thousand years. As improved chronological control becomes available, however, it would be preferred to separate these two Woodland periods.

## Database Limitations

Several database limitations were encountered in the process of data entry. The first is the archaeological survey sample of the watershed. Due to the relatively limited economic development and scholarly interest in this region, the areas systematically surveyed for archaeological sites are not representative of the entire watershed. Unfortunately, the exact boundaries of archaeologically surveyed areas have not yet been entered into the master database of the state of Ohio; however, when they are, it will be possible to make statistical extrapolations in GIS for unsurveyed areas with much greater accuracy than is available in our current study.

Two further limitations of the database are the lack of detailed chronological data for many recorded sites and the complexity of integrating multicomponent sites into the data system accurately. Related to this issue is the fact that most recorded sites on the OAI forms lack site function definitions; consequently, locating habitation sites only, for a specific time period, while possible, significantly underrepresents the true settlement for that period due to the lack of specific site function data in many site entries.

The fourth significant limitation was in the attempt to correlate archaeological sites with prime agricultural soils as a consequence of the relative spatial placement errors in these two data sets and the complexity of site function and boundary definitions, since habitation sites could be located on poor agricultural soils but adjacent to excellent ones. In addition, soils conducive to agriculture may have been attractive also to foragers. When this correlative exercise was conducted, it became clear that there were too many intervening variables and incomplete site data entries to accurately qualify the correspondence of prime agricultural soils with archaeological habitation sites. Significantly greater detail in the OAI database would be required before this type of GIS analysis becomes feasible.

## Statistical Spatial Analyses

The aim of this research is to investigate a set of questions regarding prehistoric settlement patterns in the Hocking Valley by analyzing the relationship of archaeological sites to geographic phenomena in a GIS to determine if any meaningful patterns could be inferred to address the research questions. Considering the geographic characteristics of the study area and the various attributes in the OAI coding related to changes in Middle and Late Archaic and Early and Middle Woodland period settlements, the following questions were developed and investigated.

### Archaic Demographic Trends

The first analysis is the simplest: what were the demographic trends through these centuries (see figs. 2.2–2.5)? In the Middle Archaic period, there are 22 sites in the entire valley. This increased to 140 for the Late Archaic and to 161 for the Early/Middle Woodland. Although we do not presume that all sites are equivalent in function, duration of occupation, or size, a logical inference from this significant increase in site totals is a correspondingly large internal valleywide population increase or considerable in-migration. Comparable analyses from the Cross Creek drainage in Pennsylvania (Adovasio et al. 2001), the lower Ohio Valley (Muller 1986), the Green River Valley in Kentucky (Pedde and Prufer 2001; Meindl, Mensforth, and York 2001), and the western portion of the Lake Erie Basin (Stothers, Abel, and Schneider 2001) confirm increasing Late Archaic populations within riverine or other spatially discrete regions. Since these adjacent areas portray similar demographic patterns, we infer that the Hocking Valley also experienced an internal population expansion during this time. Meindl, Mensforth, and York go as far as to state that "the first population explosion in Kentucky occurred during Late Archaic times" (87).

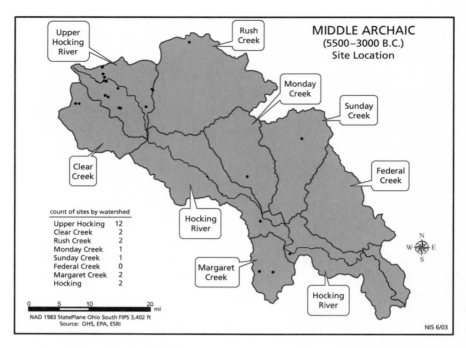

FIG. 2.2. Middle Archaic site distribution

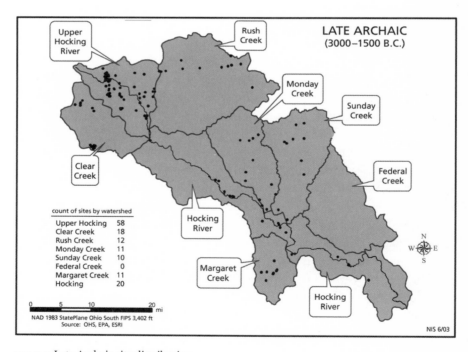

FIG. 2.3. Late Archaic site distribution

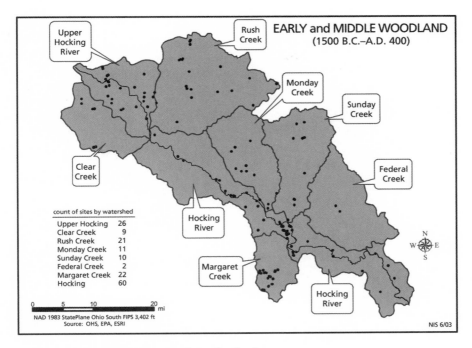

FIG. 2.4. Early and Middle Woodland site distribution

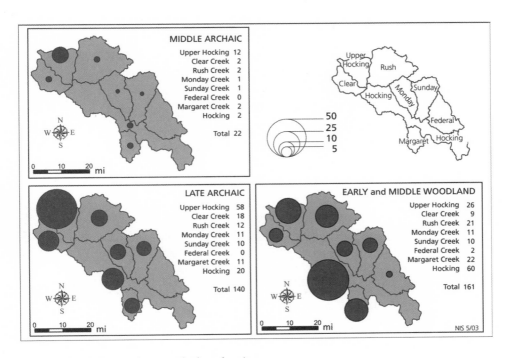

FIG. 2.5. Site distribution by watersheds and regions

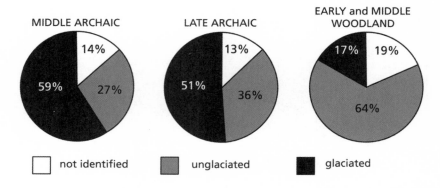

FIG. 2.6. Physiographic setting of archaeological settlements throughout the Hocking River basin

A further analytic issue involves discerning the possible rate of population growth. Although it is tempting to speculate based on these numbers, it also is premature to offer such calculations. Generating demographic rates of growth requires, at minimum, data identifying the number of people per site, habitation sites from nonhabitation sites, site size, and patterns from all adjacent riverine systems to account for migration. Lacking these data at this stage in research for the Archaic periods, we defer offering any set of specific population growth rates.

## Archaic Settlement Distribution Shifts

There are two general trends relating to shifting settlement locations through these time periods. First, there is a trend for site density to differentially increase in the unglaciated portion of the valley (fig. 2.6). Presumably, a lower percentage of people through time are residing in the upper, glaciated reaches of the valley, signifying a southern movement of population through time.

In the second trend, related to the first, we see that the stream valley physiographic setting, which includes the floodplain and terrace zones, increases considerably in percentage of sites through time (fig. 2.7). This change from 14% to 38% to 47% of sites in this collective setting indicates a heightened preference for terrace and floodplain locales, supported by previous analyses of more localized segments of the Hocking Valley (Black 1979; J. Murphy 1989; Shane and Murphy 1967; Abrams 1992a). This trend continued through the Late Woodland and Late Prehistoric periods (Wakeman, this volume).

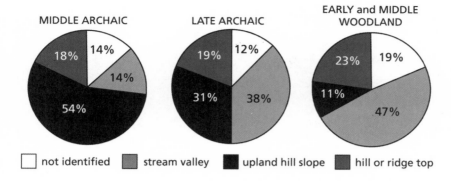

FIG. 2.7. Regional geomorphological setting of archaeological settlements throughout the Hocking River basin

## Site Clustering

In a kernel density calculation within Spatial Analysis in ArcMap, points that fall within the search area are summed and then divided by the search area to generate each cell's density value. The points lying nearer the center of a raster cell's search area are weighed more heavily than those lying on the edge, resulting in a smooth distribution of values. The values in the analysis were set at a "search radius" of 1,000 square miles, with the "cell size" set at 100 square miles. The goal of this spatial analysis is to determine whether there was a decrease in site density or clustering through the time (see figs. 2.8–2.10).

The values calculated using the kernel density method are higher in the Early/Middle Woodland periods than for the Late Archaic (the limited number of sites from the Middle Archaic precluded analysis for this period). This finding complements the previous analysis since greater clustering of sites is evident in the upper reaches of the valley during the Late Archaic period, followed by a southern shift in site density during the Early/Middle Woodland period (especially near The Plains and Margaret Creek).

The greater site density in The Plains is a function of the ritual center built there during the Middle Woodland period (as discussed in chapter 7). However, the greater site density elsewhere in the watershed encompassing the main stem of the Hocking River may reflect local community fissioning focused on prime economic locations associated with the floodplain and terrace zones, a preference confirmed above.

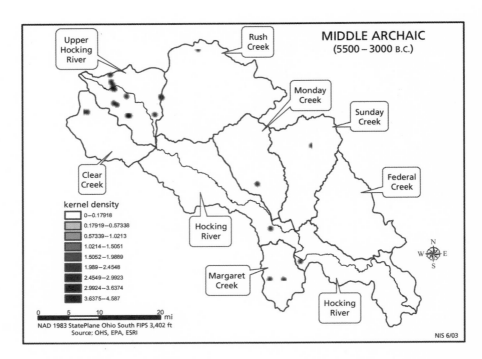

FIG. 2.8. Middle Archaic site clustering

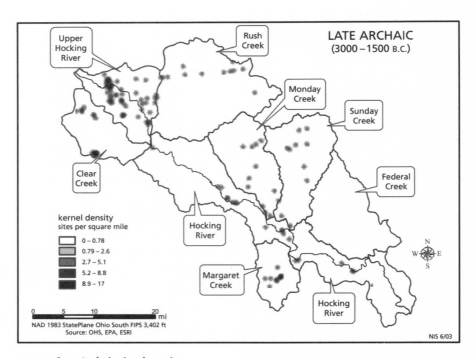

FIG. 2.9. Late Archaic site clustering

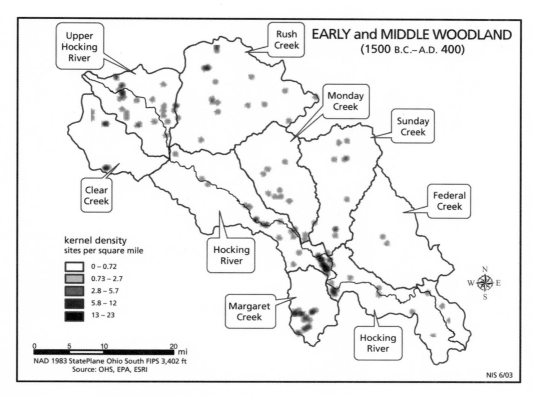

FIG. 2.10. Early and Middle Woodland site clustering

## Correlation between Settlement Shifts and Agricultural Soil Access

An analysis of site location with soils best suited for agriculture indicated that sites did not correlate with such soils through time (fig. 2.11). However, the lack of data from most sites that would have discerned site function (habitation vs. nonhabitation) makes this finding inconclusive, as does the lack of a high confidence interval between the soils and site layers in the current GIS database. The variability of site types, including ridgetop mounds and rockshelters, may partially account for a lack of correlation.

However, the settlement trend noted above strongly suggests that Late Archaic and Early Woodland communities increasingly lived near food resources of the floodplain and terrace zones, at least seasonally. In addition, residential sites may be constructed on poorer soils that lie adjacent to soils supporting such resources or suited for growing crops. Despite these qualifiers, the data indicate that a wide range of locations and physiographic zones were used in the time periods under study.

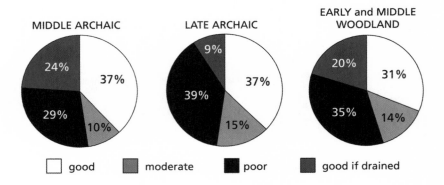

FIG. 2.11. Agricultural potential of soils for archaeological settlements throughout the Hocking River basin

One of the major cultural changes through the Archaic period is the dynamics of sedentism (Binford 1980; Brown 1985). There are many measures of the scale of sedentism. Living one's life within the confines of a single river valley as opposed to several valleys is one such measure. Another is the number of times per year the local community reestablishes its habitation site. Still another is the number of months per year that any one habitation site is occupied. These continua of change can intersect, making the issue of sedentism more complex than when simply opposed to nomadism.

From the data at hand, as well as data from surrounding valleys, we infer that the Middle Archaic population moved readily among various river valleys, while a greater sense of restriction characterized the later periods. The lower number of sites during the Middle Archaic suggests low population and thus the availability of migrating to other valleys. In contrast, the greater number of sites evidenced for the Late Archaic, supplemented by a comparably high number of sites in surveyed tributaries of the mid-Ohio Valley, suggest a greater restriction of movement. We suggest that by 2000 B.C. an individual born within the Hocking Valley was likely to live the core of his or her life within the valley. Taking this concept of scales of sedentism further, we suggest that the greater kernel density values for the Early/Middle Woodland period relative to the Late Archaic period, coupled with the overall trend toward floodplain and terrace zones, reflects a greater number of habitation sites in these zones and a greater amount of time per year spent at these sites.

Finally, we suggest that the increasing population and preference for riverine zones during the Late Archaic period corresponds with and is partially a function of the relatively high rainfall from 3000 B.C. to 1500 B.C.

(fig. 1.7). The pollen data clearly indicate an increase in nut species owing to heightened rainfall levels (Ogden 1966; Shane, Snyder, and Anderson 2001). Logically the productivity of food resources within the riverine zone was also enhanced. This environmental change is seen as contributing to the local nomadic community's decision to favor riverine zones and to remain in them for longer periods of time each year. The increased natural productivity of foods as well as an array of cultural factors may have allowed for a continuous but incremental rise in population size. Certainly future research should seek to clarify the relationship between population growth, climatic change, and natural productivity. Nonetheless, the data at hand indicate a clear positive feedback system between these factors that future GIS analysis could fruitfully explore.

## Future Research Recommendations

The OAI database lends itself to the analysis of site locations throughout the landscape. Owing to the nature of the data currently, however, going beyond information other than that related to site location is limited. Temporal comparisons of attributes of interest—such as site area and artifact assemblages relating to questions about society and culture—currently cannot be easily made. Some sites have multiple habitation periods; if one were to compare the presence of prehistoric materials at the Middle Archaic sites to those of the Early and Middle Woodland one would find ceramics in the Middle Archaic period, yet ceramics were not diagnostic of Middle Archaic sites in the Hocking Valley. No distinction in time period is made for these artifacts in the attribute data table. Other data attributes contain nested unrecorded data, which makes conclusions subject to misrepresentation if the researcher is not fully aware of the data set limitations and artifact attribute tables, which were both constructed before the application of GIS and require refinement to make more complex GIS inquires successful.

As archaeologists apply GIS to analyzing prehistoric populations and their environments, they will develop a better understanding of how the different functions and algorithms can be best applied to test hypotheses and develop models of prehistoric behavior. In our research a raster-based GIS was found to be of greater utility than vector-based analyses, and other researchers working on similar problems may also find this to be true. This approach has great potential in the field of archaeology, and as more archaeologists employ GIS as the powerful tool it is, the more the approach can be refined and the OAI database corrected and further developed.

Even with the current data set limitations, we were able to perform with confidence various preliminary investigations on the spatial patterns of site selection within the Hocking Valley during the key transition between the hunting and gathering Middle and Late Archaic populations and the later Early and Middle Woodland horticultural communities. The results of this analysis and the approaches used to arrive at our conclusions will, it is hoped, add to our understanding of both the prehistoric cultures of the Hocking Valley and the use of GIS as a tool for archaeological analysis.

# 3

# THE BREMEN SITE

## A TERMINAL LATE ARCHAIC PERIOD UPLAND OCCUPATION IN FAIRFIELD COUNTY, OHIO

Albert M. Pecora and Jarrod Burks

THE BREMEN SITE (33FA1460) is a Late Archaic period (3000–1500 B.C.) upland site about half a mile east of the town of Bremen in southern Fairfield County, Ohio (fig. 1.2). Ohio Valley Archaeological Consultants first documented the site as a lithic scatter during a Phase I cultural resource management survey in preparation for the construction of a cellular phone tower (Pecora 2000). Subsequent research at the Phase II level uncovered additional Late Archaic period remains, including stone tools, pottery, and botanical material (Pecora and Burks 2000). Two radiocarbon dates from burned nutshell within pit features containing pottery make the Bremen site the oldest known pottery-yielding context in the Hocking Valley. This chapter details the methods, data, and analytic results of these recent archaeological investigations at the site, placing these findings in the broader context of Late Archaic settlement patterns.

## Site Setting

The Bremen site covers 4,400 m² on the end of a ridge (283 masl [meters above sea level]) overlooking the confluence of Rush and Little Rush Creeks (244 masl) near the northern boundary of the unglaciated Appalachian

Plateau. The ridge consists of bedrock members of the Logan Formation covered in Wisconsin age outwash gravel and silt (Wolfe, Forsyth, and Dove 1962). At the top of the ridge the Parke silt loam has formed in silt and gravel outwash deposits (USDA 1960). The creeks below the Bremen site flow through a level valley filled in with lake sediments, making the upland-bottomland transition steep and abrupt. Chert was plentiful in the site vicinity (fig. 3.1). Not only was it available in local outcrops of Upper Mercer, Brush Creek, and Vanport, but numerous varieties would have also been readily accessible in streambeds. This is significant since the vast majority of artifacts recovered are of local chert.

Early surveyor's line descriptions suggest that the uplands around and to the south and east of the Bremen site supported an oak-maple forest while the bottoms were predominantly beech-maple (Chute 1951). Aside from oak and beech, other nut-producing species, including walnut, were also present in low numbers. Large pockets of prairie were reported from just across Rush Creek valley to the west. In general, pollen cores pulled from central Ohio contexts and dating to the Late Archaic period support the early surveyor's data (Shane et al. 2001). The Bremen site occupants likely had access to a wide variety of nut-bearing trees, floodplain resources, and the extensive edge habitat found around small prairie openings.

## Regional Culture History

In traditional culture histories of the Midwest, the Late Archaic period (ca. 3000–1000 B.C.) is depicted as the intensification of a series of culture changes that ultimately resulted in the complex societies of the Late Prehistoric period (A.D. 1000–1700; Fagan 2000). Primary changes include increased sedentism, burial ceremonialism, and a greater reliance on cultivated plants. At the same time, Late Archaic subsistence and settlement systems are the culmination of cultural trends that were set in motion in the Middle Archaic (5000–3000 B.C.). Thus, the Late Archaic represents the transition between the more nomadic hunter-gatherer groups of the early Holocene and the more sedentary gardening and farming groups of later prehistory (Phillips and Brown 1985; Prufer, Pedde, and Meindl 2001).

In general, Late Archaic populations in the mid–Ohio Valley were seasonally mobile groups who occupied base camps and special resource extraction camps. In the mid–Ohio Valley, two of the cultural phases that have been proposed for the Late Archaic period are the Maple Creek phase (1650–1250 B.C.) and the Cogswell phase (1250–750 B.C.).

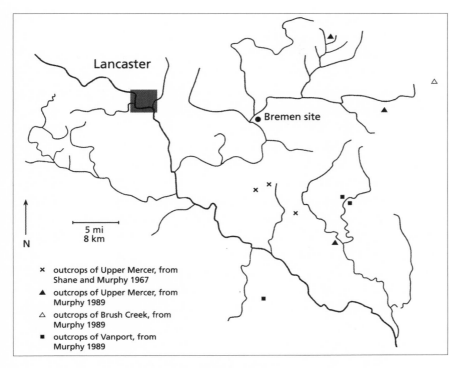

FIG. 3.1. Chert outcrops in relation to the Bremen site

The Maple Creek phase, first defined by Kent Vickery (1980) for southwestern Ohio, consists of periodically mobile groups who occupied large base camps in river valleys and smaller camps in the uplands. Chert tools used at these settlements included Merom expanding-stem and Trimble side-notched projectile points, as well as flint microtools. Numerous other Late Archaic projectile point types have been found in Maple Creek phase sites. However, dates from other northeastern Kentucky Late Archaic sites suggest that the points belonging to the Merom cluster (Justice 1987) are specific to the Maple Creek phase. Other tools used for fishing and grinding vegetable materials have also been recovered. Significantly, Maple Creek phase groups produced ceramics.

Some Maple Creek phase sites contain substantial occupation evidence. For example, the Grayson site in Carter County, Kentucky, includes two rectangular to circular structures, trash-filled pits, hearths, pits with chert caches, and a notable midden deposit, all located on a broad terrace of the Little Sandy River (Ledbetter and O'Steen 1992, 23). Overlapping of some of the Maple Creek phase features at Grayson suggests multiple occupation episodes. While this site seems to support Vickery's settlement model of larger base camps in the valleys and smaller sites in the uplands, Ledbetter and O'Steen suggest that perhaps this seeming pattern may be the result of more frequent reoccupation of the riverine settlements. Furthermore, intensive Maple Creek phase occupations have also been found along tributary streams, and deposits have been excavated in rockshelters as well. Thus, the Maple Creek phase settlement system seems to be somewhat more diversified than originally defined by Vickery in 1980.

The Cogswell phase is less well defined in the mid–Ohio Valley and represents the Terminal Archaic occupation of this region. The phase derives its name from a projectile point type (Cogswell contracting stemmed) defined by Rolingson and Rodeffer (1968) for specimens from a site in Bath County, Kentucky. Ison (1988) first proposed a Cogswell phase cultural unit for the Cumberland Plateau area based in large part on work at the Cold Oak rockshelter. Aside from a structure and various pit features at the Grayson site, most of the deposits from this phase have been found in Eastern Kentucky rockshelters (e.g., Cold Oak [Gremillion and Ison 1989] and Cloudsplitter [Cowan et al. 1981]). These rockshelter deposits hint at a significant change in Late Archaic subsistence practices, with evidence of domesticated cultigens and the use of wild varieties of starchy seed plants, including knotweed, maygrass, goosefoot, and ragweed.

## Research Methods

All research completed to date at the Bremen site took place in 2000 and 2001 as part of a cultural resource management research design. The fieldwork was limited in scope to the area impacted by the construction of the cellular phone tower. Excavation focused on the northern and southern portions of the ridgetop site area (fig. 3.2). This included the excavation of twenty-three 50 × 50 cm units (5.75 m²), seventeen and a half 1 × 1 m units (17.5 m²), and three 18.75 × 3 m plow zone removal strips (168.75 m²; fig. 3.2). The 50 × 50 cm units were excavated on a standard 10 m grid. Most of these (n = 19) were excavated in the northern portion of the site while four others were excavated in the southern portion. The 1 × 1 meter units were excavated in high and low artifact density areas in the northern (n = 14) and southern (n = 3.5) portions of the site. The 18.75 × 3 meter plow zone removal strips were limited to the northern portion of the site to identify features at the plow zone–subsoil interface. The fill from all hand excavations was screened through a ⅛ in mesh.

Overall, the 23 shovel tests produced an average of 17 artifacts per unit, with a noticeable increase in debris density (especially smaller debris) in

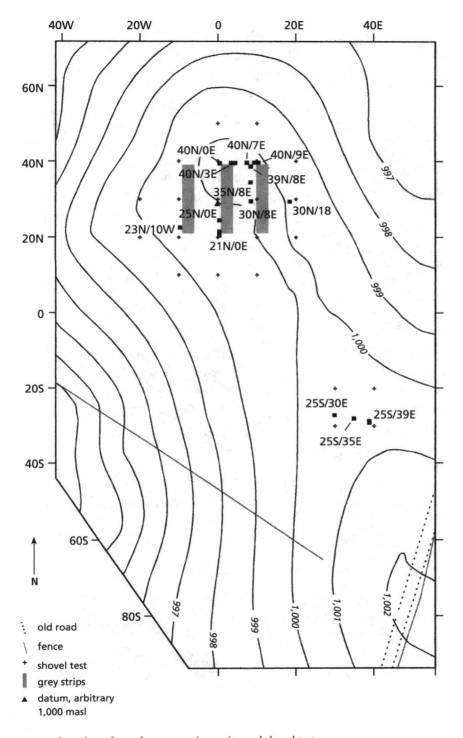

FIG. 3.2. Location of trenches, excavation units, and shovel tests

the southern area (fig. 3.3). Whether this density difference is the result of a plow-disturbed feature (e.g., feature 2) or represents the presence of a plowed midden is currently unknown. Plowing in the vicinity of features 1, 3, and 4 seems to have done little to increase that area's artifact density.

The distribution of Vanport versus Upper Mercer chert may also demonstrate the presence of site structure in the shovel test data. Both chert types appear in both areas of the site, but Vanport is nearly exclusive to the feature 2 area. While Upper Mercer objects are also present in this area, this raw material also has peaks in density in the southeast and southwest areas of the main bank of shovel tests around features 1, 3, and 4. Such a distribution could be interpreted in many ways, but may be better left until more is known about the site.

## Feature Descriptions

Four cultural features were uncovered at the Bremen site, the locations of which are shown in the context of the shovel test distribution data (fig. 3.3). All four of the features were identified at the plow zone–subsoil interface. Feature 1 appeared as a concentration of burned rock in a 1 × 1 m unit (40N/3E) excavated on the northwestern end of the site (fig. 3.3). No soil discoloration was noted in plan or profile view. Feature 1 is likely a small midden remnant or concentration of rock that survived plowing. Lithic artifacts (n = 8), burned rock (n = 89), and a very small quantity of nut charcoal (< 1 g) were recovered.

Feature 2 was identified in a 1 × 1 m unit (25/25.5S/39E) excavated near the proposed guy-wire anchor on the southeastern end of the ridge (fig. 3.3). Of the 200 L excavated from the feature, 160 L were processed through flotation and 40 L were processed through ⅛ in screen mesh. Although feature 2 was not completely excavated, the trench revealed what appears to be half of a basin-shaped feature with two distinct zones (fig. 3.4). Zone 1 is composed of the material that was initially observed. This zone extends from the top of the midden (20 cm below surface) into the basin-shaped feature (58 cmbs). It appears that the horizontal extent of the midden outside of the feature may be the result of feature fill dispersal from plowing or some other postdepositional disturbance. This is supported by the absence of a midden in an adjacent 1 × 1 m unit (25S/35E), excavated four meters to the west. The unit was excavated an additional 10 cm into the subsoil to determine if a midden was present in this area. Zone 2 (collection level 4) extends to 72 cmbs within the basin-shaped feature. The fill in zone 2 is composed

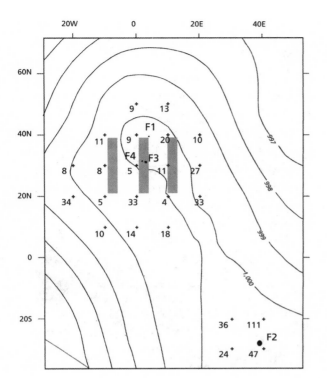

FIG. 3.3. Features and artifact distribution

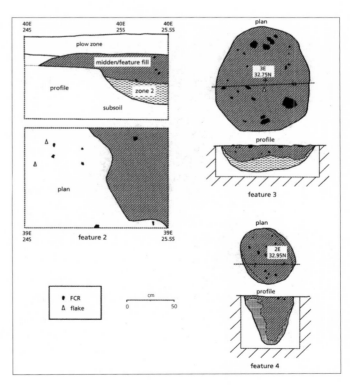

FIG. 3.4. Feature plans and profiles

of the same mottled clay (10YR4/6–5/6) observed in zone 1 (collection levels 2 and 3), but contains significantly less burned rock, charcoal, and lithic artifacts.

Nearly 31% of all lithic artifacts recovered during the project (n = 832), including two projectile point fragments, are from this feature. The majority of these (n = 804, 97%) were recovered from collection levels 2 and 3, which include zone 1 midden/feature fill material. One projectile point base from this feature resembles a Late Archaic/Early Woodland stemmed type. Nearly 40% (n = 1,403, 39%) of all burned rock recovered from Bremen was also collected from this feature. Most of this (n = 1,355, 97%) was also recovered from collection levels 2 and 3 (zone 1). In addition to the burned rock and chert artifacts, carbonized nutshell (42.5 g), grit-tempered pottery (n = 2), and burned clay were also found in feature 2. Again, most of these materials were recovered from collection levels 2 and 3. Over 90% of the nutshell (42.5 g), 11% of the pottery (n = 2), and all the burned clay (73 g) collected from this site were recovered from feature 2.

In sum, feature 2 appears to be a relatively large basin-shaped pit with abundant quantities of burned rock, lithic artifacts, and nut charcoal. Feature 2 is very similar in terms of shape and contents to feature 3. The presence of grit-tempered pottery with smooth surfaces, coupled with the stemmed projectile point, suggests that the fill in this feature dates to the Terminal Archaic/Early Woodland period. However, charred material from feature 2 dates to 2826–2302 B.C. (Beta 146168; table 3.1). This places feature 2 within the middle of the Late Archaic period in the Ohio Valley.

Feature 3 is a large, circular soil discoloration containing burned rock and lithic artifacts that was exposed in plow zone removal trench 1 near the northwestern end of the site (figs. 3.2, 3.3). In plan view the feature measures 98 cm (E-W) by 114 cm (N-S). As was observed in feature 2, feature 3 contains two distinct fill zones that extend 29 cm below the plow zone–subsoil interface (fig. 3.4). The upper fill zone is mottled, with an undulating bottom that ranges from 11 cm thick in the center to 18 cm thick on either side. Abundant quantities of burned rock, artifacts, and charcoal set off the upper fill zone from the lower.

Only the south half of this feature was excavated, and all 50 L of it was water-screened through a fine-mesh paint strainer. Artifacts recovered include burned rock (n = 417), lithic artifacts (n = 8), nut charcoal (3 g), and grit-tempered pottery (n = 17, 14 g). Although this feature is similar in shape and size to feature 2, feature 3 contains far fewer artifacts and burned rock, with the exception of pottery. All this pottery is very small (¼–½ in) and heavily eroded, to the extent that no surfaces remain intact. Charred material from feature 3 dates to 1881–1315 B.C. (Beta 146167; table 3.1). This

| Table 3.1. Radiocarbon Dates from the Bremen Site | | | | | |
| --- | --- | --- | --- | --- | --- |
| Context | Beta | Material | Radiocarbon Age | Intercept Cal. Curve | 2 Sigma Calibration |
| Feature 2, level 3 | 146168 | Charred Material | 3980 ± 60 BP | 2472 B.C. | 2826–2302 B.C. |
| Feature 3, S1/2, 20–40 cmbs | 146167 | Charred Material | 3290 ± 120 BP | 1596 B.C. 1592 B.C. 1525 B.C. | 1881–1315 B.C. |

*Note:* Calibration follows Stuiver et al. 1998.

date places feature 3 toward the end of the Late Archaic period and 800–1,000 years later than feature 2.

Feature 4 appeared as a small circular soil discoloration in plow zone removal trench 1, about one meter northwest of feature 3 (figs. 3.3, 3.4). In profile this conical pit extends 52 cm below the plow zone–subsoil interface. The feature fill observed in the profile consists of a heavily mottled clay along the margins and a darker silt and clay within the core. The heavy clay material on the feature margins is peculiar and may indicate a more recent age. However, the 30 L of processed fill produced lithic artifacts (n = 4), a small amount of nut charcoal (< 1 g), and burned rock (n = 379), the bulk of which (n = 354) is small in diameter (< 16 mm).

## Artifact Analysis

The Bremen investigation resulted in the recovery of 2,725 chipped stone artifacts, one pitted stone, 3,631 pieces of fire-cracked rock, 19 pieces of pottery, and nut charcoal (46.5 g). Since no other Late Archaic habitation site in the valley has been comparably excavated and analyzed, the detailed presentation of artifacts from the Bremen site is warranted.

## Radiocarbon Dates

Two small samples of charred nutshell were submitted to Beta Analytic, Inc., for standard radiocarbon dating (table 3.1). Both were found associated with small, exfoliated pottery sherds. The first sample was pulled from the south half of feature 3, 20–40 centimeters below surface. It intercepts the calibration curve at 1596, 1592, and 1525 B.C. ± 120. The second sample was collected in level 3 of feature 2, and intercepts the calibration curve at 2472 B.C. ± 60 (Struiver et al. 1998).

## Pottery Analysis

Pottery is rare but clearly present in the Bremen assemblage and restricted to feature 2 (n = 2) and feature 3 (n = 17). All sherds are fairly small (¼–½ in diam.), heavily eroded, and grit tempered. Without water screening, it is unlikely that any pottery would have been recovered. Unfortunately, given their small size and surface erosion, no useful information could be gleaned from the ceramic assemblage in terms of surface treatment or vessel form.

Most striking about the Bremen site pottery assemblage are its associated radiocarbon dates. Both feature 2 and feature 3 produced Late Archaic dates (table 3.1). While the radiocarbon dates may appear unusually early for ceramic production in the Midwest or Northeast, small ceramic assemblages that have not been widely published are known from a number of Late Archaic contexts in central Ohio. Seeman (1986, table 22.1) presents a list of more than 10 dates from 7 pre–1000 B.C. sites in the Middle to Upper Ohio Valley, including an 1840 B.C. ± 140 date from the Rais rockshelter in Jackson County, Ohio. Since Seeman's publication, other early dates have come to light in the region. For example, salvage excavations at the Continental Construction site (33RO348) in 1986 identified five prehistoric localities in the Scioto River floodplain in an area slated to become a shopping mall (Pacheco 1991). Locality 3 consisted of one pit feature and two postmolds (a remnant of a post), the former of which produced thick, grit-tempered pottery and charcoal dating to cal B.C. 1678 (1412) 1128 (i.e., calibrated against dendrochronology to improve accuracy). More recently, excavations at site 33MS29 conducted by the authors and Craig Keener (Professional Archaeological Services Team) in Meigs County, Ohio, have also encountered Late Archaic period pottery (Keener and Pecora 2003). This site is situated on a narrow ridge on a terrace actively eroding into the Ohio River. The two radiocarbon dates obtained to date (cal B.C. 1603 [1432] 1263 and cal B.C. 1688 [1519] 1397) come from feature contexts that also contain Merom Cluster projectile points. In light of these collective data, it appears that pottery manufacture indeed began during the Late Archaic period, and that more detailed recovery methods (e.g., water screening) are necessary to fully recover and document them.

## Lithic Analysis

Four components of the lithic assemblage are considered in this analysis: raw material types, debitage size, technological analysis, and typological analysis of temporally diagnostic tools and tool function. These components are thought to be important in that they reflect patterning that may be related to site structure and assemblage formation.

Table 3.2. Flake Sizes for Each Flint Type from the Bremen Site

| Flint Type | G1 | % | G2 | % | G3 | % | G4 | % | TOTAL | % |
|---|---|---|---|---|---|---|---|---|---|---|
| Black/gray flint | 3 | 0.1% | 103 | 4.4% | 687 | 29.5% | 1,536 | 66.0% | 2,329 | 100% |
| Vanport | 1 | 0.3% | 3 | 0.8% | 109 | 30.2% | 248 | 68.7% | 361 | 100% |
| Unidentified | – | | 8 | 44.4% | 8 | 44.4% | 2 | 11.1% | 18 | 99.9%[a] |
| TOTAL | 4 | 0.1% | 114 | 4.2% | 804 | 29.7% | 1,786 | 66.0% | 2,708 | 100.0% |

[a]Due to rounding, percentage does not total 100%.

## Raw Material Analysis

An understanding of the types of lithic raw material used for stone tool manufacture is useful for discerning how prehistoric people exploited local and extralocal resources. At the Bremen site, lithic material varieties were classified macroscopically, using known geologic hand samples or by establishing general categories according to color and texture. Raw material types follow Stout and Schoenlaub (1945) and DeRegnaucourt and Georgiady (1998). Chert varieties identified in this analysis include Upper Mercer, Vanport, and an unidentified low-quality brown variety (see fig. 3.1 for sources near the site).

## Lithic Debitage

This stage in analysis classified lithic artifacts into four general size categories (table 3.2). This was conducted by sorting all lithic artifacts through a series of nested screens: 1 in (grade 1), 1–½ in (grade 2), ½–¼ in (grade 3), and ¼–⅛ in (grade 4). Although it is generally understood that chipped-stone tool manufacture is a reductive process and that stone objects become smaller through this process, small artifacts are generated in abundance regardless of the manufacturing stage. Debitage size is not a technological indicator and should not be considered as such (Scott 1991).

All four size categories are represented in this lithic assemblage. By far, the majority of the flakes recovered sorted into grade 4 (¼–⅛ in) (n = 1,786, 67%). The relatively high percentage of grade 4 artifacts in this assemblage is not surprising. Experimental flint-knapping data collected by the senior author show that all stages of lithic reduction produce high frequencies of this flake size (Pecora 2002). But although late-stage reduction debris frequently falls within this size grade, not all debris within this grade is produced during late-stage reduction. Nearly all the pressure flakes (n = 334) identified in this assemblage are smaller than ¼ in. The use of a ⅛ in mesh for the artifact collection during this investigation was important for the recovery of this technological category and certainly elevated the recovery of this artifact size.

*Technological Analysis*

Understanding prehistoric lithic tool manufacturing processes is important for determining aspects of site function and assemblage formation. The original lithic analysis conducted for this study (Pecora and Burks 2000) assumed a technological perspective founded on experimental flint knapping (Crabtree 1966, 1967, 1972; Flenniken 1981; Collins 1975). Here these data have been grouped into relative reduction stages defined by Pecora (2002), including initial reduction, early biface reduction, late biface reduction, and pressure flake reduction (table 3.3). Although each relative reduction stage includes groups of technological flake categories, not all technological categories are diagnostic of the relative reduction stages and these categories have been excluded from this analysis.

Initial reduction techniques varied throughout prehistory and were often influenced by the quality, size, and shape of the raw material, as well as by the desired outcome (i.e., flake blank shape, size, and configuration) of the reduction process. The initial reduction process involves the preparation and reduction of cores of various types and varieties. Cores may be multidirectional, bidirectional, and unidirectional, for example. Raw material nodules may also be split into halves or sections by means of a variety of techniques. The purpose of such cores is generally to produce flake blanks, which could remain unmodified as flake tools, blades, and bladelets or be further reduced into bifacial and unifacial items.

Initial reduction produces *primary decortication* flakes, *secondary decortication* flakes, and *interior* flakes. *Alternate* flakes—those with primary decortication, secondary decortication, and interior flake attributes—are also produced during initial reduction, although these flakes are more commonly produced during the flake blank preparation stage. Initial reduction involves the preparation of flake blanks, sections, spalls, and tabular pieces of raw material. Although alternate flakes are exclusively produced from flake blank preparation, the primary decortication, secondary decortication, and interior flakes are nearly exclusive to both core reduction and flake blank preparation.

Early biface reduction is the process whereby nonbifacial forms of raw material (prepared flake blanks, sections, spalls, and tabular pieces) are converted into bifacial forms. Technological attributes identified in experimental data indicate that *biface margin removal* flakes—alternate flakes with characteristics of biface thinning flakes—and *early biface thinning* flakes

**Table 3.3.** Relative Reduction Stages Identified at the Bremen Site

| Flint Type | Initial Reduction | Early Biface Reduction | Late Biface Reduction | Pressure Flake Reduction | Total |
|---|---|---|---|---|---|
| **Gray/Black** | | | | | |
| 50 x 50s | 27 | 18 | 26 | 24 | 95 |
| | 28% | 19% | 27% | 25% | 99% |
| 1 x 1s | 108 | 33 | 72 | 49 | 262 |
| | 41% | 13% | 27% | 19% | 100% |
| Features | 76 | 28 | 87 | 43 | 234 |
| | 32% | 12% | 37% | 18% | 99% |
| Total | 211 | 79 | 185 | 116 | 591 |
| | 36% | 13% | 31% | 20% | 100% |
| **Vanport** | | | | | |
| 50 x 50s | 8 | 4 | 20 | 6 | 38 |
| | 21% | 11% | 53% | 16% | 101% |
| 1 x 1s | 13 | 5 | 31 | 40 | 89 |
| | 15% | 6% | 35% | 45% | 101% |
| Features | 1 | 0 | 14 | 6 | 21 |
| | 5% | 0% | 67% | 29% | 101% |
| Total | 22 | 9 | 65 | 52 | 148 |
| | 15% | 6% | 44% | 35% | 100% |
| **Unidentified** | | | | | |
| 50 x 50s | 0 | 0 | 0 | 0 | 0 |
| 1 x 1s | 7 | 4 | 2 | 0 | 13 |
| | 54% | 31% | 15% | 0% | 100% |
| Features | 0 | 0 | 0 | 0 | 0 |
| Total | 7 | 4 | 2 | 0 | 13 |
| | 54% | 31% | 15% | 0% | 100% |

*Note:* Due to rounding, percentages may not total 100%.

are very diagnostic of the earlier portions of this process (Pecora 2002). Both flake types accumulate in their highest quantities during the conversion of prepared flake blanks into biface blanks.

Early biface thinning flakes with remnant detachment scars are removed from the ventral surface of prepared flake blanks, sections, and spalls. Early biface thinning flakes with cortex or remnant detachment scars are highly diagnostic of the first flakes removed during the biface thinning process. Early biface thinning flakes are distinguished from late biface thinning flakes by attributes that indicate that they were detached from poorly developed, and often not fully formed, bifaces.

Late biface reduction occurs in the later portion of the percussion biface thinning process. Experimental data indicate that *late biface thinning* flakes are diagnostic of this process (Pecora 2002). The highest percentages of late biface thinning flakes are produced by converting prepared flake blanks into biface blanks. Slightly lower frequencies were recovered from converting biface blanks into preforms. Unlike early biface thinning flakes, late biface thinning flakes are removed from well-formed, developed, and nearly complete bifaces.

Pressure flaking reduction refers to the process of pressure thinning bifaces into preforms and preforms into finished notched bifaces, as well as the maintenance of notched bifaces. Pressure flakes from the Bremen site are grouped as biface pressure thinning flakes.

### Typological Analysis of Temporally Diagnostic Tools and Tool Function

Tool-stone availability and source distance is likely to have affected how lithic resources were used (Bamforth 1986; Andrefsky 1994). Such usage is likely to have involved the preparation of lithic materials for transport. Stone preparation typically involved the reduction of stone into forms suitable for transport. Flake cores, prepared flake blanks, biface blanks, biface preforms, and finished tools are examples of transportable forms.

The manner in which stone was prepared for transport imposed constraints on tool manufacture (Pecora 2002). Flake cores, for example, offer a greater amount of lithic material from which a broader range of tool forms can be produced. The potential utility of transported flake blanks, biface blanks, preforms, and finished tools decreases appreciably with each respective transport form. With this decrease in utility for each respective transport form, carrying costs (in terms of waste weight) are also greatly reduced.

Two potentially significant assemblage characteristics are likely to have been affected by the transport forms (i.e., cores, flake biface blanks, biface preforms, and finished tools). First, tool diversity is expected to be greater in assemblages created with early-reduction transport forms (e.g., cores and flake blanks). Tool diversity is expected to be greatly reduced with each consecutive transport form (biface blank, biface preform, and finished tool).

The chert type and technological analyses conducted for the Bremen lithic assemblage provide useful information on lithic material use and on lithic assemblage formation. Importantly, the technological analysis was designed to identify the type of transport forms used for each flint type. As noted, three chert types (Upper Mercer, Vanport, and an unidentified brown variety) are present in this assemblage (tables 3.2, 3.3). The dominance of the Upper Mercer within this assemblage is not surprising. James Murphy (1989) documented three Upper Mercer flint outcrops within a 20 km radius of the site and two Vanport outcrops less than 20 km southeast of Bremen (fig. 3.1).

Of the 2,329 Upper Mercer flakes, 591 (25%) are diagnostic of the relative reduction stages used in this study (table 3.3). These include initial reduction (n = 211, 36%), early biface reduction (n = 79, 13%), late biface reduction (n = 185, 31%), and pressure flake reduction (n = 116, 20%). This relative reduction stage profile indicates that a small portion of the Upper Mercer material was introduced to the site in a pre-biface form, such as in the form of a core or flake blank, represented by the initial reduction debris. In contrast, most of this flint type was introduced to the site in the form of biface blanks, reflected by the large quantities of late biface and pressure flake reduction debris. Only 13% of this portion of the assemblage (n = 79) is early biface reduction debris. The paucity of early percussion biface thinning flakes with cortex (n = 1) and remnant detachment scars (n = 6) indicates that the reduction of Upper Mercer began with the percussion thinning of premade biface forms. Thus the site occupants brought Upper Mercer material into the site in two forms: premade biface blanks dominated, followed by prepared flake cores or flake blanks.

Vanport chert objects represent just 13% (n = 361) of the debitage assemblage. Of these, 41% (n = 148) are diagnostic of the relative reduction stages (table 3.3). These include initial reduction (n = 22, 15%), early biface reduction (n = 9, 6%), late biface reduction (n = 65, 44%), and pressure flake reduction (n = 52, 35%). This relative reduction stage profile reflects a reduction trajectory that began primarily with the reduction of premade biface blanks. This conclusion is supported by the relative paucity of early biface reduction debris (n = 9) and especially the lack of early thinning flakes with remnant detachment scars (n = 1) coupled with the much higher quantities of late-percussion thinning flakes and pressure thinning flakes. Vanport chert clearly was introduced to Bremen in the form of biface blanks and biface preforms. As with the Upper Mercer material, the debris reflects the reduction of these bifaces through the later stages (projectile point manufacture, rejuvenation, recycling).

Experimental flint-knapping data for a moderately complex biface reduction system produced 12.8 late biface reduction flakes per objective piece from the middle transport stage (biface blank stage onward; Pecora 2002). Assuming that the Bremen assemblage represents a moderately complex biface reduction system that involved the reduction of biface blanks, it is calculated that the lithic assemblage from 50 × 50 cm unit data only (n = 23, 5.75 m²) represents the reduction of 3.44 bifaces of Vanport and Upper Mercer. If this sample (ca. 0.12% of the site) is representative of the site as a whole, then over 2,600 biface blanks and preforms were converted into tools by Late Archaic occupants of this upland site.

Only 18 flakes of an unidentified raw material type were collected during this investigation. Thirteen (72%) can be assigned to one of the relative reduction stages (table 3.3). These include initial reduction (n = 7, 54%), early biface reduction (n = 4, 31%), and late biface reduction (n = 2, 15%). This portion of the assemblage is too small to develop an understanding of the unidentified flint usage at Bremen. The relative reduction stage profile, however, suggests that it was generated from the earliest stages of reduction (e.g., transported nodules or cores).

Seventeen chipped-stone formed artifacts were collected during this investigation (fig. 3.5, table 3.4), including four possible projectile points or fragments. One projectile point is classified as a Late Archaic stemmed point, similar to the Karnak type (Justice 1987). A second possible projectile point is a small, narrow, drill-like biface with a flared base and severe impact fractures along both margins; it may also be Karnak-like. The impact fractures suggest that this artifact was used as a projectile point. Two other possible projectile point fragments were also recovered from feature 2 (level 3). These include a symmetrical biface blade and a square-shaped biface stem/base. The latter may be a broken Late Archaic/Early Woodland stemmed projectile point. The four small biface tips have breakage patterns consistent with impact damage, suggesting they were part of projectiles.

Only one groundstone artifact was found, consisting of a tabular piece of sandstone with three pecked and ground U-shaped pits. Pit shape is fairly uniform and ranges in size from 18.2 mm to 24.5 mm in diameter. The depth of all three pits is 6 mm. Traditionally such pits are interpreted as representing nut-processing tools.

The most common artifact from Bremen is fire-cracked rock (FCR; table 3.5). This material consists mostly of sandstone, but a variety of water-worn cobbles representing a broad range of igneous rock varieties were also present. Given the site's elevation, it is likely that all the stone used in the thermal features was introduced. While rock was commonly used in cooking, it is also possible that heated rocks were placed in pits beneath structures and sleeping areas during the cold months.

Size grade analysis shows that much of the FCR is small and may have been reused a number of times. Four size grades adapted from standard geologic particle grades (128–64 mm, 64–32 mm, 32–16 mm, and < 16 mm)

## Table 3.4. Formed Artifacts from the Bremen Site

| Artifact | Gray/Black | Vanport | Sandstone | Total |
|---|---|---|---|---|
| Bipolar core | 2 | — | — | 2 |
| Multidirection flake core | 1 | — | — | 1 |
| Biface blank | 1 | — | — | 1 |
| Projectile points | 4 | — | — | 4 |
| Drill-like biface | 1 | 1 | — | 2 |
| Biface margin fragments | 2 | 1 | — | 3 |
| Biface tip fragments | 2 | 2 | — | 4 |
| Pitted stone | — | — | 1 | 1 |
| Total | 13 | 4 | 1 | 18 |

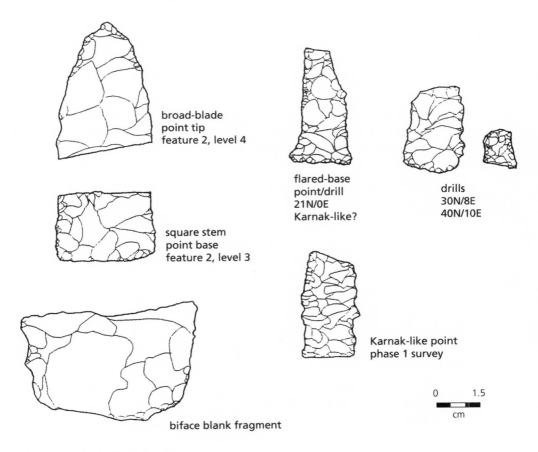

broad-blade
point tip
feature 2, level 4

square stem
point base
feature 2, level 3

biface blank fragment

flared-base
point/drill
21N/0E
Karnak-like?

drills
30N/8E
40N/10E

Karnak-like point
phase 1 survey

0    1.5
cm

FIG. 3.5. Bremen site formed artifacts

### Table 3.5. Thermally Altered Rock from Bremen

| Size | 128–64 mm | 64–32 mm | 32–16 mm | < 16 mm | Total |
|---|---|---|---|---|---|
| 50 x 50 unit | | | 132 | 11 | 143 |
| 1 x 1 m unit | | 81 | 887 | 232 | 1,200 |
| Feature 1 | | 7 | 61 | 21 | 89 |
| Feature 2 | 1 | 61 | 212 | 1,129 | 1,403 |
| Feature 3 | 1 | 8 | 58 | 350 | 417 |
| Feature 4 | | | 25 | 354 | 379 |
| Feature Total | 2 | 76 | 356 | 1,854 | 2,288 |
| TOTAL | 2 | 157 | 1,375 | 2,097 | 3,631 |
| | 0.1% | 4.3% | 37.9% | 57.8% | 100.1% |

Note: Due to rounding, percentage does not total 100%.

were used. The majority (96%) of the FCR fell into the smaller grades (32–16 mm and < 16mm). Only 157 pieces (4%) of FCR are in the 64–32 mm size range, with just two in the largest grade.

## Botanical Remains

A total of 240 L of soil collected from the four features was water screened through paint strainer mesh. This process produced 46.5 grams of nut charcoal larger than 1/16 inch. The majority of the botanical remains are from feature 2 (43 g) and feature 3 (3 g). Most of this nut charcoal appears to be hickory, though a few examples of black walnut may also be represented.

In sum, investigations at the Bremen site resulted in the recovery of chipped stone artifacts, a nutting stone, fire-cracked rock, pottery, and carbonized nutshell. In addition, four pit features were uncovered. Based on these data, site function can be inferred.

## Reconstruction of Site Function

The variety of site types created during the Late Archaic period range from habitations to a number of short-term extraction sites, each of which should display a distinctive material assemblage. The Bremen site represents a series of Late Archaic period occupations that approximate *residential camps* (Raab, Cande, and Stahle 1979; Binford 1980; Cowan 1999). That is, the site was repeatedly occupied as a habitation area by a small group of hunters and gatherers for limited periods of time. Following occupation of the site, this group would move elsewhere, placing themselves near other resources offered by the natural environment. Several lines of evidence support this inference.

Based on the Late Archaic settlement modeling by Stump et al. (this volume), communities dependent on hunting and gathering were seasonally nomadic, occupying a wide range of dispersed habitation areas. Some of the habitation sites were located in upland zones, although there was a preference for lower-lying spaces, such as terraces and floodplains. Thus we know that habitation sites could be located in upland zones some distance from the Hocking River.

Despite a low tool diversity, the features and abundance of burned rock suggest more than just a passing use of the ridge. The large number of lithic artifacts indicates a very substantial amount of tool production at this site. Since the site is not immediately adjacent to lithic outcrops, a seasonal residential function for the site is supported. Although lithic reduction debris dominates the Bremen artifact assemblage, a small quantity of pottery from the feature fill was recovered. The presence of pottery, while not definitive, suggests domestic activities associated with a habitation site. If the site is accepted as a short-term residential camp, then the presence of nut charcoal may indicate autumn and winter occupational episodes, an inference based admittedly on limited evidence.

In various models of nomadic land use (e.g., Binford 1980), it has been proposed that short-term extraction or processing sites should yield very few artifacts. Since the Bremen site produced a large number of different artifact categories, it may not have been an extraction site.

## Significance and Implications

The Bremen site is the first archaeological site excavated in the Hocking Valley with a well-detailed artifact inventory associated with the Late Archaic period. Pottery from the site is radiocarbon-dated to the Late Archaic period, representing the earliest ceramics in the valley. In fact, the Bremen pottery is some of the earliest in the entire mid–Ohio Valley. The lithic data suggest the Bremen site occupants used a variety of lithic transport and tool manufacture strategies. The primary lithic strategy appears to have involved the thinning of biface blanks from which more than two thousand tools were possibly made at the site. A smaller-scale, secondary lithic technology involved the reduction of flake cores.

In terms of settlement, the Bremen site appears to have been a short-term habitation site occupied seasonally by mobile hunters and gatherers. Within a model of highly dispersed Late Archaic communities, the site illustrates the viability of short-term occupation of upland areas by small groups. Collectively, research at the Bremen site highlights the need to excavate these small upland sites, as they are significant for our understanding of the Late Archaic period and people in the Hocking River Valley.

# 4

# THE WALKER SITE

## AN ARCHAIC/WOODLAND HUNTING-COLLECTING SITE IN THE HOCKING VALLEY

Elliot M. Abrams and Sara DeAloia

THE ARCHAIC PERIOD IN HOCKING VALLEY PREHISTORY was typified by nomadic Native American communities who created a dynamic economy based on hunting, gathering, and fishing influenced by the seasonality of resource availability. As a consequence of this type of economy and the relatively low population density in the valley, archaeological sites during the Middle and Late Archaic periods were widely distributed, across all valley physiographic zones (Stump et al., this volume).

The Walker site (33AT960) is located on the relatively flat crest of a ridge in Athens County, Ohio (figs. 1.2, 4.1, 4.2). This small site of approximately 700 m² rests at an elevation of 233 masl (765 fasl), or roughly 33.5 m (110 ft) overlooking the Hocking River floodplain. The river itself is located about 335 m (1,100 ft) from the site. The site owners, Tom and Ann Walker, had for years found points and other prehistoric artifacts on the surface of the ridge, and Tom Walker had collected several projectile points that indicate a rather long period of use of that particular section of the 200 m ridge. Since small ridgetop sites often do not receive intensive archaeological consideration (Means 1999), an archaeological field school from Ohio University, under the direction of the first author, was conducted in June 1998 to excavate the localized ridgetop artifact concentration that the landowner identified.

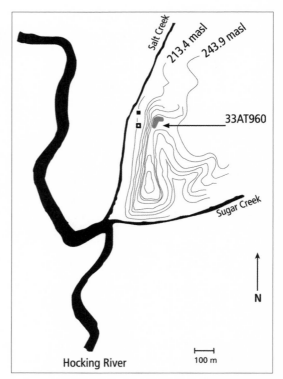

FIG. 4.1. Setting of the Walker site

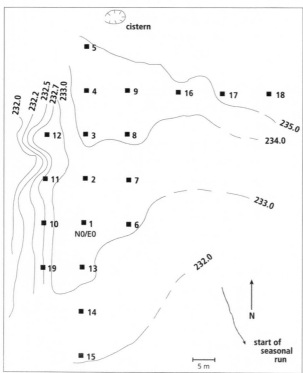

FIG. 4.2. Excavation units at the Walker site

The goal of this research was to recover the data needed to address several related site-specific issues: (1) determination of site chronology and duration of use, (2) determination of the site's general function and, related to this, (3) identification of the range of economic activities conducted at the site. Based on the data recovered and a comparison with that from the Bremen site (Pecora and Burks, this volume), we conclude that this ridgetop area was used primarily for short-term hunting and collecting activities intermittently from ca. 8000 B.C. to A.D. 400. Other ancillary activities of secondary significance were also identified.

## Physical Site Description

The center of the Walker site is located at N4359200 E404730 on the Jacksonville quadrangle. The ridge itself is about 200 m long, and the site is represented by an L-shaped concentration of artifacts abutting a depression (figs. 4.1, 4.2). Test excavations were focused along the western slope of the ridge, where the landowner defined the area of highest artifact concentration. The site area is dominated today by an oak and hickory forest. The soil on this relatively flat section of the ridge is Westmoreland-Guernsey (WhE) silt loam (Lucht, Brown, and Martin 1985). From the site's elevated aspect, a broad panorama of the Hocking River is visible. An unnamed seasonal creek runs southeast from the ridged site along the contour of the depression. Salt Creek, a larger seasonal creek named for its association with a nearby salt lick, flows just north of the site but lower in elevation by some 30 m (100 ft).

The site area over time has undergone significant modifications that affected the excavation. The forested area produced a large number of roots that prohibited some deep excavations and prevented the aligned placement of test units. Many units yielded evidence of animal burrows. In the recent past the area was plowed for farming, and trees have been cut and removed for lumber, both activities disturbing surface and subsurface artifacts and features. Today the tract is used as a sheep pasture.

## Investigation and Excavation Methods

Nineteen 1 x 1 m test units were dug at 10 m intervals. The following stratigraphic units were exposed in the test units: level 1 was an A-horizon brown silty loam averaging 8.0 cm in depth; level 2 was a yellow powdery silty loam with an average depth of 5.2 cm. Excavation ceased when the increasingly clayey B-horizon soil, lacking artifacts, was encountered. Approximately 2.7% of the total site area (19 of 700) was excavated, with roughly 2.5 m³ of soil processed through ¼ in screen mesh. In addition to the 19 test excavation units, a surface collection of artifacts about 15 m from the western slope adjoining the site was conducted. Further, seven points, one drill fragment, and one celt fragment collected by the owner from the surface of this portion of the ridge were also included in the site artifact inventory.

The owner identified a second possible site area in his lower garden along Salt Creek, where he had collected eight Lamoka points (Late Archaic) and one Kirk stemmed point (Early Archaic). Consequently, fourteen 50 cm × 50 cm test units were placed along the creek in the area he identified, but no artifacts were recovered, and thus no in situ site could be established in the lower garden. This cluster of collected points reflects either a temporary camp by hunters moving between more permanent residential sites or the secondary erosion of some artifacts from the Walker ridgetop above. In either case, due to its ephemeral nature and the lack of additional excavated artifacts in the vicinity, this was not deemed a site, and these collected points were excluded from subsequent analyses.

## Data Analysis

Only lithic artifacts were recovered from the ridgetop test excavations, the surface survey of the west slope of the site, and the owner's collection; no ceramics or ecofacts were recovered, despite screening and careful excavation. All chipped-stone artifacts were made from one of four distinct chert types: Brush Creek, Upper Mercer, Zaleski, or Flint Ridge/Vanport (J. Murphy 1989). All groundstone artifacts were either igneous rock or sandstone. The distribution of lithic debitage is not uniform across the site. Units 4, 6, 8, 9, 10, and 13 contained 73.2% by weight of all artifacts encountered. This uneven artifact distribution reflects a greater concentration of artifacts representing a site core of approximately 450 m². 

A total of 335 artifacts were recovered and analyzed. Of these, 305 were from excavation units and 30 were from surface contexts. Of the 305 excavated artifacts, 292 were chipped-stone debitage and 13 were tools. The chipped-stone debitage was classified into cores, primary flakes (containing some cortex), secondary flakes, or shatter (or irregular) flakes (table 4.1). In total, 17 of these artifacts exhibited evidence of heat treating. The majority of lithic artifacts were from Brush Creek chert, which represented 68% of lithics by count and 58% by weight (table 4.1) Fourteen projectile points were studied, six of which were sufficiently intact as to be classified within the Midwest point typology (Justice 1987). These include two Kirk stemmed points, a Lamoka point, two Adena points, and a Robbins point (fig. 4.3, a–f).

Of the 13 tools (other than projectile points), there were 8 groundstone artifacts, 2 bifaces, 2 blades, and 1 unifacial scraper. The owner's collection included a hematite celt and a drill (fig. 4.3, g, h). The 19 units at the site represent a volume of excavated soil of 2.5 m³; with 297 artifacts recovered from this soil, artifact density at the site was 119 artifacts per cubic meter.

In addition, nearly all units (17 of 19) yielded fire-cracked rock (FCR) of varying dimensions. In fact, FCR could be found at nearly any spot on the site. These fragments represent the remnants of rock-lined campfires or

FIG. 4.3. Walker site artifacts. (a, b) Kirk stemmed points, (c) Lamoka point, (d, e) Adena stemmed points, (f) Robbins point, (g) hematite celt fragment, (h) drill fragment. (Photo by Lars Lutton.)

### Table 4.1. Chipped-Stone Debitage from the Walker Site

| Raw Material | Cores Ct | Cores Wt | Primary Flakes Ct | Primary Flakes Wt | Secondary Flakes Ct | Secondary Flakes Wt | Shatter Ct | Shatter Wt | Total Ct | Total Wt |
|---|---|---|---|---|---|---|---|---|---|---|
| Brush Creek | 0 | 0 | 25 | 58.6 | 145 | 81.5 | 28 | 38.8 | 198 | 178.9 |
| Upper Mercer | 0 | 0 | 0 | 0 | 7 | 3.5 | 3 | 4.1 | 10 | 7.6 |
| Zaleski | 1 | 18.2 | 0 | 0 | 12 | 9.9 | 3 | 3.8 | 16 | 31.9 |
| Vanport/Flint Ridge | 0 | 0 | 7 | 24.0 | 53 | 27.6 | 8 | 37.3 | 68 | 88.9 |
| Total | 1 | 18.2 g | 32 | 82.6 g | 217 | 122.5 g | 42 | 84.0 g | 292 | 307.3 g |

open hearths used over the millennia of site usage, with the various transformations dispersing them from their in situ provenience. Significantly, no pit features, postmolds, or evidence of structures reflecting long-term habitation were encountered from our test excavations.

## Chronological Reconstruction

Due to the lack of preserved in situ features at the Walker site, the sole means of reconstructing the site's chronology is through cross-dating of the identified point types. The whole points are types that have been dated to the Early Archaic (Kirk stemmed), Late Archaic (Lamoka), Early Woodland (Adena/Cresap stemmed), and Middle Woodland/Late Adena (Robbins) periods (Justice 1987, 82, 128, 184, 186). In addition, the hematite celt may be associated with the Adena culture, which generally is assigned to the Early Woodland period (Converse 1978, 32). Consequently, it appears that this ridgetop was utilized from the Early Archaic through the Middle Woodland period (ca. 8000 B.C.–A.D. 400).

Significantly, no artifacts suggestive of the Late Woodland or Late Prehistoric periods (ca. A.D. 400–1450) were recovered, yet a known Late Woodland/Late Prehistoric habitation site is located along the Hocking floodplain only about 500 m south of the Walker site (fig. 1.2). Although certainly upland sites were used by these later populations for similar economic purposes, they did not include the Walker site in their seasonal rounds.

## A Functional Reconstruction of the Walker Site

Several lines of evidence indicate that the Walker site served as a short-term camp for varied economic activities. Within a generalized model of hunter-gatherer mobility proposed by Binford (1980), the Walker site would represent a *location* for foraging and collecting groups. Binford described a location as a place where only resource procurement occurred, serving as a satellite site to residential base camps in a foraging settlement-subsistence system (9). This postulated function is based on several aspects of the artifact assemblage recovered, including the relatively low overall number and density of artifacts at the site. The test excavations yielded a total of only 297 artifacts. By contrast, the Late Archaic Bremen site yielded 2,725 lithic artifacts (Pecora and Burks, this volume). Second, the absence of other material residue is equally telling of site function. There was a complete absence of pit features and postmolds, both generally associated with any type of Ohio Valley residential base camp. Additionally, no ceramics were recovered despite the fact that the site chronologically spans periods when ceramics were commonly in use throughout the valley. This suggests that restricted economic activities were conducted at the site and that food preparation was limited. Collectively, these three factors that characterize the Walker artifact inventory—low numbers/densities of artifacts, lack of architectural or pit features, and limited variation of artifact types—parallels that from other small sites in upland zones that similarly are interpreted as resource procurement sites (Means 1999). Importantly, these procurement activities were probably short term. Groups of people may have climbed up to the site, procured food, fiber, or minerals, and left. There is limited access to water from the site, and although it is often difficult to determine the duration of occupation at these types of sites, the low number of artifacts is consistent with short-duration extraction sites.

The site's classification as a food extraction site does not preclude other activities from having occurred. Some people at the site may have been involved only in processing rather than procuring food. While others were out hunting or collecting, activities such as basketry, leather working, or the manufacture of stone or wooden tools may have taken place. The lithic tools and the presence of groundstones for processing plants and nuts suggest that a wide range of economic tasks were performed during different short-term occupation episodes, perhaps conducted by distinct age and gender groups.

## Implications for Future Research

The Walker site was the locus for the processing of hunted and gathered foods and materials procured by different indigenous populations between ca. 8000 B.C. and A.D. 400. The site was used for very short periods of time. It afforded access to forest species as well as views to the broad floodplain below. The site was used by foraging societies during the Archaic period and continued to be used as the valley population became increasingly sedentary through time. This speaks to the enormous continuity across generations in the transmission of information concerning valued upland procurement sites in the Hocking Valley.

These small, dispersed, nonhabitation sites are a critical component of the Archaic/Middle Woodland landscape, representing significant economic activities. Unfortunately, they are rarely excavated, and when they are their artifact assemblages are seldom published. As our models of these nomadic tribal systems become more detailed (Binford 1980; Adovasio et al. 2001; Abrams and Freter, chapter 12 in this volume) and our GIS technological abilities to map them across landscapes and time continue to improve (Stump et al., this volume), it is hoped that these small but critical sites will become the focus of renewed research.

# 5

# LATE ARCHAIC COMMUNITY AGGREGATION AND FEASTING IN THE HOCKING VALLEY

Marjorie Heyman, Elliot M. Abrams, and AnnCorinne Freter

THE LATE ARCHAIC PEOPLE OF THE HOCKING VALLEY lived in small, dispersed communities, each composed of between two and four families. They lived a nomadic life, moving seasonally from one ecological zone to another as economic and social needs required—a flexible settlement pattern exemplified by Late Archaic populations elsewhere in the Midwest, such as along the Wabash River (Winters 1969, 131). As population density within the valley increased during the Late Archaic period (Stump et al., this volume), movement became incrementally more restricted. Against this backdrop of gradually increasing population density and sedentism, organizational cultural changes were instituted, providing greater opportunities for formal negotiation and dialogue among and between kin groups. This chapter defines one such Late Archaic organizational change—periodic community aggregation mediated through feasting.

In the ethnographic and archaeological records, group aggregation is often correlated with variability in seasonal food access (Dietler and Hayden 2001b). The process of aggregating is seen as adaptive, enhancing the overall quality of life of the participants, specifically by offsetting some of the difficulties inherent in seasonal food resource fluctuations. This might include the direct sharing of food, the transmitting of information about foods, and the organizing of larger communal work groups to process foods needed for both fall and winter (e.g., gathering quantities of short-harvest-season nut species, or the smoking or salting of fish and meats). Much of the literature relating to seasonal tribal aggregations describes feasting as the primary mechanism that formalizes the communal practice and in the process creates greater tribal solidarity and integration (Parkinson 2002a).

Data necessary to address the question of incremental sociopolitical change during the Late Archaic period in the Hocking Valley have been limited by the lack of carefully excavated habitation sites. However, data relevant to this issue recently have been obtained from the terminal Late Archaic (ca. 1500 B.C.) component of the County Home site (33AT40), excavated as part of Ohio University's 1998 archaeological summer field school (figs. 1.2, 5.1, 5.2). The site was chosen for excavation for several reasons. In the 1970s archaeologists from the University of Michigan dug a 2 × 2 m test unit in the center of the floodplain knoll on which the site was built, recovering Woodland artifacts and encountering a hearth. Additionally, two Early Woodland (Adena) burial mounds are located approximately 0.5 km northeast of the site, and The Plains complex of sacred circles and burial mounds are located 1.7 km to the west-southwest (fig. 5.2). Finally, the specific area was scheduled to be bulldozed for the construction of a dog shelter; therefore, systematic archaeological survey and excavation of the site was undertaken to provide an accurate record of features and ecofactual and artifactual data before the site's destruction.

The County Home site is located near the Hocking River and Sunday Creek confluence, atop a slight topographic rise that slopes gently to the south and west. It is within the Hocking flood zone, but owing to its elevation on the knoll, experiences flooding only once every 50 years rather than every few years. Its proximity to the array of natural resources associated with the main river, a creek tributary, and a nearby salt lick make the location of this site perhaps optimal for a small Late Archaic community dependent on an economy based on hunting and gathering.

## Feasting

The aggregation of small nomadic communities is well documented in the ethnographic and archaeological record. Early Archaic bands, for example, assembled for large-scale bison hunting, most notably at the Olsen-Chubbuck site in Colorado (Wheat 1972). Based on research in the Tehuacan Valley, Mexico, MacNeish (1981) documented the presence of aggregations

FIG. 5.1. The County Home site (facing north). (Photo by Elliot M. Abrams.)

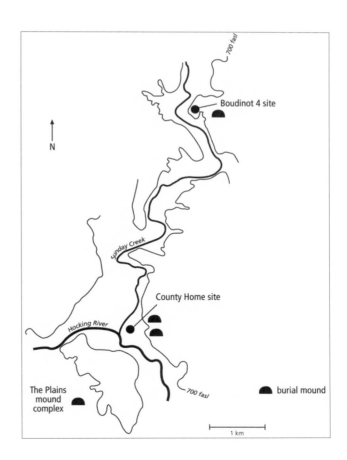

FIG. 5.2. Location of the County Home site

of small, nomadic groups on a seasonal basis. MacNeish introduced the concept of "macrobands" as aggregates of smaller "microbands" who not only periodically assembled but did so in the most productive environmental zone. Importantly, the loci for these macroband assemblies eventually became the places where more permanent tribal villages were later established (Winters 1969).

A consistent aspect of the formation of episodic macrobands is their participation in feasts, the "communal consumption" of food or drink or both (Dietler and Hayden 2001, 3). Its impact on social change transcends the physical process of consumption. Feasting is often the impetus for increased economic production, the arena for the enactment of collective rituals, and the means of creating central places for the conduct of a range of economic and other social acts not possible within the daily realm of life. Its significance is reflected in the contemporary feasting practiced by the Shawnees (Howard 1981).

There are many archaeological signatures of feasting, each specific to the scale of cultural complexity being investigated. Hayden (2001, 40) outlined the multiple identifiers of feasting, noting that one major material reflector of feasting is the unusual size of food preparation facilities. That is, cooking units would be expected to be significantly larger at those sites where feasts were held. The archaeological recovery and analysis of large features relating to the Late Archaic component of the County Home site identifies their role as cooking units indicative of feasting and, by inference, the episodic formation of aggregate communities.

## Field Excavation Methods

The excavation methods involved surveying the 100 × 60 m cornfield upon which the site is located. A pedestrian survey was conducted and surface artifact distribution was mapped to determine the possible area for houses and domestic activities. Based on topography and artifact distribution, a zone measuring 25 m by 25 m was designated for the placement of eight 2 × 2 m units for hand excavation using shovels and trowels (fig. 5.3). After the base of the plow zone was reached, twenty-three distinct cultural features were identified within seven units, based on form and interior contents. The soil within the 2 × 2 m test pits was incrementally shaved off, sieved through 0.64 cm (¼ in) screen mesh, and changes in feature shape, soil character, and artifact composition were noted. Soil from features was collected separately and floated to recover small associated artifacts and ecofacts.

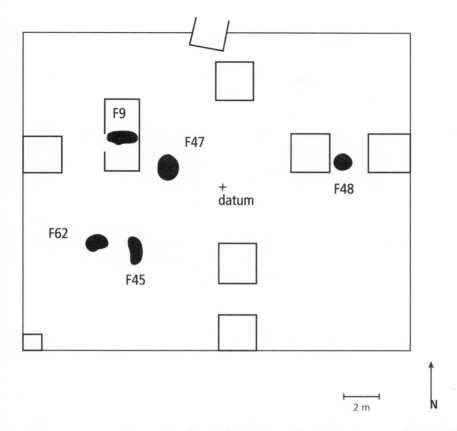

F9

F47

F48

+
datum

F62

F45

2 m

N

FIG. 5.3. Plan map of the largest cooking features at the County Home site

Sixteen 1 × 1 m units were dug, radiating from the residential zone center. These units yielded only one feature, allowing us to spatially define the residential zone within this hamlet. Finally, due to construction time constraints, a bulldozer stripped the plow zone from the 25 × 25 m domestic area, revealing the presence of additional post and pit features. A total of 78 features were recorded at the site.

As the size of pit features was measured, it became evident that five features were significantly larger than all others and exhibited unique archaeological signatures in both feature form and contents. These five unusual features and their implications are the focus of this chapter, while the other features of this chronologically multicomponent site serve as the basis for later Woodland demographic reconstructions (see Crowell et al., this volume). The following description of feature form, content, and volume is the basis for our inference that these features were communal roasting pits used during feasts at the County Home site toward the end of the Late Archaic period (Heyman 2000).

# The Archaeological Signature of Community Cooking Features

The five features (figs. 5.3 and 5.4) generally contain similar assemblages: chert debitage fragments, groundstone artifacts, rounded clay pieces, botanical ecofacts (grass and twigs, carbonized nut shell fragments and seeds), charcoal, coal (only found within some features), animal bone fragments, and fire-cracked pebbles and rocks. All contents were weighed and described for comparison. The presence or absence of coal, abundance of clay fragments, type of faunal and floral remains, and lithic fragment content and provenience were noted. Since these features are the core data for inferring feasting, the artifact inventory for each feature is presented (table 5.1). Four chert types—Brush Creek, Upper Mercer, Zaleski, and Flint Ridge/Vanport—were located as secondary deposit within all five features. Table 5.2 lists the weights for each of these chert types per feature.

Fire-cracked rock (FCR) was usually found lining the edges of the features, or in the case of feature 47, located immediately adjacent to the wood charcoal lens. These rocks are generally reddish, subangular, and occasionally encrusted with small bits of charcoal. In all cases, fire-cracked rocks are micaceous sandstone, found abundantly in nearby outcrops. A few pieces of FCR are rounded, composed of quartzite (a rock type much harder than micaceous sandstone), with some surficial scratches. Reddish, rounded granitic cobbles also were recovered from features 47 and 48. It is possible that these were used as both groundstones and heating rock elements. Heating rock elements, in addition to being placed in the features directly, often were placed in the interior cavity of an animal to aid in the cooking process (Wandsnider 1997).

Groundstone also was recovered from all five features at the site. These are reddish, rounded, occasionally broken granitic or quartzite cobbles (ranging up to 84 mm in length). Since granite is a material that does not outcrop within the immediate vicinity of Athens, it is likely that these were recovered already worn from stream beds. Though not as hard as granite, quartzite is significantly harder than micaceous sandstone, and therefore rounded quartzite cobbles could have been recovered from streambeds or been slowly reworked into the rounded cobbles during grinding. Faint parallel lines are observed on the surface of some (but not all) of these, consistent with light grinding stone wear patterns. Others were apparently used as rock heating elements during cooking. It is probable that some of the larger cobbles, likely collected from the nearby riverbeds, may have doubled as both grinding stones and heating elements.

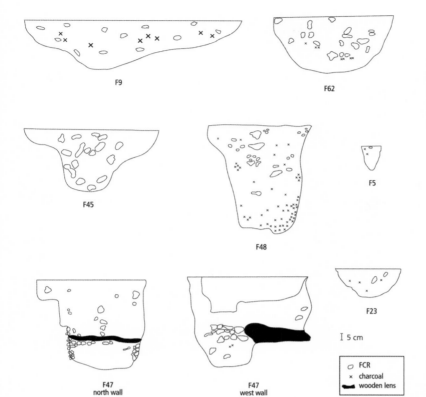

FIG. 5.4. Profile of the five features in this study, in contrast to other County Home site features

F9

F62

F45

F48

F5

F47
north wall

F47
west wall

F23

I 5 cm

- FCR
× charcoal
▬ wooden lens

## Table 5.1. Artifact Inventory from the County Home Site

| Feature | F9 | F45 | F47 | F48 | F62 |
|---|---|---|---|---|---|
| Artifact | Weight[a] | Weight | Weight | Weight | Weight |
| Sorted material | 7,027.3 | 1,003.8 | 2,270.0 | 3,016.3 | 1,833.6 |
| Fire-cracked rock | 4,191.1 | 2,205.8 | 3,591.4 | 2,101.9 | 1,627.4 |
| Bone | 25.8 | 4.4 | 5.1 | 14.6 | 3.9 |
| Botanicals | 5.4 | 0.4 | 0.2 | 0.1 | 0.3 |
| Ceramic pellets | 41.6 | 8.3 | 44.9 | 54.4 | 18.2 |
| Charcoal | 90.7 | 5.8 | 5,679.3 | 366.4 | 1,606.6 |
| Chert | 223.0 | 80.4 | 329.3 | 377.0 | 45.8 |
| Coal | 1.6 | 2.0 | 8.4 | — | 15.3 |
| Groundstone | 420.1 (13)[b] | 166.2 (1) | 680.6 (2) | 944.1 (1) | 31.7 (2) |

[a]Weights are given in grams.
[b]Numbers in parentheses represent count.

## Table 5.2. Chipped-Stone Inventory from the County Home Site

**Feature 9**

| Artifact | BC | FR | UM | Z |
|---|---|---|---|---|
| Cores | — | — | — | — |
| Primary flakes | 4.4 (8)[a] | — | 20.6 (2) | — |
| Secondary flakes | 52.6 (42) | 17.3 (14) | 25.5 (17) | 6.3 (6) |
| Debitage | 23.4 (320) | 2.7 (71) | 2.8 (79) | 0.7 (14+) |
| Points | — | — | 4.4 (2) | — |
| Unifaces | 19.2 (2) | — | 10.8 (1) | 51.6 (1) |

**Feature 45**

| Artifact | BC | FR | UM | Z |
|---|---|---|---|---|
| Cores | — | — | — | — |
| Primary flakes | — | — | — | 23 (3) |
| Secondary flakes | 17.7 (4) | 1.1 (1) | — | 8.5 (3) |
| Debitage | 6.0 (105) | 0.5 (29) | 3.1 (36) | 0.3 (9) |
| Points | — | — | — | — |
| Unifaces | 20.1 (1) | — | — | — |

**Feature 47**

| Artifact | BC | FR | UM | Z |
|---|---|---|---|---|
| Cores | 144.4 (2) | — | — | — |
| Primary flakes | 79.1 (7) | 2.2 (1) | 19.8 (1) | 1.1 (1) |
| Secondary flakes | 2.4 (3) | 3.1 (2) | 0.9 (1) | 4.2 (3) |
| Debitage | 11.5 (112) | 1.2 (1) | 3.3 (4) | 0.5 (16) |
| Points | — | — | — | — |
| Unifaces | 9.5 (1) | — | — | — |

**Feature 48**

| Artifact | BC | FR | UM | Z |
|---|---|---|---|---|
| Cores | — | — | 318.6 (1) | — |
| Primary flakes | — | — | — | — |
| Secondary flakes | 3.1 (5) | 14.7 (2) | 2.2 (1) | — |
| Debitage | 33.1 (38) | 1.2 (17) | 3.6 (14) | 0.5 (5) |
| Points | — | — | — | — |
| Unifaces | — | — | — | — |

**Feature 62**

| Artifact | BC | FR | UM | Z |
|---|---|---|---|---|
| Cores | — | — | — | 12.7 (1) |
| Primary flakes | — | — | — | — |
| Secondary flakes | 9.9 (3) | — | 2.2 (1) | — |
| Debitage | 12.7 (1) | 0.5 (1) | 1.2 (1) | — |
| Points | — | — | — | — |
| Unifaces | — | — | — | — |

Key: BC = Brush Creek; FR = Flint Ridge; UM = Upper Mercer; Z = Zaleski.

[a]Numbers represent weight in grams. Numbers in parentheses represent count.

Numerous round, yellow to reddish-brown, baked clay pellets were observed within all five features. These clay pellets, ranging between 0.25 to 1.5 cm in diameter, are untempered, indicating that they are not fragmented remains of ceramic vessels but instead served another function. As will be discussed later, it is possible that small game were coated with a clay slurry and then baked in a roasting pit. The clay would harden, effectively sealing in nutrients and moisture. At times, fire-cracked rocks may have been placed adjacent to the clay-covered game to evenly distribute the heat from the fire. One fire-cracked rock was recovered with clay adhering to its surface from the interior of feature 47, a roasting pit, further supporting this reconstruction.

Bird, mammal, and possibly fish bone fragments are found within all five features. Most of the recovered bone fragments are calcined, chalky white, and soft, while other bone material is dark gray and has retained its original bony structural framework, including haversian systems and external striations of tendenous attachments. Sutton and Arkush (1998) state that calcined bone has generally been directly exposed to high heat, whereas darker-color bone generally has been cooked for shorter periods and has not come in contact with a direct heat source. While no positive species identification has been made of the bones, several have been identified as bird (thin, hollow long bones), mammal (bones with vesicular appearance; possibly white-tailed deer in two cases), and possibly fish (small, thin vertebrate disks) remains. No large bone fragments were preserved within the five pit features; however, the reconstructed diameter of some of the long bones suggest that they are from larger mammals. Based on bone fragment size, it is likely that many are from smaller mammals such as rabbit or squirrel.

Charred nutshell fragments, possibly hickory, are present in features 47, 48, and 62. Other botanical remains are preserved within all features, generally comprising small seed hulls that are frequently carbonized. No positive species identification has been made to date, but the diverse set of food remains confirms that extensive exploitation of resources, typical of the Late Archaic, occurred at the site; further, the total assemblage of attributes associated with these features clearly attests to their function as large cooking units for an array of foods including large animals.

One conspicuous attribute of the five features is their comparatively large absolute volume. Matching their interior measurements with volumetric formulae for various shapes (Heyman 2000), the interior volume for these features is calculable (table 5.3). The mean volume of the features is 0.421 m³. In contrast, the mean volume of cooking units from another Late Archaic/ Early Woodland hamlet in the Sunday Creek tributary, the Boudinot 4 site (33AT521—see figs. 1.2, 5.2; Abrams 1989b), was 0.024 m³. Effectively, the

| Table 5.3. Dimensions and Volumes of Features from the County Home Site | | |
|---|---|---|
| Feature | Dimensions (l × w × d) | Volume (m³) |
| F9 | 1.85 m × 90 cm × 50 cm | 0.421 |
| F45 | 2.0 m × 1.1 m × 52 cm | 0.363 |
| F47 | 96 cm × 86 cm × 75 cm | 0.418 |
| F48 | 85 cm × 83 cm × 97 cm | 0.552 |
| F62 | 1.0 m × 95 cm × 47 cm | 0.350 |

five Late Archaic cooking units from the County Home site were 15 to 20 times the size of those built at a comparable site some 4.6 km up-tributary from the County Home site. Thus the comparative volumes strengthen the argument that not only were these five features used for cooking but that they were used in the preparation of quantities of food beyond the ordinary level of consumption.

## The Reconstruction of Food Preparation Methods

Although all five are identified empirically as cooking or roasting features, the morphology of the roasting pits indicate differences in cooking function. The presence of side shelves in two of the features (45 and 47; see fig. 5.3) suggests a function comparable to the upper shelf in a barbeque grill, as it effectively removed the meat or plant material from direct heat, thereby allowing for slower cooking over an extended time.

In feature 47 burned tree branches were found near the base of the pit, overlying fire-cracked rocks. The presence of fire-cracked rocks both below and above the tree limbs indicates that the rocks were used to distribute heat evenly over the area of the pit. It is unclear whether the rocks were heated first, to ignite the fuel wood, or heated after the meat had been added. However, historical accounts of the Plains Indians (Wandsnider 1997) describe them cooking bison by placing heated rocks in the base of a roasting pit, overlaying these with green boughs, and covering the wood with more hot rocks. Slabs of bison meat were then placed on the rocks, sprinkled with water, and again overlain with green tree boughs. This was repeated until the hole was filled. The animal's hide was placed over the filled hole and covered with gravel, and then a fire was built and kept burning for up to twenty-four hours. By sealing the pit, moisture was retained during cooking, and the cooking time was extended. Kintz (1990) describes a similar technique for the Yucatec Mayas, wherein a larger animal is butchered, buried in a deep pit, and slowly roasted over an extended time.

Both archaeological and ethnographic analogs provide examples of clay being used to coat small hunted game or shelled animals prior to being baked, effectively sealing in the moisture and nutrients that would otherwise be lost in the cooking process. For example, in present-day China, duck is cooked by covering the bird with lily pads, then coating it with a clay slurry. A hammer is used to break the hardened clay coating. Ozker (1982) observed a similar phenomenon at the Early Woodland Schultz site in the Saginaw Valley, whereby a single layer of mussels were steamed by covering them with a clay slurry and placing them under rocks that were then heated with fire. Afterward, the baked clay jacket had to be broken to recover the cooked mussels. Similarly, at the County Home site, the presence of clay pellets interspersed with fire-cracked rock and charcoal flecks suggests that a comparable cooking technique was utilized by this community. A few clay pellets retained charcoal smudges on their surfaces. Additionally, a few pieces were not reddish, as would be expected in an oxidizing environment, but instead were whitish-gray, a color that results when firing occurs in a reducing environment. Covering a clay-slipped game animal with rock, dirt, and leaves may have locally created reducing conditions within the larger cooking environment.

Consequently, based on both empirical data and analogs, cooking of large portions of meat in these Late Archaic County Home site features began with preparing the meat. This involved placing small rocks inside or against the meat and then wrapping the meat in leaves and clay. Layers of rocks and fuelwood were placed at the base of the cooking units. The meat was then placed on this layer and covered with another layer of fuelwood and rocks. This was repeated as desired and the entire unit was covered.

According to Purdue (1986), the average deer in Late Archaic and early Early Woodland periods was smaller than those living today. He analyzed deer size changes from Archaic through the Historic period using data from eighteen archaeological sites in central Illinois. Changes in body weight and sex determinations were made by examining and measuring changes in the size of the deer astragalus (ankle bone). These data indicate that male deer body weight was up to 24% less, and female deer size up to 15% less, in the Middle and Late Archaic than during the Woodland and later periods, likely due in part to a complete complement of top predators in the ecosystem during this time period. With this as a guide, the typical yield per deer can be estimated.

Using an average deer size of 125 lbs. (modern white-tailed deer range between 100 and 180 lbs.), the deer, once dressed and dismembered, would contain approximately 80 lbs. of consumable meat as a reasonable estimate (E. White, pers. comm., 2000; cf. Jefferies et al. 1996, 22). This amount can be cooked in an oven hearth of approximately 0.3 m³ (an estimate consistent with the volumes of the cooking features under study), which is sufficiently large to accommodate rocks, wood, leaves, or other cooking materials and allows space for steam and smoke to develop. Drying the meat or cooking it over an open fire on a spit would be done over a wider, shallower hearth of smaller volume.

## Feature Chronology

Chronometric dates for the five cooking features indicate a terminal Late Archaic/early Early Woodland age (see table 5.4). A Late Archaic Trimble point, Middle Woodland Steuben expanded stem point, and Woodland cordmarked potsherd were recovered from feature 9, indicating continuous use of the site as it evolved from a temporary campsite to a more sedentary hamlet (Crowell et al., this volume). It also indicates the continued use of large cooking features beyond the transitional Late Archaic/Early Woodland period.

## Discussion

As late as the 1980s, archaeologists knew very little about the Late Archaic societies in the Hocking Valley (J. Murphy 1989, 345–46). It was known that the Late Archaic was characterized by small communities of nomadic hunters and gatherers who exploited a wide range of resources and landscapes, preferring terraces as zones for habitation sites (Shane and Murphy 1967; J. Murphy 1989). This is typical of Archaic groups in the Midwest (Farnsworth and Emerson 1986). However, it was recognized (J. Murphy 1989, 122; D. Anderson 2002) that some of the antecedents to institutions characterizing tribal society would be found in the Late Archaic period. The data and analysis in this chapter confirm that statement, providing a specific archaeological signature for one such institution.

An observation from the present research on cooking features from the County Home site is that Late Archaic base camps may yield different archaeological remains based on seasonality of occupation and proximity to

Table 5.4. Radiocarbon Dating of Large Cooking Features
        from the County Home Site

| Beta Lab Number | Feature | RCYBP | Calibrated Age[a] B.C. | Cal. Intercept B.C. |
|---|---|---|---|---|
| 141234 | F45 | 3080 ± 80 | 1518–1126 | 1334 |
| 136254 | F47 | 3070 ± 60 | 1488–1130 | 1338 |
| 139636 | F48 | 2820 ± 70 | 1210–826 | 956 |
| 141235 | F62 | 3220 ± 70 | 1682–1320 | 1500 |
| 143697 | F9 | 2960 ± 40 | 1368–1019 | 1177 |

[a]The 2-sigma range, based on Stuiver et al. 1998.

riverine resources. We have argued that feasting took place at a base camp located directly on the floodplain at the confluence of the Hocking River and Sunday Creek, perhaps one of the best locations for resource acquisition. For the County Home inhabitants, the ecological setting was especially appealing since the settlement is on a small rise above the floodplain, offering some protection from periodic flooding but still conveniently close to water. It is close to annually renewable floodplain plant life (including wild seed-bearing plants) and forests that provided nuts such as hickory. The preponderance of mast trees, including hickory and acorn, and a nearby salt lick attracted mammals that could be easily hunted. The presence of the large cooking features suggests that feasting, in addition to other possible communal activities, took place differentially (but not exclusively) at those sites in prime locations—a hypothesis for future testing.

Data from the Hocking Valley indicate that institutions often associated with tribes, such as mound construction and horticulture, were established during the first millennium b.c. (Crowell et al., this volume). The research in this chapter indicates that the creation of seasonal communities of macro-bands, or composite groups, occurred by 1500 b.c., supporting the argument that greater degrees of sedentism occurred before other cultural patterns associated with tribal structure (Brown 1985, 1986).

By 1500 b.c., population in the valley had increased, demonstrating a conspicuous preference for habitation on the terrace and floodplain zones (Stump et al., this volume). Seasonal movement by local communities was more restricted and sites in the best locations (such as the County Home site) were likely occupied for longer periods of time each year. Significantly, the pollen profiles from areas adjacent to the Hocking Valley (Shane et al. 2001; fig. 1.7, this volume) indicate a considerable decline in rainfall ca. 1500 b.c. This new condition of lower rainfall would have affected the normal fluctuations of annual resource productivity. Collectively, these factors may have made food access more difficult, a situation that might have encouraged greater communication and negotiation among local communities. It is within this context that we find the large cooking pits being built and the inferred feasting taking place. Moving beyond these possible environmental changes, there is considerable debate about the sociopolitical context of feasting and communal aggregation. Stothers, Abel, and Schneider (2001) suggest that Archaic communities assembled for competitive economic exchange in the context of debt relations, while Mensforth (2001) offers evidence of Late Archaic intercommunity violence in the Green River Valley, Kentucky, which influenced local community interaction and integration.

Unfortunately, Late Archaic skeletal data from the Hocking Valley are virtually nonexistent; thus we currently lack the data to address the question of community violence. Similarly, we have no way of directly testing the hypothesis of competition and unbalanced debt among Late Archaic communities, although the data indicate that local communities established base camps in loci of differential resource access in the Hocking Valley. Ethnographic analogues illustrating competitive feasting among Northwest Coast societies (Hayden 1990) and the precontact Kayapos of Brazil (Werner 1990) are matched by noncompetitive feasting by Algonquian hunters who would sometimes sponsor a feast for the village or freely give away their kill, gaining "a vanity" from the act (White 1991, 99). Ultimately, competition and cooperation are two sides of the same coin, but what is clear is that the data from the Hocking Valley indicate a greater degree and more formalized type of interaction among local communities beginning ca. 1500 B.C. than was experienced by previous generations.

The activities that may have taken place during these communal gatherings included trading, sharing information, resolving intercommunity conflicts, or seeking mates; in effect, the same stimuli for later communal feasting associated with mound construction. One intriguing possibility is that the different microbands typically met before migration to the winter camps to hunt deer and preserve it by salting and smoking it within the large roasting pits. It is likely that no single group, especially at this time period, controlled access to salt resources, but that various microbands met intermittently at a common area, probably in the early fall, when deer were at their greatest weight, to engage in the time-consuming process of preserving meat for later consumption during the winter. These gatherings were ideal settings for the larger macroband to exchange stories and individual histories, obtain mates within the larger group, visit with distant kin, exchange trade items, and reinforce the sense of a larger community identity with shared ideologies, patterns exemplified by the Shoshone Paiutes (Steward 1938). Marriage between members of different communities helped to spatially expand kinship ties that would continue to strengthen group cohesiveness. While there, the larger macroband engaged in communal meals prepared at the site, with the cooking of large quantities of food in the roasting pits. The roasting pits are large enough to cook meat for at least 60 people over the course of several days, or more if several roasting pits were being used at the same time.

Regardless of causality, from the perspective of processual historical theory we note that one of the prime components of cultural evolution is that of contingency—that instituted behaviors emerge only after preconditions have been established. While the notion of leadership in a small nomadic community may have been muted by various factors, the context for the expression of greater leadership may have existed during the aggregation of those small communities. Organizational requirements, scheduling, and food procurement and preparation may have all prompted a greater assumption of leadership. Accordingly, the skills demanded of a more formalized tribal leader, as well as the cultural or social psychological acceptance of such a leader, began in the Late Archaic period, supporting the position that feasting may be central to the tribal evolutionary process (Dietler and Hayden 2001a, 16).

## Implications

Tribal formation is a protracted and incremental process. In the history of various societies, episodic and seasonal aggregation by small groups forming macrobands was evident. The formation of such larger communities, however, is often difficult to observe archaeologically. The identification of possible feasting pits and the analysis of their form, content, chronology, and location may be our best archaeological means in the Midwest of identifying macroband formation. Future analyses of Late Archaic habitation sites should further test and refine the implications offered here regarding the role of feasting and community aggregation in the establishment of larger tribal communities.

# 6

# WOODLAND COMMUNITIES IN THE HOCKING VALLEY

David Crowell, Elliot M. Abrams, AnnCorinne Freter, and James Lein

THE FIRST MILLENNIUM B.C. WAS A TIME of great change within the Hocking Valley. Local communities of seasonally nomadic hunters and gatherers were establishing longer-term base camps on the terraces and floodplains of the main stem of the river and its tributaries ca. 1500 B.C. These same communities were manufacturing crude pottery to expand the uses of nuts and wild seeds (Pecora and Burks, this volume). In addition, the periodic aggregation of these typically dispersed small bands into larger temporary communities, such as at the Late Archaic component of the County Home site (Heyman, Abrams, and Freter, this volume), is evidenced at this time.

What followed during the first millennium B.C. was the formation of increasingly sedentary communities who eventually converted wild seeds into garden grown domesticates and built earthen burial mounds predominantly on ridgetops overlooking the community hamlet. These changes in the Hocking Valley were part of broader regional change in Midwest riverine societies, including "the appearance of permanent habitations, food storage, domestication of plants, multiregional exchange of valuables, cemeteries, intragroup ranking of individuals, and the elaboration of art in a social context" (Brown 1985, 201).

Few habitation sites have been intensively surveyed and excavated in the Hocking Valley; consequently there are limited direct data delineating these significant changes. Two sites, however, have yielded the data on which we reconstruct this major transition in ecological and social relations within the Hocking Valley. These two sites—the Boudinot 4 site (33AT521) and the Woodland component of the County Home site (33AT40; figs. 1.2, 5.1, 5.2, 6.1)—collectively provide the majority of data for this chapter. Each, however, provides different types of data: the Boudinot 4 site has yielded data that better address the issues of settlement and gardening while data from the County Home site more directly speak to Woodland community demography.

FIG. 6.1. The Boudinot 4 site (facing west). The site is on the rise behind the small center tree. (Photo by Elliot M. Abrams.)

## The Chronology of the County Home and Boudinot 4 Sites

The primary technique used to date both the County Home and the Boudinot 4 sites was radiocarbon assays funded by the John Baker Foundation of Ohio University (see tables 6.1 and 6.2). These radiometric dates indicate a significant occupation span for both sites, minimally from the Late Archaic through the onset of the Middle Woodland period. Certainly these sites overlap in terms of general period of occupation, although the County Home site was occupied two or three centuries longer than the

Table 6.1. Radiocarbon Dates from the County Home Site

| Beta Analytic No. | Feature | RCYBP | Calibrated Date[a] | Cal. Intercept |
|---|---|---|---|---|
| 169747 | 30 | 3340 ± 70 | 1861 B.C.–1449 B.C. | 1673 B.C. |
| 169749 | 54 | 1810 ± 80 | A.D. 28–414 | A.D. 236 |
| 169751 | 68 | 3970 ± 90 | 2859 B.C.–2201 B.C. | 2470 B.C. |
| 178823 | 40 | 3250 ± 40 | 1676 B.C.–1430 B.C. | 1519 B.C. |

[a]The 2-sigma range, based on Stuiver et al. 1998.

Table 6.2. Radiocarbon Dates from the Boudinot 4 Site

| Beta Analytic No. | Feature | RCYBP | Calibrated Date[a] | Cal. Intercept |
|---|---|---|---|---|
| 27478 | 16 | 2900 ± 60 | 1291 B.C.–916 B.C. | 1104 B.C. |
| 26743 | 14 | 2610 ± 80 | 911 B.C.–519 B.C. | 799 B.C. |
| 27479 | 11 | 2370 ± 90 | 787 B.C.–204 B.C. | 403 B.C. |
| 26752 | 5B | 2070 ± 60 | 348 B.C.–A.D. 65 | 81 B.C. |

[a]The 2-sigma range, based on Stuiver et al. 1998.

Boudinot 4 site. Additional evidence for Late Archaic occupation at the County Home site comes from the previously discussed radiocarbon date array from the site's five large roasting features (Heyman, Abrams, and Freter, this volume, table 5.4).

Beyond radiocarbon dating, Middle Woodland occupation of the County Home site is confirmed by artifactual evidence. The first testing of the site, by archaeologists at the University of Michigan, revealed a feature that was assessed as Middle Woodland (according to the Ohio Archaeological Inventory). In addition, two obsidian flakes (fig. 6.2) were recovered in 1998 during the surface survey of the site, and this nonlocal raw material is associated with the Hopewell Interaction Sphere of the Middle Woodland period (Seeman 1979).

## The Demography of an Early/Middle Woodland Hamlet

An increase in population density has long been cited as a primary and independent factor prompting societal change (Boserup 1965). Despite the importance of monitoring changing population density within regions, there have been few attempts to reconstruct the demographic scale of Woodland communities. However, data from the Boudinot 4 site can be used to

generate such a demographic model. The survey of the Boudinot 4 site yielded artifact distributions that identified the natural rise on the terrace as the main area of habitation, measuring about 20 × 20 m (fig. 6.3; Abrams 1989b). Excavation of this habitation area revealed 19 subsurface features, which were identified primarily as cooking units, generic pits, and architectural posts. Only three postholes were exposed; thus no discernable pattern of housing was detected. Based solely on the limited areal extent of features on the rise, it was estimated that a community of 10 to 20 people inhabited the site (Abrams 1989b).

To more solidly reconstruct the population size of a community, several field and analytic steps must be taken: (1) the site must be identified by archaeological data as a habitation site, (2) chronometric samples must confirm placement in time, (3) the site must yield a significant number of architectural features, such as posts from houses, (4) these features must be confirmed as posts, and (5) spatial analysis must define the outlines of houses or, minimally, the clusters of posts. Once all those steps have been taken, a probable number or range of people per house can be multiplied by the number of houses determined to have been simultaneously occupied at the site. The number of people per house is drawn from the ethnographic or ethnohistoric record, which generally will yield an estimate of the *range* of community size. Fortunately, the data from the County Home site satisfy these requirements.

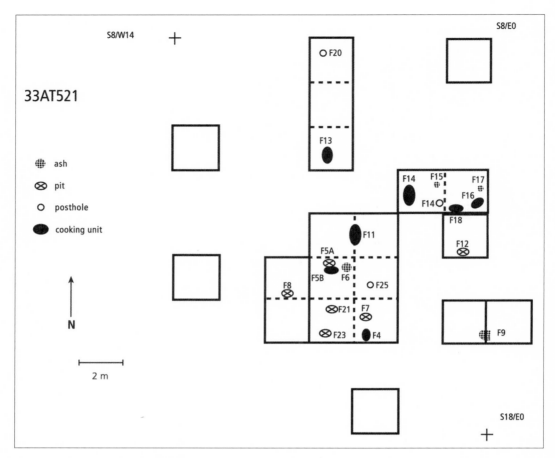

FIG. 6.3. Plan map of the excavations at the Boudinot 4 site

A key element of the excavation of the County Home site was the mechanical stripping of the plow zone over the 25 × 25 m habitation area, defined through a systematic transect survey and test excavations. A total of 78 features were recovered (fig. 6.4). One of these was a midden and five were very large cooking units (these were the analytic focus of chapter 5). The remaining 72 pit features were recorded in terms of location, dimensions, shape, and interior contents. The attributes of shape and dimension alone served as the bases for generating four classes of pit features: (1) circular, inward-slanted sides, tapered to rounded bottom; (2) basin shaped, straight to inward-slanted sides, flat bottom; (3) straight sides, flat bottom; and (4) ovate, shallow to deep, irregular flat to basin-shaped bottom.

Interior contents were examined to refine this feature typology. Features designated in the fourth category consistently contained fire-cracked rock, charcoal, coal, and, in some cases, animal bone, suggesting that broader pit features with ovate openings functioned as hearths. Features in the second and third categories contained few cultural materials beyond small amounts of lithics as secondary deposition. For these features, content was less informative than shape and size, both of which suggested a functional designation of generic pit, perhaps used in part for storage or refuse disposal.

The first category of features contained charcoal but little else. On occasion, rocks were found along the edge of the feature. These 29 features are identified as postmolds, the remnants of domestic architecture (fig. 6.5). The rocks seem to be chinking used to enhance stability within the larger hole dug for the post. The charcoal remnant at the base of the wooden post is interpreted as the result of intentional charring. This technique is still used by farmers in Athens County today to strengthen wood posts and reduce the wood's susceptibility to weathering and decomposition.

The next step in defining population size involved mapping the 29 postmold features at the site (fig. 6.5). Although the emergence of nicely circular

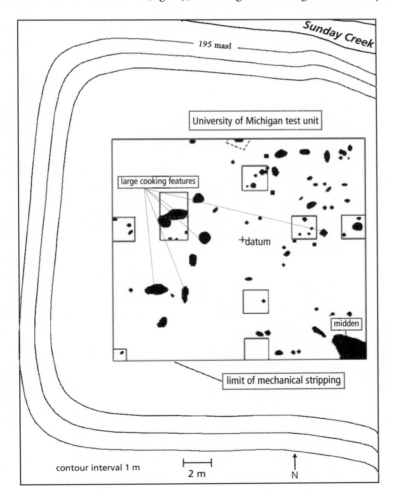

FIG. 6.4. Plan map of all features at the County Home site

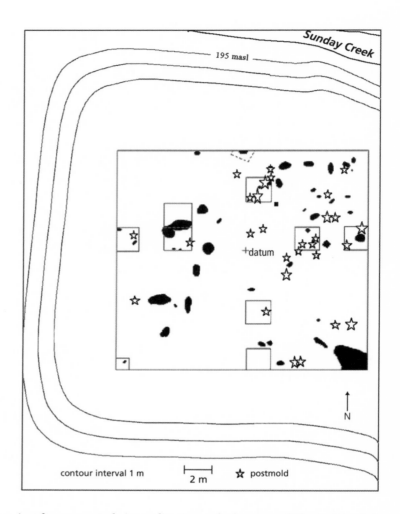

FIG. 6.5. County Home postmolds

contour interval 1 m    2 m    ☆ postmold

outlines is often expected, in reality it rarely happens (Clay 1986, 584). Thus, a statistical analysis was conducted on the spatial distribution of the posts in order to generate *domestic architectural clusters*. A point pattern analysis was deemed the most appropriate method to discern clustering. This was done by establishing a 5 × 5 cm grid over the feature distribution mapping. This created a grid of 71 rows and 79 columns. The next step involved identifying those cells that contained posts. These data were recorded and entered into the IDRISI software package, which creates a digital representation of the distribution of postmolds. A statistically based quadrat analysis was then performed. The distribution of postmolds deviated significantly from randomness, indicating that spatially clustered alignments of posts once existed at the hamlet (see Crowell 2002 for fuller statistical details).

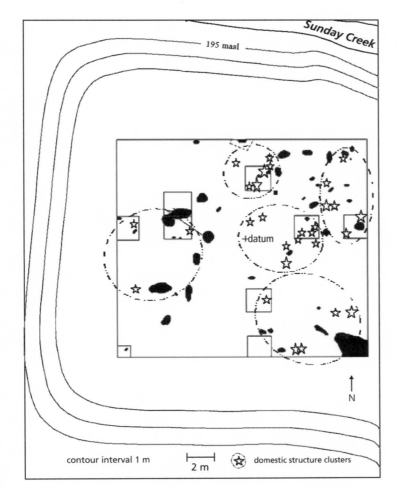

FIG. 6.6. County Home architectural clusters

Another statistical step required identifying the actual domestic structure clusters at the site. This was done using the IDRISI software and consisted of a pattern analysis that "uses variability in a 3 × 3 pixel window or a 5 × 5 or 7 × 7 octagonal pixel window to assess several different measures and to show relations between each window" (IDRISI v. 2.00.000, 1987–1997, Clark University). In this case, the 5 × 5 octagonal pixel window was chosen as the operating template and an image was produced that showed affiliations between postmolds. The resulting image of this patterning was integrated into the base map of the site, thus identifying the clusters of domestic architecture (fig. 6.6).

It must be remembered that the site was occupied for many centuries and thus these clusters represent discrete but not absolute entities with fixed boundaries. In addition, clusters may represent posts not affiliated with housing. For example, the cluster located on the western periphery of the site—spatially separate from the other domestic structure clusters and closely associated with several large roasting features—may represent the remnants of racks used in drying and butchering game.

A final step in this method is estimating the number of people per house. The size of each domestic cluster at the site ranged between 3 × 4 m and 6 × 6 m. Although speculative, this size suggests that each house may have been occupied by from five to seven people. With five such houses, we arrive at a normative maximal population of 25 to 35 for this Middle Woodland hamlet.

## Residential Settlement Patterns

Whereas data from the County Home site provided the basis for estimating community size at its latest occupation, research at that site did not extend far beyond the confines of the habitation area. In contrast, research on the Boudinot family farm involved excavation of the Boudinot 4 site as well as a survey of the surrounding 6 ha area (Abrams 1989b, 1992b). The results of prior surveys on the Boudinot property were included in our reconstruction of residential mobility and sedentism between 1000 B.C. and 200 B.C. in the region.

The Boudinot property was surveyed in the summer of 1986 and 1988 by the Ohio University field school directed by Abrams, confirming the presence of sites identified on the Ohio Archaeological Inventory forms and testing areas between known sites. Shovel testing and larger-scale excavation of this area confirmed the presence of several small habitation sites—including the Boudinot 4 site—surrounding a small burial mound (fig. 6.7). The residential pattern revealed by this research indicates that a small community inhabited one of the sites on a seasonal basis, perhaps the fall and spring. Parts of the summer may see the population living on the floodplain. Rockshelters in the ridges east of the site may have been occupied during the harshest winter months, although no rockshelters have specifically been excavated to test this hypothesis. The terrace area was then reoccupied by the same group at either the same site or at a nearby site within what might be called the *homestead* of that community.

Here the homestead is defined as the land repeatedly used for residential purposes and adjacent resource procurement by a *local community* over multiple generations with reoccupation reinforcing a priori access if not some form of ownership. In effect the homestead is that centripetal core of

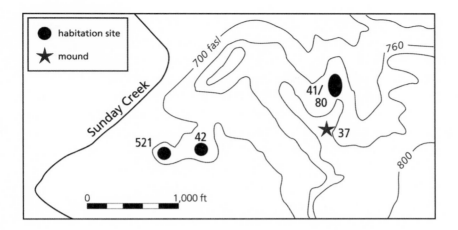

FIG. 6.7. Map of the Boudinot sites, showing OAI designations (numbers accompanying symbols).

a local community's "territory" used directly for housing and resource acquisition; by definition, it transcends the area of any single habitation site. Hypothetically, a local community of, say, 18 people occupied the Boudinot 4 site in 800 B.C., abandoning the site in the winter and reoccupying the site in the spring. In other years, they might return instead to rebuild the Boudinot 2 (33AT42) habitation site (fig. 6.7).

One of the key aspects to settlement in the Early Woodland Period in the Hocking Valley is that sites with access to a wide range of food resources during the Late Archaic period continued as loci for increasingly settled seasonal camps or hamlets. This is evidenced at the County Home site, Boudinot 4 site, site 33FA1640, the Hope site, the Chauncey site, and the Children's Home site (Abrams 1989b, 1992b; Shane and Murphy 1967; J. Murphy 1989; Pecora and Burks, this volume). In fact, the majority of Late Archaic sites continued to be occupied during the Early Woodland period. Unfortunately, these sites also are in prime locations for construction and agriculture and these transforms make it difficult to separate the components and thus the behavioral patterns that distinguished these two periods.

The continued occupation of these sites reinforces the observation by Stump et al. (this volume) that terraces and floodplains remained the focus of habitation and resource exploitation during the Early Woodland period. Although food and raw materials were strategic resources for hunting-gathering populations, the terrace zone itself was one of the most crucial yet limited resources in the Hocking Valley since they were elevated above the impact of seasonal flooding and located between two or more major sets of resources. Situated between the floodplain and upland zones, the terrace provided access to wild and garden foods for six or more months of the year. Proximity to creeks offered a steady flow of water and in many cases access to salt. Salt licks are located in Sunday Creek directly north of the County Home site and in the small seasonal creek just north of the Boudinot 4 site. Natural licks provide salt for consumption by both humans and animals such as white-tailed deer, and the salt can also be used to preserve foods. The salt curing of fish and other meat during the fall may have been essential for survival during the winter.

Less than 5% of the Hocking Valley is composed of elevated floodplain and terrace zones (Abrams and Freter, chapter 1 in this volume), and some of these are too narrow for long-term habitation. In addition, upward of 94% of these zones are along the main stem of the Hocking River, where they are dissected by seasonal creeks, further reducing their habitability. As local communities increasingly resided for longer periods on the terraces, we speculate that there was a heightened scale of environmental modification of this zone. In some respects, one could describe the increased modification of the terrace, being the center of a homestead, as a process of terrace domestication. Further, as these desired terrace zones increasingly were settled for longer habitation by some groups, other groups may have been prompted to become increasingly sedentary and territorial, given their perception of the growing scarcity of prime habitation space.

## Burial Mounds and Homesteads

The Boudinot Mound (33AT37) was located at the center of the distribution of the Boudinot residential sites (figs. 6.7, 6.8). Several comparable site clusters with associated mounds have been identified in the Hocking Valley (Abrams 1992b; J. Murphy 1989) and the Muskingum Valley (Carskadden and Morton 1997). In the Hocking Valley there are hundreds of small, conical earthen mounds, usually built on ridgetops. Saxe (1970) and Charles and Buikstra (1983) proposed that the burial mounds symbolically linked homestead territories with specific local communities and the Woodland community settlement pattern in the Hocking Valley supports this model.

These mounds were relatively easy to build and demanded little labor. The quantification of a representative mound sample yielded labor expenditures from six to ninety-six person-days (Abrams and LeRouge 2004). The Boudinot Mound required an estimated eighteen person-days. If built in a single construction effort, this translates to six to ten people working two to three days. Each mound typically had one or more burials placed at its base, with subsequent layers of soil added, none of which generally con-

FIG. 6.8. The Boudinot Mound (33AT37). (Photo by Elliot M. Abrams.)

tained further interments. The limited sample of skeletons from Hocking burial mounds (J. Murphy 1989) indicates that males and females, children and adults, were interred in mounds, a range paralleled elsewhere in the Midwest (Milner and Jefferies 1987).

Despite early archaeological investigations of earthen mounds and the presence of over two hundred mounds in Athens County alone (Black 1979), few of the small mounds of the Hocking Valley have been chronometrically dated (the dating of the cluster of larger mounds in The Plains is presented in chapter 7). Murphy (1989, 371) lists only three small ridgetop mounds from which radiocarbon dates have been obtained: the Rock Riffle Run Mound (440 B.C. ± 60 years), the Bob Evans Mound (430 B.C. ± 60 years), and the Daines Mound II (280 B.C. ± 140 years). To our knowledge, no other ridgetop mounds have been dated since Murphy's writing.

Although these mounds were first and foremost religious features that bore a special emotional and psychological place in the lives of past people, they may have additionally served as markers of territory or communication. A GIS analysis of forty-two mounds in Athens County indicated that any mound was visible from any adjacent mound (Waldron and Abrams 1999); consequently an individual standing near a ridgetop mound could see one or more mounds within that or the adjacent drainage system. We suggest that this indicates some form of communication among local communities.

# Theoretical Implications of Woodland Settlement Patterns

The central issue relating to habitation for this and other periods in Midwest archaeology is that of the degree and types of sedentism. Sedentism—the degree of permanence of living place—can be expressed by various indices: the distance traveled yearly by a community; the length of time per year that a community resides within a single site; the number of sites occupied through the year; the number of times a community reoccupies the same site. Archaeologically, the degree of sedentism can be measured through the form and number of elements such as substantial structures, storage pits, and midden deposits. Seeman (1986, 1992a), Clay (2002), and Clay and Creasman (1999) emphasize that Early Woodland residences were not permanent settlements; periodic abandonment of the residential site was the typical pattern. Clay (1998, 2002) specifically cites the ephemeral post patterns at Early Woodland sites as evidence for a dispersed and still somewhat nomadic population, akin to the Late Archaic pattern. Yerkes (1994, 2002) similarly observes that the relatively meager evidence of long-term architecture at Middle Woodland Hopewell sites indicates seasonal occupation. He systematically notes (2002, 231–35) the absence of substantial domestic architectural remains, thick middens, concealed storage pits, and ecofactual data that would indicate year-round occupation of Hopewell habitation sites (cf. Dancey 1991; Pacheco 1996a, 1997).

In the Hocking Valley, the post patterns at the Boudinot 4 site, as well as those at the Early Woodland Duncan Falls site (Carskadden and Gregg 1974), are in fact ephemeral, and we agree that this indicates seasonal abandonment. Groups who anticipate short use-life of their house tend to use low-quality, less durable building materials for their residence (Abrams 1989a; Kent and Vierich 1989). In addition, the Boudinot 4 site lacked any midden or deep storage pits. The inference that the Boudinot 4 site intermittently was occupied for roughly six months per year was based on the presence of seeds that could have only been collected or grown in the fall and the spring (Abrams 1989b).

Our general reconstruction does not point toward permanent (i.e., year-round) occupation of any habitation site. Rather, it suggests that seasonal movement, typified by fall and spring habitation on the terrace, winter occupation in rockshelters, and summer habitation on the floodplain, was restricted within spatially defined homesteads territorially distinct from those of neighboring communities.

## Horticultural Subsistence

These increasingly sedentary local communities ultimately supplemented their hunting and gathering with the gardening of select indigenous plants —squashes, chenopods, erect knotweed, sumpweed, and maygrass, constituting members of the Eastern Agricultural Complex (EAC). This was a protracted process involving several incremental stages before the actual gardening of domesticated species (Ford 1985; Harlan 1995). Archaeologists have long recognized the multiple processes that led to domestication (Smith 2001). First, the eventual planted species must become part of the diet as a wild species. Then, selective methods to enhance the plant's natural productivity in the wild may occur. The intentional or unintentional transplanting of the wild species follows. It is only then that reproductive control of the desired species may occur, often intermingled with wild versions of the same species.

Currently we lack data to indicate that any of the EAC species were consumed during the Late Archaic period (ca. 3000–1500 B.C.) in the Hocking Valley. However, we do have archaeobotanical data documenting this process for the Early Woodland period (ca. 1000 B.C.) from the Boudinot 4 site. Based on the analysis of archaeobotanical species from Boudinot 4 site features (Abrams 1989b; Wymer and Abrams forthcoming), one unidentified species of squash was evident ca. 1092 B.C., with chenopods, erect knotweed, and sumpweed becoming part of the plant inventory ca. 400 B.C. and maygrass joining this array of species ca. 200 B.C.

Several aspects of the botanical data indicate that these species entered the diet as wild species but subsequently underwent a domestication process and were later grown in gardens, probably in close proximity to the actual housing area. First, as the seeds of these plants were being collected and grown for consumption, more species of nuts were collected (Wymer and Abrams forthcoming). Hickory nuts decrease from a high of 95% of all nuts collected ca. 800 B.C. to 78% by 100 B.C., with hazelnuts, black walnuts, and butternuts added to the nut inventory (ibid.). Second, maygrass is considered nonlocal to southeastern Ohio and its presence in the archaeobotanical inventory suggests an intentional desire to manage or grow the plant. This is significant also in that maygrass is available in the spring, one of the leanest seasons for available foods (see Abrams and Freter, chapter 1 in this volume), as opposed to all the other managed species, which are available in the relatively abundant fall.

Third, the Boudinot 4 features yielded several plant species such as tick trefoil and pine that grow in open areas and are classified as invasion species. Coupled with the technology of axes (or Adena celts) for clearing, the picture is one of cleared terraces with recurrently used houses forming the hamlet in proximity to one or more gardens within which seed-bearing plants were managed, eventually resulting in morphological changes connoting domestication. Although none of the potential domesticates in the valley has been subjected to micromorphological or genetic analysis, the constellation of these data suggests a gardening component by at least 500 B.C. that supplemented the essential hunting and gathering economy of the Early Woodland period.

The analysis of the archaeobotanical remains from the County Home site is ongoing. However, preliminary analysis indicates the presence of wild chenopodium ca. 1500 B.C. (Jennifer DeMuria, pers. comm., 2004). Although further analysis and data are required, it is hypothesized that by 1500 B.C. the wild form of this seed-bearing plant became part of the diet.

## Woodland Social Organization

A final topic relating to these local Woodland communities is that of social structure—specifically, community membership. A basic ethnological model assumes that social organization was kin based—that some members of each local community were direct blood (consanguineal) relatives and that others married into the village as affinal relatives (Keesing 1975). This assumption is supported in part by the relatively small number of community members of marital age, a demographic condition that encouraged if not required *local community* or, from a spatial dimension, *homestead* exogamy, the cultural prescription to obtain a mate from outside one's immediate community. Thus the *local community* of 25 to 35 people was composed of four to five *households,* and each included married adults, one of whom was probably born in a different *homestead.*

A *lineage* is a social corporate group that links local communities through descent from a common male or female ancestor (Keesing 1975, 17). In tribal societies, it is "an adaptive solution, in different ecological settings, to the problems of maintaining political order and defining rights over land and other resources across generations" (18). Although it is empirically unconfirmed that social identity was recognized through lineages, it is hypothesized that lineage affiliation bound the dispersed Hocking Valley local communities residing within their respective homestead, creating the sociospatial organization that is at the core of tribal society. If accepted, then there would have been a mosaic of lineages nonrandomly distributed across watersheds serving as the foundation for tribal interaction.

Archaeological data potentially can confirm this basic model. DNA analyses of skeletons from known proveniences in the valley could identify marital boundaries, interpreted as paralleling social boundaries. Based on the comparative morphology of skeletons from Adena burial mounds, Taxman (1994) has already shown that the Ohio River served as a boundary between genetically distinct marital populations. Taxman's research is the first empirical data that indicates selective marital patterns for Early Woodland period populations. This concept of regional diversity strengthens the position that Woodland populations represented a culturally pluralistic set of societies (Clay 2002, 165). We concur and suggest that a large part of that pluralism was reflected in distinct lineage membership units dispersed across the Hocking Valley political landscape, an important subject for future research.

# 7

# WOODLAND CEREMONIALISM IN THE HOCKING VALLEY

Jeremy Blazier, AnnCorinne Freter, and Elliot M. Abrams

FOR THOSE NATIVE AMERICANS LIVING in the Hocking Valley ca. 100 B.C., the structure of life had changed considerably from that of their Late Archaic predecessors. Now communities of two dozen or more members were relatively sedentary in prime areas within the valley—especially terraces near bottomlands with an abundant supply of water. Gardening was an integral part of the economy, supplementing seasonal hunting and gathering activities, which still provided the majority of the local community's nutritional needs. Pottery was well established, representing a major technological advancement in terms of cooking, storage, and food processing. Although speculative, lineage affiliation was crystallized as part of the social identity of individuals, with lineage units within and across watershed regions of the Hocking Valley structuring marriages to a degree not evidenced in the Late Archaic (Crowell et al., this volume).

Although the construction of small, usually ridgetop burial mounds began in the Hocking Valley ca. 500 B.C. (J. Murphy 1989; Abrams 1992a; Crowell et al., this volume), earthwork construction beginning ca. 50 B.C. and continuing for over three centuries is evidenced in larger mounds as well as circular earthworks clustered predominantly in what is now The Plains, in southeastern Ohio (fig. 1.2). This chapter details the development of this new religious architecture and situates these mounds in the context of a broader sociopolitical and economic model for Woodland societies.

## The Plains

The Plains is an Illinoian outwash terrace approximately 3.75 km (NW to SE) in length and 1.4 km (SW to NE) in width (fig. 7.1). It is surrounded by ridges; the three natural passages to The Plains are through a 250 m northern break in the ridges from the floodplain of the Hocking River, a southern passage along an elevated plateau, and a roughly 250 m wide eastern entrance connecting The Plains with the floodplain of the Hocking River. Although there are a few seasonal runs within The Plains, there is no permanent flow of water, a factor that, while not precluding short-term occupation, certainly made all but the periphery of The Plains untenable for permanent settlement.

Upon or overlooking this area were built approximately 31 earthworks— nine "sacred circles" and 22 conical mounds (figs. 7.1, 7.2). In *Description of the Antiquities Discovered in the State of Ohio and Other Western States* (1820), Caleb Atwater mentions the Hocking Valley only briefly, but he is the first to note the presence of three large earthworks in The Plains (J. Murphy 1989, 47). In 1836, Samuel P. Hildreth produced the first map of The Plains (fig. 7.3), which appeared in the classic *Ancient Monuments of the Mississippi Valley* (Squier and Davis 1848). Hildreth's map, however, is extremely inaccurate and his work did little to stimulate research in the Hocking Valley (J. Murphy 1989).

The negligible impact of Hildreth was counterbalanced by the tremendous role played by E. B. Andrews, who "spear-headed the first organized investigation of archeological sites along the Hocking River. Sponsored by the Peabody Museum of Harvard University, he conducted fairly extensive mound explorations in Fairfield, Hocking, Perry, and Athens counties during 1875 and 1876" (J. Murphy 1989, 51). His map of earthworks in The Plains (fig. 7.4) is more accurate than that of Hildreth. Andrews's greatest impact was his trenching of at least 14 of the 22 (64%) conical mounds.

In the wake of Andrews's massive trenching efforts, several mound-specific projects were conducted. In the 1930s Emerson Greenman (1932) excavated the remnants of the Coon Mound and, in doing so, helped shape the definition of the Adena culture. William E. Peters, from Athens, confirmed and added to the map of mounds in the Athens vicinity including The Plains mounds as they existed in the 1940s. In the 1970s Nancy Wilson

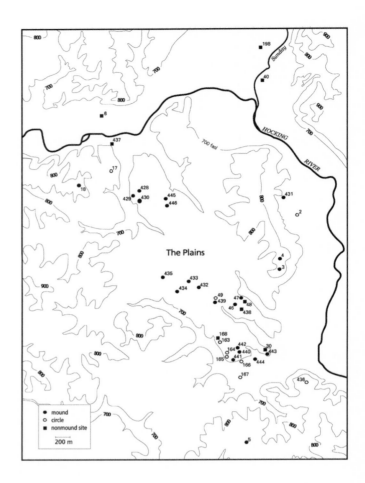

FIG. 7.1. Earthworks in The Plains

The Plains

- mound
○ circle
■ nonmound site

200 m

FIG. 7.2. The Hartman
Mound. (Photo by
Zachary Abrams.)

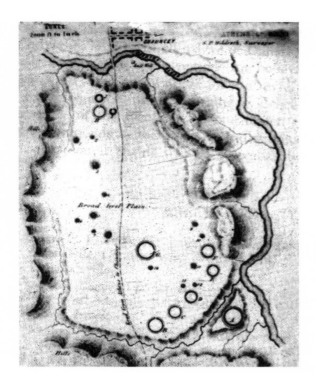

FIG. 7.3. Hildreth's map of The Plains

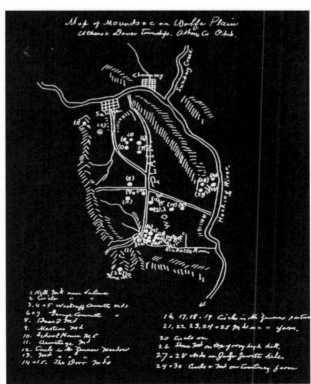

FIG. 7.4. Andrews's map of The Plains

excavated several of the mounds as well as the first circle (33AT17) in The Plains, but unfortunately those data were lost to archaeology due to her untimely death and the subsequent destruction of her fieldnotes. Mounds 428 and 429, already trenched by Andrews, were reexcavated by Shaune Skinner and colleagues in the 1980s, bringing more scientific rigor and analysis to The Plains research (Skinner and Norris 1984; Wymer 1984). It was not until this research that the first radiocarbon dates were assigned to any of the mounds. Mound 434 was excavated (Abrams 1992a) and mound 441 was retested (Blazier 2002), the latter having been previously trenched by Andrews. This long and generally unarticulated series of excavations has the dubious distinction of having generated perhaps one of the most tortured nomenclatures of archaeological sites in the United States. We have tried to reconcile all the labeling of past investigators (table 7.1) and have recommended that the Ohio Archaeological Inventory (OAI) number be included as the primary reference in any scholarly discourse.

In addition to earthworks, there are five recorded nonmound sites in The Plains (fig. 7.1). None have been excavated, although they are classified on the OAI forms in general as Late Archaic/Early Woodland. Site 33AT48 is the Cottingham 1 site and is identified as the approximately 15 acres (6 ha) surrounding 33AT47 (Dorr Mound 2). Wilson conducted fieldwork at this site but, as noted above, all data and notes have been lost. Site 33AT438 (the Hamlin Garden site) is within 50 m east of 33AT46 (Dorr Mound 1), but little is known of this site. Site 33AT30 (the Fourth Street site), close to mound 33AT443, was surveyed at 10 m × 40 m and yielded one small pot sherd. Site 33AT168 (Michaels 1 site) is simply recognized as an area where large amounts of worked chert were recovered and it too is near site 33AT163, a large circle. Despite the scant data from these four sites, their association with earthworks suggests to us that these sites were used exclusively during the time of earthwork construction—that they functioned specifically as "mortuary sites" (Seeman 1986; Clay 1986; Clay and Niquette 1989) rather than more generalized, longer-term habitations.

Site 33AT437 (Hartman campsite) yielded projectile points and other debitage and it too is close to an earthwork (site 33AT17). However, it is not directly adjacent to the earthwork and, unlike the other nonmound sites, this site directly overlooks the Hocking River floodplain. This site could have been a more permanent living site. Furthermore, the Gabriel site (33AT6), just across the floodplain from site 33AT437, was occupied through every period in Hocking Valley prehistory (J. Murphy 1989).

In sum, we infer that during the Woodland period The Plains was a true "vacant ceremonial center"—a center used exclusively for the performance

## Table 7.1. Labeling of Earthworks in The Plains

| OAI | Local Name(s) | Hildreth | Andrews | Greenman | Peters |
|---|---|---|---|---|---|
| *Circles* | | | | | |
| 33AT2 | Courtney Works | — | 29 | — | Fort 2 |
| 33AT17 | Hartman Circle | H | 2 | — | Fort 3 |
| 33AT49 | — | G | 12 | — | — |
| 33AT163 | — | E | 16 | — | — |
| 33AT164 | — | D | 17 | — | — |
| 33AT165 | — | C | 18 | — | — |
| 33AT166 | — | B | 19 | — | — |
| 33AT167 | Slater Gravel Pit Site | A | 20 | — | — |
| 33AT436 | Aerial Circle | — | — | — | — |
| *Mounds* | | | | | |
| 33AT3 | Judge Jewett Md. 1 | — | 29 | — | — |
| 33AT4 | Judge Jewett Md. 2 | — | 28 | — | — |
| 33AT5 | Signal Hill 1; Stone Md. | — | 26 | — | — |
| 33AT18 | Mound near Salina | — | 1 | — | Md. 4 |
| 33AT46 | Dorr 1 | 10 | 14 | 11 | — |
| 33AT47 | Dorr 2 | 9 | 15 | 10 | — |
| 33AT428 | Connett 3 | 2 | 3 | — | — |
| 33AT429 | Connett 4 | — | 4 | 5 | Md. 2 |
| 33AT430 | Connett 5 | 1 | 5 | 6 | Md. 1 |
| 33AT431 | Courtney Md. | — | 30 | — | Md. 3 |
| 33AT432 | School House Md. | 8? | 10 | 8 | — |
| 33AT433 | Martin Md. | 7 | 9 | — | Md. 7 |
| 33AT434 | Armitage Md. | 6 | 11 | 3 | — |
| 33AT435 | Coon Md.; Beard/Baird Md. | 5 | 8 | 1 | — |
| 33AT439 | Haymer Md. | 14 | 13 | — | — |
| 33AT440 | — | 12? | 22 | — | — |
| 33AT441 | — | 13? | 21 | — | — |
| 33AT442 | — | 11 | 23 | — | — |
| 33AT443 | — | — | 24 | — | — |
| 33AT444 | — | — | 25 | — | — |
| 33AT445 | Hartman Md. /Connett 6 | 3 | 6 | 2 | — |
| 33AT446 | Connett 7 | — | 7 | — | — |

*Sources:* Based on Andrews 1877, Greenman 1932, J. Murphy 1989, Peters 1947, Skinner and Norris 1984, and OAI forms available at the Ohio Historic Preservation Office, Columbus.

of ritual activities by the surrounding population (Thompson 1954). Following Prufer's model (1965) of Middle Woodland settlement, the settlement pattern in the Hocking is typified by a vacant, nonresidential religious center surrounded by small, dispersed, and semisedentary local communities who aggregated periodically at that center (Pacheco 1996b, 1997).

## Earthwork Content and Construction

An unfortunate lesson learned from the history of archaeological research in The Plains is that the excavation of an earthwork does not always translate into accessible artifacts or construction data. Much information has been lost over the years of research. Attempts to relocate some of the data once shipped to the Peabody Museum at Harvard University have proven unsuccessful. None of the nine circles today have provided any excavation data. However, there are data of varying quality from eleven of the twenty-two mounds from which to infer general cultural patterns relating to the builders of these architectural works.

### The Mounds

All the excavated mounds evidence a construction pattern of multiple stages, and much has been written describing the interment of a central burial(s) on which a small mound was built, to be followed over time by the addition of layers of soil, accompanied by ritual (Skinner and Norris 1984; J. Murphy 1989; Abrams 1992a; Greber 1991).

One of the more intensively studied profiles comes from site 33AT441 (Blazier 2002; Blazier and Freter 2002; see fig. 7.5). This mound, trenched initially by Andrews, was until 2002 incorrectly thought to be Andrews's mound 24, but is in fact his mound 21. Given the inaccuracies of Andrews's original map, this type of mislabeling is common and understandable. First, the original location of mounds by Andrews is questionable. Second, mound 21 is listed on the Ohio Archaeological Inventory as "partially destroyed" by house construction, whereas the reexcavated mound was in no way impacted by house construction. Third, mound 21 is described as being 14 ft 8 in (4.3 m) tall by Andrews (1877), whereas mound 24 is listed as being 8 ft (2.4 m) tall. Since the mound which was reexcavated was 8 ft in height, it was assumed to be mound 24. However, a recent GPS reading was obtained on the mound through the generous services of Ralph Moran and Joe Wakeman and this reading confirms that the mound described below is Andrews's mound 21.

FIG. 7.5. Mound 33AT441 (facing southwest), showing our trench profile. (Photo by Jeremy Blazier.)

Andrews trenched through the mound, stating only that he found ashes, "kitchen refuse," and bones of a small animal (1877). No skeletal data are reported from the mound. The goal of reexcavation was to understand the stratigraphy as well as the chronology of construction. Before the excavation of a 1 × 1 m trench along an interior exposed wall of Andrews's old trench (fig. 7.6), a series of photographs of the mound and surrounding area were taken, then surface foliage (primarily poison ivy) and pine litter were cleared. Where possible, excavations were conducted in cultural levels, facilitating Harris Matrix analysis. When features were encountered, a profile was drawn and soil samples were taken. Excavation continued until premound sterile soil was reached. No burials were encountered during excavation.

Forty-nine chipped-stone artifacts were recovered; 60% were Brush Creek chert, which was widely used in southern Athens County and is abundant in the alluvial deposits along the lower Hocking River. Upper Mercer chert represented 24% of the total chipped-stone inventory, while Flint Ridge/Vanport material (including a small thumbnail scraper) comprised 11%. The remaining 6% of chipped-stone artifacts have sources yet to be identified. A total of 24 groundstone artifacts were recovered, the majority being poorly preserved burned fragments. Evidence of burning within mound episodes is reinforced by the large amount of fire-cracked rock (FCR) distributed throughout levels 3 through 9 found in close association with the burned groundstone. Unlike other burial mounds, no ceramic artifacts were recovered, and only one possible gorget fragment was

FIG. 7.6. Trench, 33AT441. (Photo by Jeremy Blazier.)

encountered. Two postmolds were exposed in the profile wall, one in level 6 at a depth of 160 cm, the second in level 7 at 177 cm. The FCR and the charcoal lens encountered in level 7 indicate that the posts were burned. A charcoal sample from this charcoal lens (feature 3) from the base of mound 33AT441 yielded a radiocarbon date of 168 B.C.–A.D. 54 (table 7.2).

There were at least six episodes of construction (fig. 7.7) for mound 33AT441. At the base, 210 cm from the mound surface, is level 10, a sterile subsoil of yellow clay. Above this is a layer of darker soil—level 9; compact, with charcoal and a few FCR, this is most likely the original ground-level humus. The first stage of construction was the clay subfloor encountered in level 8. It was 10 to 15 cm thick, very compact, with a few FCR and some oddly shaped clay nodules. This subfloor appears to have been a prepared level, with clay brought in and purposely formed into a cap on which funerary rites took place. There is evidence for similarly prepared subfloors

### Table 7.2. Chronology of The Plains Mounds and Earthworks

*Radiometric Dating*

| Site | Lab No.[a] | RCYBP | Calibrated Date[b] | Cal. Intercept |
|------|-----------|-------|--------------------|----------------|
| 33AT428 | DIC 2873 | 1920 ± 310–320 | 789 B.C.–A.D. 764 | A.D. 78 |
| | DIC 2955 | 2180 ± 55 | 388–53 B.C. | 342, 324, 202 B.C. |
| 33AT429 | DIC 2859B | 1790 ± 50 | A.D. 88–384 | A.D. 240 |
| | DIC 2860 | 1930 ± 45 | 39 B.C.–A.D. 213 | A.D. 75 |
| | DIC 2861 | 1200 ± 145 | A.D. 597–1158 | A.D. 815 |
| 33AT434 | SMU 2161 | 1810 ± 45 | A.D. 83–340 | A.D. 236 |
| | Beta 27705 | 1880 ± 90 | 50 B.C.–A.D. 380 | A.D. 128 |
| 33AT441 | Beta 160109 | 2040 ± 40 | 168 B.C.–A.D. 54 | 46, 6, 4 B.C. |

*Cross-Dating with Diagnostic Artifacts*

| Site | Artifacts |
|------|-----------|
| 33AT5 | Copper; bear tusks |
| 33AT428 | Copper; shell beads; pipes |
| 33AT429 | Log crypt |
| 33AT430 | Copper; tubular pipes |
| 33AT432 | Copper |
| 33AT435 | Copper; marine shells; mica; log crypt |
| 33AT446 | Copper; shell beads |

*Sources:* Abrams 1992a; Blazier and Freter 2002; Skinner and Norris 1984.

[a]Beta = Beta Analytic, Inc.; DIC = Dicarb Radioisotope Co.; SMU = Southern Methodist University.

[b]The 2-sigma range, based on Stuiver et al. 1998.

in many mounds in the area, including the Rock Riffle Run Mound, the Daines II and III Mounds, and the Armitage Mound (33AT434) (J. Murphy 1989, 156, 174; Abrams 1992a, 103).

The second stage of construction—level 7—revealed the greatest number and density of artifacts and features. Level 7 contained a much darker soil than the clay subfloor, 30 FCR, 12 chert flakes, and 10 burned/cracked pieces of groundstone. This second construction episode appears to be a result of the ritual burning incorporated in the funerary process. Excavation of the Connett Mound 4 (33AT429) uncovered a similar lens of charcoal, and analysis yielded wood species not found in The Plains, suggesting that they were transported to the mound. Consequently, it appears that this lens was not merely the result of burning local undergrowth to clear the area for mound construction (Skinner and Norris 1984:63; Wymer 1984). Construction episodes 3, 4, and 5 are each defined by changes in the soil and artifact distribution. The existence of FCR in each level suggests the

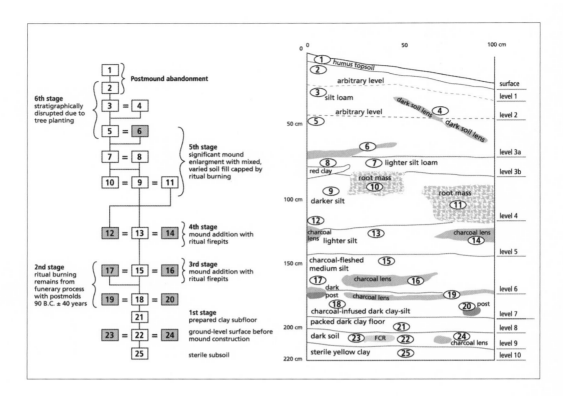

FIG. 7.7. Profile and Harris Matrix of 33AT441

ritual burning of fire pits, and subsequent construction of mound levels (Abrams 1992a). Levels 3b, 3a, and 2 are determined in arbitrary increments of 18 cm and collectively represent the last stage of construction. They do not show distinctive layering, perhaps because of the amount of root destruction and root masses present. Level 1 and the humus ground cover represent soil accumulation since the mound's disuse.

In order to fully explore the relationships between construction levels, the stratigraphic profile was converted into a Harris Matrix (fig. 7.7). The Harris Matrix method allows only three possible relationships between two units of stratigraphy: (1) the units have no direct stratigraphic connection, (2) they are in superposition, or (3) the units are correlated as parts of once whole deposits or a feature interface. Harris states that the primary object of archaeological stratigraphy is to place the units—the layers and features —into a relative sequential order from which their full interrelationships and interfaces can be better evaluated (1989, 36).

The matrix of mound 33AT441 shows a clear pattern of burning throughout, but in discrete stages restricted to specific levels. Like the profiles from 33AT435 (Greenman 1932), 33AT428 and 33AT429 (Skinner and Norris 1984), and 33AT434 (Abrams 1992a), the greatest amount of funerary activity in

33AT441 occurred at the initiation of the placement of the skeleton. Second, certain units or features are clearly superpositioned, visually clarifying the multiple stages of construction. Last, cell 17, the radiocarbon-dated charcoal lens, can be easily placed into context and its relationship to surrounding layers is more easily understood. The Harris Matrix thus becomes a valuable methodological tool for archaeological interpretation.

Despite the number of mounds investigated, very few actual skeletons exist. Greenman (1932) identified the single interment in the Coon Mound (33AT435) as an adult male and Abrams and Dorothy Humpf (Abrams 1992a) also identified the single Armitage (33AT434) skeleton as an adult male. Two skeletons were identifiable from Connett Mound 3 (33AT428), both of which were adult females (Skinner and Norris 1984). This sample of three mounds, while limited, does represent a 14% sample of mounds from The Plains. The balance between adult men and women suggests an egalitarian ethic to status recognition, consistent with that from earlier times (Crowell et al., this volume).

Finally, an analysis was conducted comparing the labor expended in the construction of mounds in The Plains with that expended in the smaller ridgetop mounds (Abrams and LeRouge 2004). It was shown that the largest mound—33AT445—required approximately 2,612 person-days of work as a multiyear collective effort. This figure is roughly one hundred times that of the smaller ridgetop mounds built by earlier generations outside The Plains, suggesting that larger numbers of people were involved in mound construction in The Plains.

## The Circles

Although no artifactual data are available from any of the nine earthwork circles, their size is well documented. Murphy (1989, 197), following Hildreth, notes that they range in diameter from 110 (33.5 m) to 210 ft (64 m). The 1998 Ohio University field school remapped the Courtney circle (33AT2) at 207 ft (63 m) in diameter, which is in line with the OAI diameter of 200 ft (61 m) and Peters's measured diameter of 195 ft (59 m). The average of 200 ft, then, is a fair approximation. One interesting aspect of these circles is that repeated plowing has lowered all of them to near invisibility. Owing to the conscientious efforts of the present landowner, however, the Courtney circle is still visible. The main wall creating the circle is approximately 10 m wide. In the center of the circle was a rise of earth 20 m in diameter. Based on local information relating to the earlier days of plowing this area, it was ascertained that the exterior wall rose at least 7 ft (2.1 m), whereas today it gradually inclines on average less than 40 cm. With an estimated height of the wall at 2.1 m, its width at 10 m, and the diameter of the entire circle at 61 m, the volume of earth in the surrounding wall was estimated at 3,365 m³ of earth. If we divide that by 2.6 m³ of earth dug per person-day (Erasmus 1965), then it required roughly 1,294 person-days to dig the earth for the exterior wall of this circle. The Coon Mound (33AT435) was calculated to have required 1,306 person-days (Abrams and LeRouge 2004), making the Courtney Circle (33AT2) comparable in construction labor requirements to all but the largest of construction projects in The Plains.

One final aspect to this circle follows James Murphy (1989, 200), who notes that soil testing of the Courtney Circle (33AT2) indicated that its soil was different from that of the outwash soil on which it was built. We have been unable to locate any soil report relating to this circle. However, given the volume of earth in the circle, we would expect to find sizeable barrow pits had all its soil been from the immediate field. In the absence of such pits, it is possible that soil from the Wisconsin terrace, about 200 m to the west of the circle, may have been the primary soil source. If so, the collective labor expenditure in its construction would far surpass that quantified for solely digging the earth due to the additional soil transportation costs. This indicates that considerable collective effort was required in the construction of such circles.

## Chronology

To date, four mounds have yielded radiometric dates from which to base chronology. In addition, of the eleven mounds providing artifactual data of interior contents, seven contain artifacts diagnostic of the Middle Woodland period (table 7.2). Skinner and Norris (1984, 94) suggest that sample DIC 2860 (recalibrated here with an A.D. 75 intercept) is most reflective of initial construction of the mound since it comes from the central burial of 33AT429. Sample DIC 2861 comes from a feature at the periphery of the mound and is unlikely (as they state) to be a reliable date. The two dates from 33AT428 were from wood charcoal from the same feature (1984, 123); that one is very early, in conflict with the artifactual data of a construction after A.D. 1, and the other has a relatively large error range (a one-sigma error of over 600 years), which suggests that this context produced a mixed or contaminated radiocarbon sample yielding unreliable results. The two regular radiocarbon dates from the Armitage Mound site (33AT434) were processed by two different labs from the same context—one was a piece of bark taken directly from the kneecap of the central burial at the base of the mound and one was burned bark from directly under the central burial (Abrams 1992a, 88). The one date from 33AT441 has great integrity; it was obtained from a deep feature toward the base of the mound and dated through AMS radiometric dating.

Cross-dating—the use of dated formal or stylistic artifact attributes from elsewhere to assign chronology—is a second means of assigning a general chronology to The Plains earthwork complex. Many artifacts made outside the Hocking Valley, with sources outside Ohio, enter the area through what is termed the Hopewell Interaction Sphere (Seeman 1979). These include such exotica as copper artifacts from the upper Great Lakes region, mica from Tennessee, and bear claws and teeth, as well as obsidian, from the Rocky Mountain region. These are dated as entering Ohio ca. 50 B.C. From table 7.2 we see that the vast majority of mounds that have yielded artifacts contain evidence of that long-distance sphere. In addition, Clay (1991; also Dragoo 1963) has analyzed Adena mounds and circles in Kentucky and concluded that circles were in general built later than mounds. Further, the three largest mounds in The Plains (33AT439, 33AT445, and 33AT446) logically required the greatest amount of time to construct, suggesting late dates be assigned for at least some of their construction.

Collectively, all available lines of analysis indicate that the earthworks in The Plains were built from ca. 50 B.C. to A.D. 250, making this center coeval with the larger Hopewell complexes found elsewhere in Ohio (Potter 1971; Otto 1979; J. Murphy 1989; Greber 1991). Whether the first wooden shovelful of dirt was dug at 89 B.C. or 46 B.C. is both irrelevant and unknowable. The significance of this chronology is that this wider regional scale of ceremonialism and its associated social and political implications occurred *after* the establishment of homestead-based, gardening communities bound by shared identities memorialized by small ridgetop burial mounds.

## Discussion

The earthworks and associated artifacts from The Plains were created by Native Americans first and foremost as an expression of grieving, honor, and memory of the dead, a significant component of their ideational or religious system. As such, these data present the first real opportunity to consider archaeologically the religious beliefs and practices of an indigenous population in the Hocking Valley.

Although there is great diversity of interior contents within the mounds, several ritual acts relating to interment are consistently evidenced from the archaeological record. Earthen mounds served as funerary structures, repositories for a limited number of individuals. Interment, cremation, and possibly excarnation—the exposure of the dead to the elements for some time prior to burial—were part of the burial process. Most placement of the dead occurred at the base of the mound. Burning also was part of the funerary ritual. Blankets of bark were often placed beneath and above the central interment with signs of having been burned. Cremated burials also are found in mounds, as are pits within which burning occurred. The profiles of mounds reveal that burning within pits took place at the initial interment as well as at subsequent construction events. Further, animal remains have been recovered from some of the mounds. These include eagle, bear, and wolf. Pendants from similar mounds elsewhere depict birds of prey (Dragoo 1963). An eagle beak was recovered from the Connett Mound 3 (33AT428). These animal representations conceivably reflect totemic or ancestral descent imagery.

Collectively, the funeral rite itself emphasized several aspects of indigenous religion. Animism—the belief that the soul or spirit of the dead survives the physical body and "animates" nature by residing within the landscape—was likely the core religious principle. One critical dimension of animism is the concept of transformation. The presence of animal remains may reflect the spiritual guidance of a shaman, who is often portrayed in Native American religious literature as one who is transformed from human to animal as part of their communicative liaison with the spiritual world (Hall 1997). One could further argue that the various acts of burning—cremations, bark layers, and pits used during the building of new episodes of construction—reflect another form of transformation, from solid to fragile, from earth to sky, from corporeal to spiritual.

If this broad picture of animism is accepted, then by extension the entire landscape of The Plains was conceived of as an interactive part of the ideational system once mounds began being built. As part of a "constructed landscape" (Knapp and Ashmore 1999), The Plains served as the spiritual center for these Native Americans. The fact that there are no habitation sites in The Plains perhaps is a result of this area being conceptualized as sacred and thus prohibitive to more secular activities, with access being scheduled or restrictive.

The funeral of any one individual is ultimately a social act involving a wide range of living individuals. The participation of a larger social unit in the funerary act is evidenced in many ways. The logic of shamanistic guidance demands societal participation. The effort expended in some of the larger construction episodes, described above, indicates participation by multiple local communities or, as Clay (1992) notes, an aggregation of "allied groups." The pattern of discontinuous but recurrent construction of a single mound further indicates the return by the same communities over some period of time. Finally, the burial pattern from the Armitage Mound (33AT434) reveals the central burial of a full skeleton of a fifty- to sixty-year-old man surrounded by at least fifteen cremated skeletons wrapped in bark (Abrams 1992a).

Although there are varied interpretations of these data, one model of sociopolitical organization inferred involves several communities of shared social affiliation periodically meeting to bury and then honor their dead. Following Clay (1991, 1992), we support the concept that the collective act of burial was as significant for the participants as it was to honor the specific individual buried in the mound. Accordingly, the periodic aggregation of villagers to honor an individual who symbolized the shared identity (and possibly genealogy) of the participants served to solidify the relations among these individuals, reinforcing their common kinship or lineal bonds.

We further hypothesize that lineage members from various local communities were those who collectively participated in the funerary rituals described above. By doing so, an array of other activities—including negotiating marriage partners, sharing economic information and goods, and conversing on many topics for innumerable social and psychological reasons —took place, just as was argued for feasting and aggregation in Late Archaic times (Heyman, Abrams, and Freter, this volume). The diversity of the specific burial forms (Hays 1994)—from log crypts to bark blankets, burials with exotic artifacts to those with none, unburned extended burials to bundled cremations—may in part be understood as reflecting the expression of different lineages associated with different mounds, or alternatively as representing the relative importance of individuals within the lineage based on differences of age, gender, social office, or ancestry.

The ability of these small local communities to organize into larger regional political units centered at The Plains is an example of what Sahlins (1961) termed the "segmentary lineage," the organizational ability to unify dispersed communities. It is one of the key definers of tribal society and appears to have been part of the structure of societies in the Hocking Valley at least by 50 B.C.

One model that may embrace these large but temporary political units is the "peer polity" model (Braun 1986; also Pacheco 1996a, 1997). Within this model, political units of roughly equal size represent a mosaic of comparable and balanced political strength, thus preventing any one unit from expanding. This model may characterize the Middle Woodland political landscape. A further dimension of the peer polity model is that the establishment of one such regional unit may inspire the creation of other such units. Hypothetically, as larger regional units periodically assembled in the Scioto or Licking Valleys, a comparable scale of organization may have been created in the Hocking Valley centered in The Plains.

THE PLAINS WAS LARGELY an unoccupied ritual center serving a dispersed population of small horticultural/hunting and gathering communities. These communities, who occupied several residential locales across the year contained within a homestead area (Crowell et al., this volume), periodically aggregated at The Plains for the conduct of religious, social, and economic purposes, a practice that began in a different form at least as early as the Late Archaic period (Heyman, Abrams, and Freter, this volume). This pattern of settlement and ceremonial activity in the Hocking Valley articulates with that evidenced elsewhere in the mid–Ohio Valley (Dancey 1991; Pacheco 1996a, 1997; Yerkes 1994). In our opinion, this center represents the largest regional extent of political inclusiveness in the Hocking Valley since the building of earthworks in The Plains ended ca. A.D. 250 and was never resumed.

# 8

# THE SWINEHART VILLAGE SITE

## A LATE WOODLAND VILLAGE IN
## THE UPPER HOCKING VALLEY

John F. Schweikart

SOUTH OF BUCKEYE LAKE IN FAIRFIELD COUNTY, Ohio, and northwest of the unglaciated Plateau lies a 600 km² area that marks the physiographic transition between the till plain of the Central Lowland Province, the Allegheny Plateau, and the unglaciated portions of southern and eastern Ohio (figs. 1.1, 1.2, 8.1). This region contains second-order upland head-water streams that flow into the Scioto, Hocking, and Muskingum drainages. Despite its distinctive ecological diversity relative to other portions of the valley and its central position and gently rolling topography, this crossroads for populations moving between the Scioto, Hocking, and Muskingum drainages has received little consideration by archaeologists. Typically, this area and other hinterlands have been viewed through the cultural-historical lenses of one of the three surrounding, more intensively researched drainages. However, to fully appreciate the tribal social process, all portions of the Hocking Valley must be investigated.

## Description of the Swinehart Village

The Swinehart Village (33FA7) is located on the boundary between the Central Lowland till plain and the Allegheny Plateau, and is situated on a

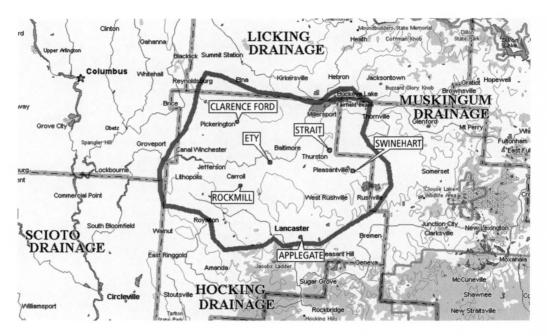

FIG. 8.1. Location of the Swinehart Village and nearby sites

steep bluff-edge terrace above the eastern bank of Little Rush Creek, an upland headwater tributary in the Hocking drainage (fig. 8.2). While this site is in the Hocking drainage proper, it is also only a few kilometers from upland tributaries of both the Scioto and Muskingum Rivers. This sloping bluff-edge promontory is flanked on three sides by fertile Wisconsin-age lacustrine floodplains. The northeastern side of the village is connected to rolling uplands some 30 m above Little Rush Creek (Meeker, Petro, and Bone 1960; Wolfe, Forsyth, and Dove 1962).

An earthen embankment 50 cm high surrounds the promontory and is separated from adjacent uplands by a linear depression 1 to 2 m wide and 15 m long. The embankment encloses 1.4 ha, with an effective use area of approximately 1 ha. Inside the enclosure there is an upper and a lower terrace of roughly equal size, separated by a 10 m wide and 3 m high talus slope. There are three openings or gateways in the embankment. The largest was originally 4 m wide and is associated with the linear depression to the northeast. The other openings are along the western edge of the lower terrace embankment above Little Rush Creek, and appear to have undergone some erosion.

Although the Swinehart Village site has yielded diagnostic materials ranging from the Early Archaic through Late Prehistoric periods, the bulk of materials recovered from the site dates to the Middle through early Late Woodland (ca. A.D. 300–800) and include (1) a limited amount of bladelets

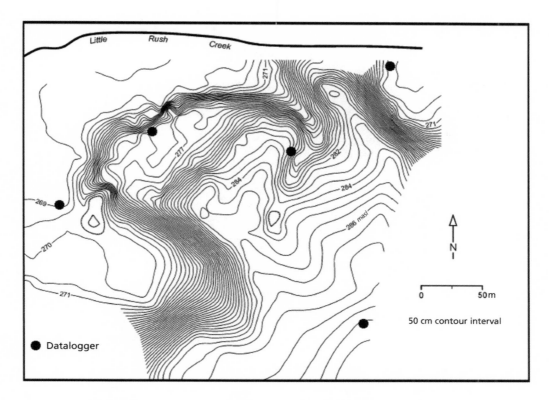

FIG. 8.2. Topographic map of the Swinehart Village

made of high-quality Flint Ridge/Vanport flint, (2) Chesser-Lowe series points (McMichael 1984), and (3) Chilton gorgets (Converse 1978; see also fig. 8.3). The Swinehart Village site conforms to a pattern found through much of central and southern Ohio between ca. A.D. 250 and 400. These sites are characterized by the appearance of amorphous aggregated settlements located on terraces adjacent to secondary streams (Burks and Dancey 1999; Converse 1993; Ericksen, Sprague, and Almstedt 2000). This pattern was soon followed by the development of 1–4 ha nucleated C- or D-shaped villages situated on bluff edges and often demarcated by ditch features, embankments, or evidence of encircling posts (or all three) (Dancey 1998; Seeman and Dancey 2000). Examples of these Middle Woodland and transitional Late Woodland settlements include (1) the Strait Site, an expansive (6–7 ha; Burks and Dancey 2000) terminal Middle Woodland site located along a headwater tributary of Walnut Creek that appears to date to ca. A.D. 220–260 (Jarrod Burks, pers. comm., 2002) and the Ety site, a small (0.8 ha) enclosure along a tributary of Big Walnut Creek. With the possible exception of the Applegate Fort near Lancaster (J. Murphy 1989, 352), there are no other known examples of aggregated early

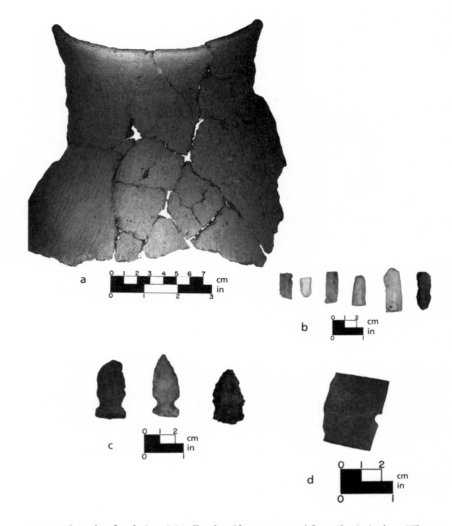

FIG. 8.3. Sample of early Late Woodland artifacts recovered from the Swinehart Village: (a) Newtown-like ceramic vessel, (b) bladelet fragments, (c) Chesser-Lowe hafted bifaces, (d) fragment of a Chilton-style gorget. (Photo by John F. Schweikart.)

Late Woodland enclosed sites, except for the Swinehart Village site, in the entire Hocking drainage. Of significance is that these enclosed village sites have *not* been found in the central and southern portion of the Hocking Valley, strengthening the observation that societies in the broad upper Hocking Valley north of the Hocking Hills were in some ways culturally distinctive from tribal communities elsewhere in the valley.

# A Preliminary Demographic Model for Aggregation at the Swinehart Village

A primary goal of research at the Swinehart Village site is to generate an estimate of community population size. All the means to estimate population size from an archaeological database are fraught with problems. Nevertheless, researchers have attempted to estimate the population size for some of these early Late Woodland aggregated settlements. William Dancey (1992, 24), for example, identified eleven household clusters at the 3.13 ha Water Plant site, suggesting that each cluster housed 10 individuals per household, for a total maximal estimate of 110 people.

In early research at the Swinehart Village site, Robert Goslin identified a series of six large "ash pits" during his 1927–28 investigations of the upper terrace. Jarrod Burks and I recently subjected this same terrace to a magnetometry survey yielding what may be at least five building or structure patterns. Given that Swinehart, at 1.4 ha, is less than half the size of Water Plant, and that five to six distinct clusters of activity were evidenced in contrast to the 11 at Water Plant, it is a reasonable suggestion that the Swinehart Village housed at most approximately fifty people, or less than half the population of the Water Plant site, assuming that all clusters were occupied simultaneously.

As for the demographic makeup of these groups, in the absence of a representative skeletal database from the site, we must refer to a standard age-sex pyramid for a hypothetical tribal population. Specifically, figure 8.4 represents an age-sex pyramid for what Chagnon (1997, 155) called an "undisturbed" Yanomamö population where the characteristic shape of the pyramid is wide at the bottom and then rapidly narrows toward the top due to high birth rates coupled with high death rates for younger individuals. This age-sex pyramid is consistent with extensive ethnographic data from many sources from the Human Relations Area Files (HRAF) in reference to tribal societies.

If the late Middle Woodland/early Late Woodland population living at the Swinehart Village generally conformed with the HRAF dataset, then at any given time the village was represented by a tribal population dominated by infants and young children, followed by some teenagers, fewer young adults, and even fewer people over age forty. Specifically, nearly 40% of the people alive at the village at any given time would have been children under the age of ten. Rephrased, nearly half of these children would not have lived to see their twentieth birthdays, and more than a third of the twenty-year-olds would not have lived to see their thirtieth birthdays.

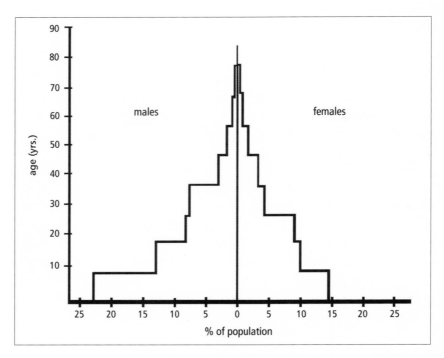

FIG. 8.4. Generalized demographic pyramid for a preindustrial horticultural society. (From Chagnon 1997.)

This demographic profile for the local community occupying the Swinehart Village site is significant in suggesting that marriage partners were limited in each community and thus intercommunity relations had to maintain the flow of marriage partners in the absence of centralizing multicommunity aggregation at ritual loci such as The Plains in the Hocking Valley.

## Two Possible Reasons for Aggregation: Productivity and Defense

Despite their widespread distribution across central and southern Ohio and their wide range of sizes (0.8 ha to over 4 ha), nucleated sites like Swinehart Village are remarkably consistent in terms of their site settings. Specifically, nearly all of them included artificially enhanced enclosures intentionally placed to take advantage of prominences above fertile floodplains in areas that otherwise exhibit moderately low relief. In light of this fact, two hypotheses can be tested concerning this preference for terraced landforms surrounded by an enclosure. The first is that the people at Swinehart Village chose their site location in order to maximize their resource productivity, testable by examining climatic conditions on the terrace for expanded productivity as well as through analysis of the paleoethnobotanical or faunal assemblages from the site. The second hypothesis is that site selection was influenced by an overriding concern for defense, testable by examining the improved visibility to surrounding areas from the elevated location of the Swinehart Village.

## Resource Productivity: Estimating the Growing Season

Based on preliminary analyses of limited paleoethnobotanical and faunal assemblages from the Swinehart Village site, it appears that the occupants continued the mixed horticultural, hunting and foraging subsistence economy attributable to their Middle Woodland predecessors (Simon 2000; Styles 2000; Wymer 1996, 1997). One avenue for increasing subsistence productivity would be to extend the growing season. Today the growing season for Fairfield County averages 170 days (April 26–October 13; Meeker, Petro, and Bone 1960, 2). However, the potential for early and late frosts can be influenced by local microclimatic conditions (see table 1.5). Plant cover also influences local temperatures and affects the risk of early or late season frosts. Air over meadows or weedy crops may be markedly colder than over bare soil due to heat loss through evaporation, while tall screens of vegetation like trees can provide protection from radiant heat loss (Geiger 1959, 397–99).

In order to obtain temperature data for the Swinehart Village over a full growing season, five HOBO® Temp data loggers were placed at various elevations within and surrounding the Swinehart Village site. These devices were launched using BoxCar® 2.06 software on April 20, 1997, and recorded surrounding air temperatures every 3 hours and 12 minutes for a 240-day cycle until December 16, 1997. Results from four of the five data loggers indicate a growing season of 157 days (May 11–October 15, 1997; fig. 8.5). (Only Data logger no. 4 deviated from this in that the autumn season extended six more days, ending around midnight on October 21.) Thus the growing season in 1997 at Swinehart Village was nearly two weeks *shorter* than the 50-year average of 170 days for Fairfield County. This is surprising since 1997 was the second year of a pronounced el Niño effect, bringing warm weather to the region. It also suggests that if modern climatic trends are in any way analogous to those of the past, there would have been little or no advantage —or even a possibility at Swinehart Village—to extending the growing season.

In sum, temperature data from Swinehart Village for the 1997 growing season suggest that the surrounding locale does *not* afford a positive extension of the growing season, found to be well below the 50-year county

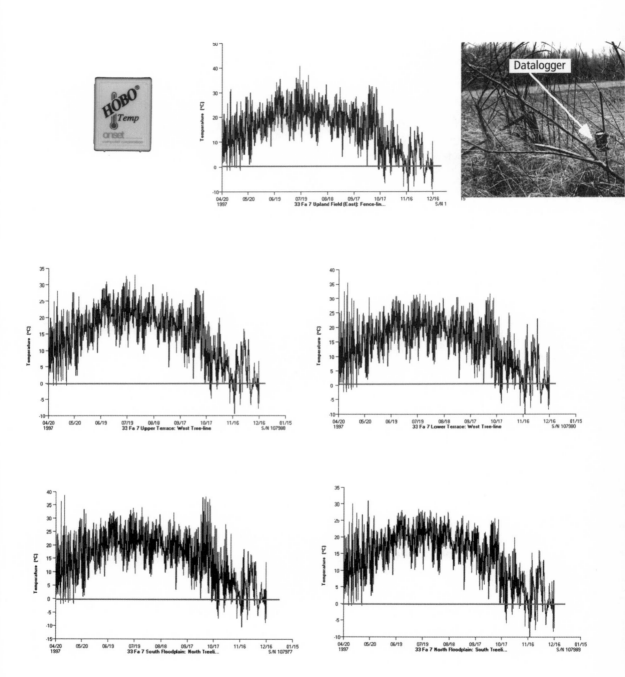

FIG. 8.5. Hobo® Datalogger data taken at the Swinehart Village during the 1997 growing season

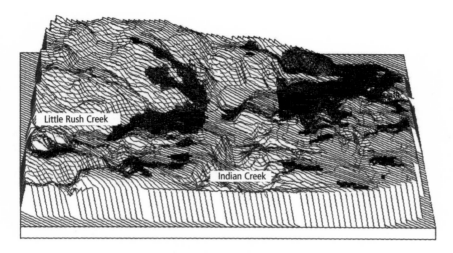

FIG. 8.6. Wire frame digital terrain model of the Swinehart Village (looking south, with a 4× exaggeration of terrain). Areas in black are visible from the center of the enclosure at an eye level 1.5 m above the ground.

average. However, other microclimatic variations of this terraced location, such as proximity to well-drained upland soils adjacent to fertile lacustrine or alluvial soils, certainly were important in site selection. A consideration of these varying soils could have been used as a means to even out crop losses from unpredictable droughts or flooding.

## Defense

Frequently the evaluation that a given early Late Woodland enclosure possesses defensive attributes is largely based on anecdotal information. In order to evaluate the potential defensive aspects of the Swinehart Village, a digital terrain model was employed (fig. 8.6). In this case contour data from the Rushville, Ohio, topographic quadrangle (1961, photorevised 1985) was digitized and analyzed using ArcInfo® at the Center for Mapping at the Ohio State University. Once digitized contour data had been entered, a three-dimensional model of the terrain was generated. Next, a visibility study was conducted. Initiating this study, a value of 1.5 m was given for the sighting height and a point was chosen to approximate the viewing height of a single adult standing at or near the center of the Swinehart Village. Then, a view of all the areas that could be "seen" was "draped" over the three-dimensional model.

Assuming tree cover was not an obstructing element, results of three-dimensional modeling of the Swinehart Village indicate that areas to the south and east of the enclosure were in clear view for an observer near the center. Areas to the west, north, and to a lesser extent to the south of the enclosure could be seen for much of the Little Rush Creek Valley. The only area not visible was behind a bend on Indian Creek to the north. Therefore, if concerns centered on observing movements along the Little Rush Creek Valley, this study indicates that the placement of the Swinehart Village would offer a strategic advantage over placement in the floodplain.

In sum, defensive aspects of the Swinehart enclosure provided a strategic advantage for an observer overlooking Little Rush Creek and appears to be a significant influence on site settlement in conjunction with other factors such as access to land conducive to growing cultigens. Further evidence of defense at Swinehart Village may come from the fact that Robert Goslin is reported to have identified postholes "around the edge of the embankment" at the site, features also recovered from the Scioto Trails site (Don Aplomad to Goslin, October 3, 1957; Dancey, pers. comm., 1992). The Scioto Trails site on the south end of the city of Columbus holds the dubious distinction of being the only early Late Woodland site in central Ohio with human remains exhibiting signs of a lethal wound from a projectile (Erika Keener, pers. comm., 2001).

## Discussion

Based on these analyses, communities chose to build their villages on terraces overlooking the floodplain to provide a broad visual panorama of their horticultural fields, as well as any intruders who may have entered the area. Thus we see settlement patterns influenced by political as well as economic concerns. If so, then this period in the upper Hocking Valley may have been characterized by political tension between communities, expressed as raiding or more formalized conflict.

Although speculative, these new intercommunity tensions emerged after A.D. 350, just when the local and regional Middle Woodland ceremonial and mortuary centers were apparently abandoned. With the cessation of regional aggregation in centers, local dispersed populations in the upper Hocking Valley would have lost an important opportunity to find suitable marriage partners. Given the demographic structure that would have limited the number of marriageable partners within a community, the breakdown of this mechanism may have exacerbated tensions between communities that were already focused on limited agricultural land resources, resulting in the tense political climax archaeologically expressed by the location and defensive enclosure typified by the Swinehart Village site.

RECENT RESEARCH AT THE SWINEHART VILLAGE SITE illuminates several aspects of Hocking Valley prehistory. First, it demonstrates that settlement decisions by local communities ca. A.D. 350–500 in the upper Hocking Valley were influenced by political as well as economic factors. Second, political concerns took the form of intercommunity conflict, which prompted settlements to be located on available elevated, defensible terraces rather than floodplains. Third, each community actively responded to threats of violence by constructing a defensive embankment for protection. These patterns further suggest that occupants of the upper Hocking Valley were quite distinct from those residing in the central and southern valley, since no such defensive embankments have been found outside of the upper valley. This may have implications when considering tribal affiliation of communities through the entire valley. The Swinehart Village exemplifies the diversity evident in tribal communities in the Hocking Valley.

# 9

# THE ALLEN SITE

## A LATE PREHISTORIC COMMUNITY IN THE HOCKING RIVER VALLEY

Elliot M. Abrams, Christopher Bergman, and Donald A. Miller

THERE ARE SEVERAL KNOWN LATE WOODLAND and Late Prehistoric (A.D. 700–1300) villages from the central Hocking Valley, including the Graham site (McKenzie 1967), the McCune site (J. Murphy 1989), and the Gabriel site (J. Murphy 1989). Unfortunately, none has received the scale of intensive horizontal excavation needed to address questions relating to the demography and domestic economy of these late communities in the valley. With that in mind, an Ohio University field school directed by Abrams was initiated to survey and intensively excavate the Allen site (33AT653), a habitation site along Margaret Creek, a tributary of the Hocking River (fig. 1.2).

## Allen Site Background

The Allen site (figs. 9.1, 9.2) rests on an upper terrace overlooking Margaret Creek to the west. It is at approximately 700 fasl (213 masl) and is in an ecotone setting intermediate to the resources of the creek and floodplain and those of the gently rolling ridges to the east. An opportunistic survey by David L. Hudnell in 1986 identified two distinct clusters of surface artifacts on the terrace, Allen 1 and Allen 2, which our research confirmed as habita-

tion sites (fig. 9.3). These two locations could be deemed sites unto themselves, although they were considered operations within the broader Allen research.

FIG. 9.1. The Allen site (facing east). The main residential area (Allen 1 area) is on the rise by the central lone tree. (Photo by Elliot M. Abrams.)

There were three major divisions of field research at the Allen site. The sequence of field research began in the summer of 1990 with test excavations conducted over a six-week period at the Allen 1 area. Intensive excavation in this area resumed for an additional six weeks during the summer of 1992. The second stage of research involved the systematic survey of the Allen terrace during the summer of 1994: 77 1 m × 50 cm shovel test units were placed every 20 m along seven east-west transects, and 95 2 × 2 m excavation units were placed in areas of high artifact concentration. The third stage of research, in 1996, involved the test excavation of the Allen 2 area. Collectively, some 21 weeks of full-scale survey and excavation were conducted at the site.

## Site Boundary Definition

One of the requisites for understanding the domestic behaviors of this past society is defining the areal extent of the village. This is not necessarily a straightforward exercise since there are several measures that can be used to define the boundary of a site and certainly, like the edge of a kingdom and the extent of an empire, the boundary of a tribal community fluctuated over

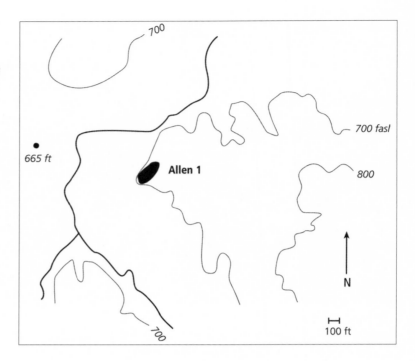

FIG. 9.2. Location of the Allen site, with Allen 1 stippled.

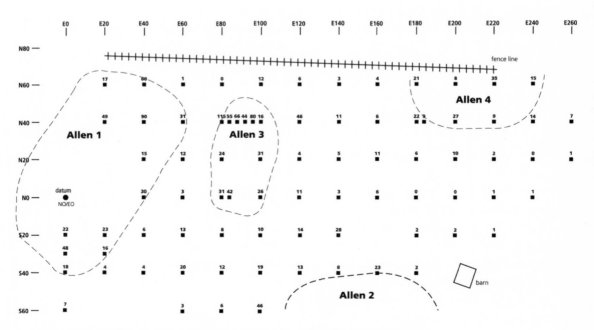

FIG. 9.3. Areas within the Allen site, showing test units and artifact counts per unit.

centuries of occupation. Based on the ubiquity of artifacts (fig. 9.3) and the natural contours of the terrace, an area of approximately 3.12 ha (240 m E-W by 130 m N-S) could represent the total Allen site. This figure, however, is not the most reflective of site size and demography, since artifacts are not uniformly distributed across the terrace and housing (as reflected by feature distribution) did not cover the entire area.

Two major areas of habitation and artifact concentration—Allen 1 and Allen 2—were confirmed by the relative density of artifacts in the survey. For both areas, there is a clearly defined boundary of artifacts (fig. 9.3). The Allen 1 area extended from roughly N70 to S40 and from W20 to E40, or approximately 110 × 60 m (0.66 ha). The village plan of the Allen 1 area paralleled the natural edge of the terrace. The Allen 2 area extended from approximately S40 to S70 and E120 to E180, or 30 × 60 m (0.18 ha). Its southern edge was defined in part by the presence of an unnamed seasonal spring. If both areas were occupied simultaneously, the total area of habitation covered 0.84 ha.

In addition, two other areas on the Allen terrace yielded high densities of artifacts signaling potential loci of human activity. The Allen 3 area extended from E80 to E120 and N40 to N0, roughly 40 × 40 m (0.16 ha). We excavated a line of 2 × 2 m units at 4 m intervals along the N40 transect in this area, yielding data from which we conclude that pottery was being fired in at least portions of the Allen 3 site area. In addition, an area in the northeastern edge of terrace—Allen 4—yielded a relatively high density of artifacts, but this area was particularly disturbed by plowing and no further excavations could be productively expended.

# Chronology

## Radiocarbon Dating

Of the 126 features excavated at the Allen 1 area, 11 (9%) were selected for radiocarbon dating. Wood charcoal from two features at the Allen 2 area were also radiocarbon-dated. The charcoal from these pit features was analyzed by Beta Analytic, Inc., through funds generously provided by the John Baker Foundation at Ohio University. Table 9.1 presents the chronological results of the radiometric dating. Discarding the dates from F70 and F122, which were affected by modern intrusion, the dates of primary occupation effectively range from A.D. 600 to 1310, placing the site's initial occupation at the end of the Late Woodland and continuing through the Late Prehistoric.

### Table 9.1. Radiocarbon Dates from the Allen Site, Areas 1 and 2

*Area 1*

| Beta Lab No. | Feature | RCYBP | Calibrated Date[a] | Cal. Intercept |
|---|---|---|---|---|
| 66177 | 12 | 1490 ± 90 | A.D. 395–687 | A.D. 598 |
| 66178 | 61 | 5330 ± 90 | 4346 B.C.–3963 B.C. | 4118 B.C. |
| 66179 | 70 | 90 ± 60 | A.D. 1665–1955 | A.D. 1908 |
| 75187 | 51 | 880 ± 70 | A.D. 1018–1281 | A.D. 1173 |
| 75188 | 86 | 790 ± 70 | A.D. 1042–1379 | A.D. 1259 |
| 75189 | 98 | 1100 ± 80 | A.D. 723–1152 | A.D. 910 |
| 75190 | 23 | 1140 ± 80 | A.D. 688–1025 | A.D. 925 |
| 75191 | 118 | 1000 ± 80 | A.D. 889–1216 | A.D. 1021 |
| 75192 | 17 | 1300 ± 60 | A.D. 642–886 | A.D. 689 |
| 77729 | 101 | 1090 ± 60 | A.D. 780–1030 | A.D. 979 |
| 77730 | 122 | 330 ± 70 | A.D. 1436–1945 | A.D. 1573 |

*Area 2*

| | | | | |
|---|---|---|---|---|
| 75193 | 228 | 1300 ± 100 | A.D. 561–977 | A.D. 689 |
| 75194 | 208 | 650 ± 80 | A.D. 1223–1431 | A.D. 1372 |

[a]The 2-sigma range, based on Stuiver et al. 1998.

## Ceramic Seriation

Two diagnostic types of sherds were recovered from the Allen 1 excavation. Described below, these are sherds similar to Chesser cordmarked, a type dated through association with one radiocarbon date at A.D. 1070 ± 140 years (Prufer 1967), and one Feurt sherd, a type identified as Fort Ancient (Griffin 1966). Thus the chronological placement of the pottery is consistent with the results of radiocarbon dating.

## Lithic Point Type Seriation

The lithic inventory collected from the surface by Hudnell from the Allen 2 area consists of 221 Late Woodland and Late Prehistoric points (Hudnell 1994). Of these points, 18 were Jack's Reef pentagonals, 105 were Hamilton incurvates, and 98 were Levannas (based on Justice 1987), falling within the radiocarbon range of roughly A.D. 600–1310.

The point types recovered from the Allen 1 area (described below) reflect a far greater range of use, extending to Paleoindian/Early Archaic use of this area. However, of the 46 points, nearly 50% are classified as either

Late Woodland or Late Prehistoric, lending confidence that the analysis of features and artifacts from the Allen 1 area reflect behaviors performed by people during the later portions of prehistory.

## Demography of the Allen Community

The first goal of this research is to generate a population estimate through the following analytic steps: (1) identify architectural postholes, (2) reconstruct the number and size of contemporary houses, (3) estimate, based on ethnographic analogs, the number of people who might reside within houses of that size, and (4) multiply houses by numbers of people. This technique, in general form, has been successful in generating population estimates at rural and urban Classic Maya sites (Webster and Freter 1990).

### The Allen 2 House

The excavation of the Allen 2 area yielded an alignment of posts that were part of the walls of a house (figs. 9.4, 9.5). Fourteen postholes were found forming the outline of this house (structure 1). On average the posts were 8 cm in diameter and extended 10 cm below the base of the plow zone. Posts were spaced about 35 cm apart and the approximate dimensions of the structure were 5 × 3 m, for an interior area of 15 m². Another set of posts was found directly below the first set, indicating that the structure had been rebuilt at the same location at least once. Structure 1 was rectilinear and may serve as the template for residential architectural form for this time period. Based on the areal extent of artifacts and pit features recovered from the survey and excavation of the Allen 2 area, we infer that three to four such houses would have existed in this portion of the Allen site.

### The Allen 1 Features

Although no house as conspicuous as structure 1 was encountered at the Allen 1 area, 126 pit features were located in that part of the site (fig. 9.6). Pit features were identified in the field on the basis of three variables: (1) a curvilinear form of darker soil relative to the surrounding soil matrix when viewed in plan, (2) a distinct conical or tapered profile, and (3) interior contents indicative of human use, such as charcoal, fire-cracked rock, lithics, or pottery. Of the 126 features, 100 (79%) contained charcoal flecks, 36 (29%) contained lithics, and 30 (24%) contained pottery.

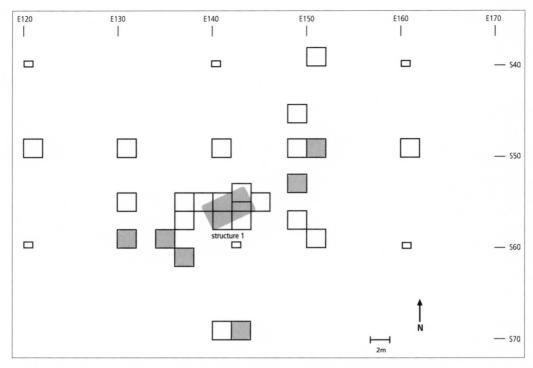

FIG. 9.4. The Allen 2 area, showing the location of structure 1. Shaded units yielded features.

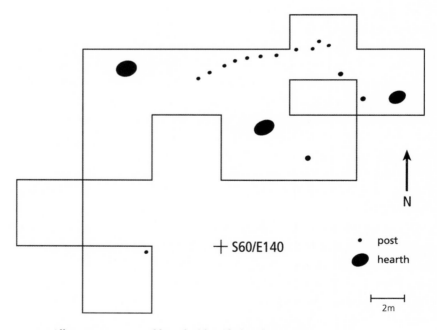

FIG. 9.5. Allen 2 area posts and hearths identified with structure 1

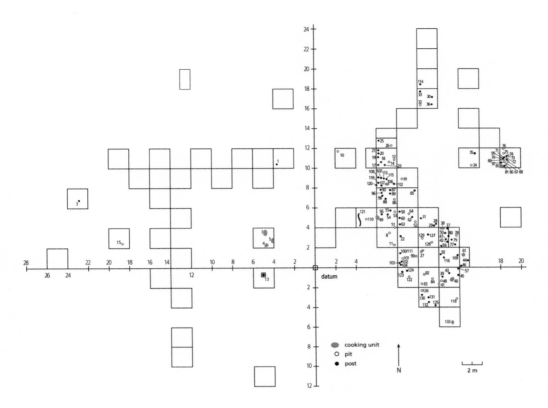

FIG. 9.6. Features from the Allen 1 area

To identify architectural posts from other functional features, a hierarchical cluster analysis based on maximal aperture length of the feature was conducted. This single formal variable is most diagnostic of function, given that size will, in most cases, distinguish architectural posts from larger utilitarian and multifunctional pits and these from even larger cooking features. The obvious problem is that length is a continuous variable and this statistic divides length into discrete clusters. In fact, there was an overlap in the sizes of various "types" of features; for example, larger architectural posts may have been equivalent in size to small heating units within a house. From this, seven categories of features were identified (table 9.2).

A second analytic step in the identification of architectural postholes involved examining the profile of features within the more ambiguous 13–22 cm range. It was decided that those with distinctively tapered profiles were likely architectural posts and those lacking this tapering were classified as generic pits. Although there may be some misclassified features in this analysis, we are fortunately not seeking typological purity.

## Table 9.2. Clustered Lengths and Associated Functions from the Allen Site

| Length Range (cm) | Function |
|---|---|
| 7–12 | Architectural post |
| 13–22 | Either larger architectural post or generic pit |
| 23–34 | Generic pit |
| 38–44 | Small cooking unit |
| 48–55 | Medium cooking unit |
| 64–65 | Large cooking unit |
| 138 | Roasting unit (F93) |

## Architectural Posts

We identified 53 small (7–12 cm) postholes and designated 17 larger features (13–22 cm), based on form, as architectural posts at the Allen 1 area. Thus, 70 features (56% of all features) were identified as postholes, the majority of which probably were remnants of structural elements of housing.

Observing any possible alignments of architectural posts is the best means of defining the form and size of domestic architecture. Fig. 9.7 maps the 48 small and large posts found at the base of the plow zone, revealing several straight lines, which are interpreted as portions of walls: (1) features 25, 21, 20 and 19; (2) features 108, 107, 113, and 115; (3) features 58, 60, 63, and 22; and (4) features 80, 79, and 77. Three observations emerge from this distribution. First, there are perhaps as many as eight clusters of posts localized to this area of the site. Second, the presence of four distinct straight lines of posts indicates that houses were rectilinear. Third, it is evident that houses were not uniformly distributed over the 0.66 ha area defined as the Allen 1 village. Rather, there is a distinct clustering of houses within the village.

## Population Size Estimate

From the distribution of posts and artifacts at the Allen 1, it is argued that from five to eight houses at the site were occupied at any one time. The Allen 2 site probably contained four to five structures. If these two areas were occupied simultaneously, then a maximum number of thirteen houses were in use. If viewed as noncontemporaneous, a minimum number of houses is estimated to be five. A realistic range of six to ten houses was probable given the flexible membership in tribal communities. Pollack and

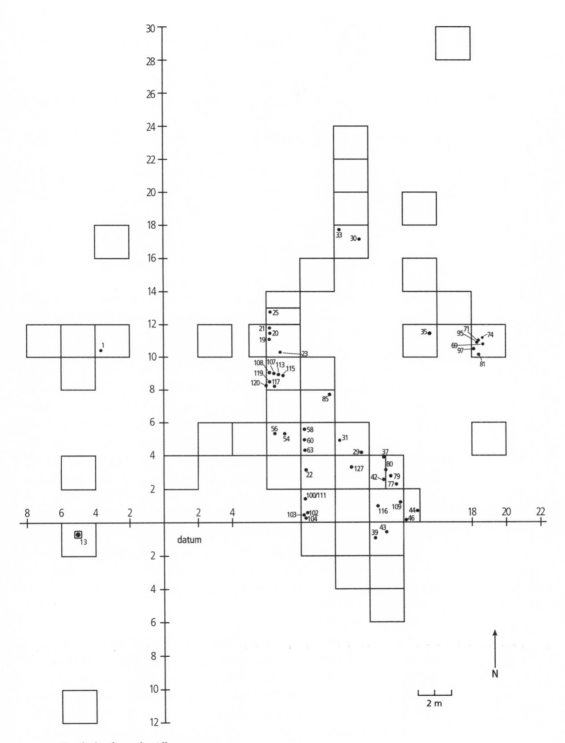

FIG. 9.7. Postholes from the Allen 1 area

Henderson (1992, 284) state that early Fort Ancient villages in general were composed of between six and ten structures.

A house is a static material entity which serves a dynamic household developmental cycle. However, given the average house size of 15 m², we assume that each house was occupied by between five and seven individuals, or slightly higher than the three to six people per house suggested by Henderson, Pollack, and Turnbow (1992, 261). If so, then the Allen site community was composed of between twenty-five and ninety people, with an average of about fifty-five, the exact number fluctuating throughout the period of occupation but increasing through time. Presumably, the lower range best models the Allen community at its inception, around A.D. 500–600.

This demographic estimate is consistent with those generated elsewhere. Henderson, Pollack, and Turnbow (1992, 261) cite a range of three to six people per structure with early Fort Ancient communities composed of between twenty-four and forty people. The population for the Muir site in Kentucky (Turnbow and Sharp 1988a, 272) was estimated at a mean of sixty people but again with a considerable range. The Graham site in the Hocking Valley (fig. 1.2) was estimated at between fifty and eighty people (McKenzie 1967), although the very small size (0.02 ha) of that habitation area casts doubt on the upper end of that estimate.

A further similarity in village structure is the localization of a residential core within the site. On a terrace with artifacts spanning 3.14 ha, the spatial extent of the actual Allen 1 village was 0.66 ha., paralleling the western edge of the terrace. Within this 0.66 ha, houses were clustered within a smaller space of approximately 30 × 20 m (0.06 ha). The Allen 2 area, also serving residential purposes, was approximately 100 m away and measured 0.18 ha.

Other Hocking Valley sites reveal similar patterns of intrasettlement structure. The Graham site covers some 65 × 65 m (0.42 ha; McKenzie 1967, 65). The location of pit features, including posts, is localized to a small 20 × 10 m (0.02 ha) knoll of the site. The same is true for the Sims site (Skinner and Norris 1981), also on the Hocking floodplain. The total area of the site is 0.92 ha, but the main artifact concentration is localized to a space about 50 × 40 m, or about 0.2 ha.

The Park site, located in the floodplain of the Hocking Valley (Skinner and Norris 1981), also displayed this general pattern. The total site, based on artifact distribution, was recorded at 0.55 ha. However, a discrete habitation zone of the total site measuring approximately 0.15 ha was evident, spanning the Archaic to the Late Prehistoric periods. Another habitation area, measuring about 0.05 ha and separated from the first habitation zone by 30 m, was exclusively Late Prehistoric. Thus we have evidence for localized habitation zones far smaller than the total "site" area.

## Reconstruction of Houses

Based on the alignment of architectural posts, the houses at the Allen 1 and 2 areas were 4 to 5 m long and perhaps 3+ m wide, for an internal area of about 15 m². Henderson, Pollack, and Turnbow (1992, 261) state that Fort Ancient houses from A.D. 950 to 1200 ranged in size from 9.8 m² to 15 m². Consequently the Allen domestic structures fall at the high end of the established size range of houses of the early second millennium A.D. in the region.

In the mid–Ohio Valley during this general period, houses were built in various forms. Those excavated from the Philo II site (Carskadden and Morton 1996, 2000) were generally rectilinear but widely varied in size. The Muir site dwellings were effectively rectilinear (Turnbow and Sharp 1988a), while those from the Blain Village appear to be intermediate between a curvilinear and rectilinear form with a decided emphasis toward the latter (Prufer and Shane 1970).

That these Allen houses are rectilinear is significant from an anthropological perspective. Rectilinear house form tends to evolve from a curvilinear form under the broader conditions of increased sedentism and more permanent horticultural/agricultural production (Abrams 1989a). These growing communities tend to build houses that lend themselves to internal divisions and ease of expansion. Rectilinear structures meet both social requirements better than curvilinear structures, and this pattern of shifting form is evident in regions as diverse as the southwestern United States (Gilman 1987) and the Near East (Redman 1978).

## The Allen Site Pottery

The primary analyses of Woodland ceramics from southern Ohio have focused on taxonomy as it relates to chronology and regional connectivity (Griffin 1966; Prufer and McKenzie 1966; Prufer 1967; J. Murphy 1989). Unfortunately, the sherds recovered from the Allen site were limited in various ways, making taxonomic classification difficult. No whole vessels were recovered. Further, the sherds were in generally poor condition and very small. Potsherds were labeled fragments if they were less than 2 cm². If the baseline of 4 cm² had been used, as is often the case in Midwest archaeology, the total number of analyzable sherds out of the 247 recovered would have been fewer than 5. Potsherds equal to or larger than the 2 cm² baseline were labeled sherds rather than the common term sherdlets. These sherds were divided into body and rim sherds.

Of the 247 potsherds recovered from our entire excavation, 82 (33%) were larger than 2 cm², and 165 (67%) were fragments less than 2 cm². The average sherd weighed 3.0 g, and the average fragment 0.67 g. Of the 82 sherds greater than 2 cm², only 5 were rims. Since a total of 83 m³ of soil was excavated, the 82 sherds represent a density of about 1 sherd per cubic meter of soil; the total sample of 247 ceramic artifacts represents a density of about 3 sherds per cubic meter of soil. Of the 247 potsherds, 166 (67%) were recovered from features and 81 (33%) were from soil levels.

The number and density of sherds is extremely low in comparison with other late sites within the mid–Ohio Valley. For example, the Graham Village yielded 6,039 sherds (McKenzie 1967, 67). The Muir site yielded 23,328 sherds (Turnbow 1988, 97). The Water Plant site in central Ohio, dated to the sixth century A.D. (Dancey 1988), yielded 1,640 sherds from both surface collection and excavation. Even earlier sites, such as the Middle Woodland Murphy site (Dancey 1991), yielded 858 sherds. Rockshelters in Athens County have yielded larger amounts of pottery than the Allen 1 area. Chesser Cave (shelter A) yielded 1,132 sherds, with a density of roughly 8.7 sherds per cubic meter of excavated soil (derived from Prufer 1967).

## Ceramic Typology

The typology of pottery used during the Late Woodland and Late Prehistoric periods in southern Ohio is defined on the basis of exterior decoration (typically cordmarking) and tempering material (Griffin 1966; Baby and Potter 1965; McKenzie 1967; Prufer and McKenzie 1966; Prufer 1967; Prufer and Shane 1970; J. Murphy 1989). The distinction between various ceramic types is often, however, vague. For example, Peters cordmarked, as defined by Prufer and McKenzie (1966, 241) from Peters Cave in the Scioto River Valley, is tempered most commonly with flint and chert debitage, this being the sole attribute distinguishing it from Chesser cordmarked found at Chesser Cave in Athens County, which is predominately limestone tempered (Prufer 1967, 12). James Murphy (1989, 326), however, correctly observes that sherds from the Carpenter Shelter in Athens County are tempered with a mixture of limestone and chert.

The Allen sherds were difficult to place within this typology. Certainly their small size made identification difficult, and the more diagnostic sherds (i.e., rims) were extremely few. In addition, the tempering agent had been leached from most sherds.

Given these obstacles, most sherds were simply defined as either plain or cordmarked with no typological identification. However, five sherds could be placed within the existing typology. Four cordmarked sherds (fig. 9.8a)

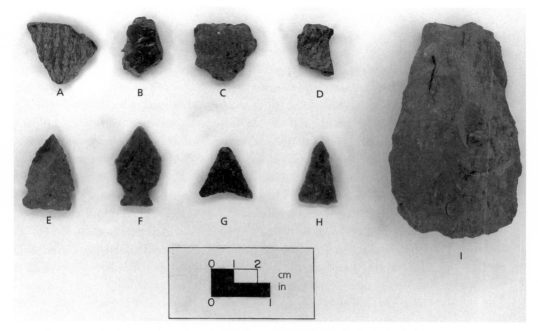

FIG. 9.8. Allen site artifacts: (a) Chesser cordmarked-type sherd, (b) Hudnell sherd, (c) plain sherd, (d) unidentified cordmarked sherd, (e) Matanzas side-notched point, (f) Jack's Reef point, (g) Levanna point, (h) Hamilton incurvate point, type 5 Fine Triangular, (i) chert hoe. (Photo by Lars Lutton.)

closely resemble Chesser cordmarked pottery (Prufer and McKenzie 1966; Prufer 1967). One sherd has thin incisions, possibly linking it with Feurt incised pottery as illustrated in Griffin 1943 (plate 24). Although the McCune site yielded 5,007 Feurt sherds, representing 80.5% of all sherds (J. Murphy 1989, 293), the Graham site, like the Allen site, yielded only one sherd "vaguely reminiscent of Feurt Incised" (McKenzie 1967, 71).

In addition, four sherds and seven fragments were distinguished by their burnished and possibly painted exterior (fig. 9.8b). This treated exterior may reflect a higher-quality vessel perhaps used for different purposes than the utilitarian plain and cordmarked vessels. For working purposes, these sherds are designated as Hudnell sherds; however, with such a small sample, no new typological designation can yet be offered.

In sum, the sherds from the site are rather modest in quality and exterior ornamentation (fig. 9.8c, d). The only established types that are evident are four that resemble Chesser cordmarked and one that is likely a Feurt sherd. All sherds represent the remnants of essentially utilitarian pottery vessels. There were likely several different styles and forms of pots at the site at any one time.

## Ceramic Chronology

Ceramic types are often relied upon to establish or confirm site chronology. Here again there are difficulties owing to the overlapping characteristics which define types as they relate to chronology (Griffin 1966, 55; J. Murphy 1989, 232–33; Prufer and McKenzie 1967, 246). Nonetheless, the resemblance of four of the Allen sherds with Chesser cordmarked confirms a Late Prehistoric date. The one radiocarbon date from Chesser Cave was A.D. 1070 ± 140 years (Prufer 1967), and all four of these sherds came from features dated at A.D. 1180 (feature 51) and A.D. 1260 (feature 86). In addition, the one possible Feurt sherd came from within feature 118, radiocarbon dated to A.D. 1020. Prufer notes that in southern Ohio "a distinctive, local Woodland pottery complex which appears during Adena times, remains essentially intact . . . into Late Woodland times" (1967, 10). This statement established the notion of continuity in cordmarked pottery spanning several centuries, an observation supported by the Allen research.

## Pottery Manufacture

A sample of eight sherds from the Allen site were subjected to x-ray diffraction, x-ray fluorescence, and optical petrography to determine the potential source of clay used in their manufacture (Pitts 2001) These techniques have proven successful in various other archaeological contexts (Beck 1981; Pillay et al. 2000; Douglass and Schaller 1993; Stout and Hurst 1985). The seven sherds analyzed were a mix of Chesser cordmarked, other cordmarked, plain, and "Hudnell" sherds, with the one possible Feurt sherd completing the sample.

Pitts (2001) collected samples of clays from the vicinity of the Allen site, determining the chemical composition of three sources: clay from a paleosol of the Upper Grenshaw formation located on the terraces and upland slope, clays from the Teays River system also located on the terraces and upland slopes, and clay from an ancient lake located in the floodplain of Margaret Creek.

When laboratory analysis was completed, Pitts concluded that seven sherds in the sample (all but the Feurt sherd) were chemically identical— that is, they were made from the same clay. Further, she concluded that the Teays clay located principally in seams on the slopes adjoining the terraces and upland zones was the likely clay source for the Allen site ceramics and consequently that they were of local community manufacture. The one outlier was the Feurt sherd, confirming its nonlocal manufacture.

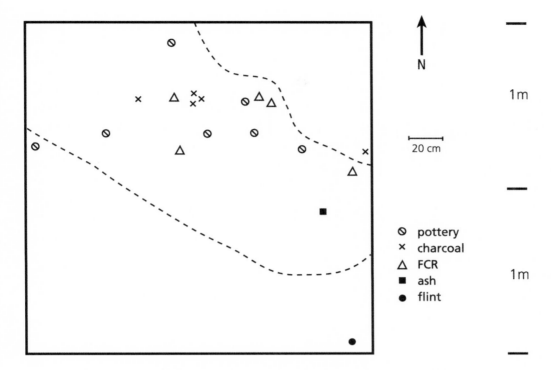

FIG. 9.9. Feature 200, a pottery-firing surface at the Allen site

pottery
charcoal
FCR
ash
flint

In the course of the 1994 survey of the entire Allen terrace, our 1 m × 50 cm units along the N40 transect revealed a surface of level 2 soil that was conspicuously harder than any of the other level 2 soils. In addition, small flecks of charcoal were evident on level 2. We then expanded our initial survey units and excavated an additional four 2 × 2 m units. This surface was designated feature 200 within the Allen 3 area (figs. 9.3, 9.9). In addition to its hardness, several characteristics defined this feature surface: (1) a darker soil (10YR 5/6) compared to the typical level 2 soil matrix (7.5YR 4/6), (2) mottling of ash deposits, and (3) soil marked with scattered bits of fire-cracked rocks, charcoal flecks, and possible ceramics.

This feature is inferred to be the archaeological remnants of a pottery firing area. If one deductively considers the archaeological expectations for such a feature as opposed to a house or midden, they would match the data described above: a hard, burned surface pocked with charcoal, ashen remnants of firing, bits of burned sandstone, and very small fragments of ceramic flecks, the barest remains of waster sherds that did not survive the firing process. This feature suggests that a technique called hearth firing (Sinopoli 1991, 31) was practiced. In hearth firing, the surface on which the pots are fired is effectively flat.

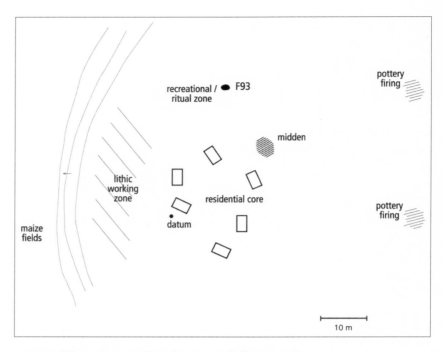

FIG. 9.10. Schematic map of activity areas and village zonation

Spatially, the potsherds from the Allen 1 excavation were found in the residential core—that area where architectural posts were recovered. This indicates that cooking activities took place near houses. Further, the firing of pottery took place some 30 m away from the "edge" of the village. The smoke generated from the firing process likely compelled the potters to conduct such activities away from houses and living areas where children would be playing and other economic activities would be performed, paralleling the placement of pottery firing areas away from residential courtyards in the Maya region (Freter 1996). Thus we begin to reconstruct the activities and spatial dimension to such activities as performed by the Allen site villagers (fig. 9.10).

## The Lithic Industry

A sample of 14,860 lithic artifacts from both feature (778 specimens) and nonfeature (14,082 specimens) contexts at the Allen 1 area were recovered. The vast majority of the recovered lithics (95%) were from plow zone contexts.

## Sources of Lithic Raw Materials

There were various sources of lithic raw materials available to the inhabitants of the Allen village. The local Brush Creek chert is very abundant and easily accessible. A relatively high quality Brush Creek chert can be quarried about 2 to 3 mi (3–5 km) southwest of the site while a poorer quality Brush Creek chert is located just south of the site along Bailey Run. Upper Mercer and Zaleski cherts are 20 to 30 mi (30–50 km) away from the site. Flint Ridge/Vanport chert occurs about 75 mi (120 km) north of the site and is well known for its distinctive coloration and high quality (Stout and Schoenlaub 1945).

These chert types were identified solely on the basis of visual attributes, particularly color and internal homogeneity. Brush Creek, by virtue of its yellow/tan coloration and fossiliferous character, was readily identifiable. No attempt was made to distinguish between qualities of Brush Creek. Upper Mercer and Zaleski, while visually conspicuous in some cases, were cautiously combined as "black." High-quality chert displaying a spectrum of colors was classified as Flint Ridge/Vanport.

A sample of artifacts from 33.6% of the 294 excavated lots at the Allen 1 area were examined. This sample included lithics from all features as well as a random selection of nonfeature contexts. A total of 3,267 artifacts were weighed and classified (table 9.3).

From this preliminary investigation, it is clear that Brush Creek chert was the raw material preferred by the occupants of the Allen site, with the mean flake size being heavier than those of more distant raw materials.

## Lithic Analysis

The sample of lithic materials from the Allen 1 site consisted of 14,657 pieces of debitage and 203 retouched tools. The retouched tools are comprised of flake tools, such as end scrapers, retouched flakes, and bifaces, including finished preforms and tools broken during manufacture, as well as drills and projectile points. The sample of projectile points is varied and comprises

Table 9.3. Lithic Raw Materials from the Allen Site

| | Brush Creek | % | Black (UM/Z) | % | Flint Ridge | % | All Materials |
|---|---|---|---|---|---|---|---|
| Total count | 2,284 | 69.9 | 565 | 17.3 | 418 | 12.8 | 3,267 |
| Total weight (g) | 2,571.0 | 78.2 | 388.6 | 11.8 | 328.7 | 10.0 | 3,288.3 |
| Mean wt./artifact (g) | 1.1 | | 0.7 | | 0.8 | | 1.0 |

specimens dating from the Late Paleoindian to Late Prehistoric periods. The most prevalent projectile points include Late Archaic types (Matanzas, Lamoka, and Merom clusters), Middle /Late Woodland types (Snyders and Lowe clusters), and Late Prehistoric triangular points. The Allen 1 sample, therefore, reflects a multicomponent occupation spanning most of the Midwestern prehistoric sequence.

The debitage categories were based on classification schemes employed by both Old and New World prehistorians (Bordes 1961; Frison 1974; Tixier, Inizan, and Roche 1980). The first level of analysis involved separating the debitage into flakes, cores, and fragments (shatter and "chunks" of raw material). The flakes were then further subdivided, as much as possible, into groups that would more specifically identify the reduction sequence to which they belonged. The terminology used in the classification of lithic artifacts recovered from the Allen site is further based on the work of Newcomer and Karlin (1987), Sonneville-Bordes (1960), Newcomer (1971), Callahan (1979), and Bradley and Sampson (1986).

The material was analyzed according to attributes that would describe certain aspects of the flaking technology. The artifacts were first sorted into two major classes: retouched tools and debitage. The tools were further subdivided into subclasses that included bifaces/preforms, projectile points, knives, scrapers, and miscellaneous tools. The debitage was divided into unretouched flakes, cores, and pieces of shatter.

After the first sorting, into tools and debitage, a second series of attributes were used to describe raw material type and any relevant technological traits. Projectile points and other retouched tools were separated by type and subsequently categorized according to morphological and technological characteristics.

Finally, the flakes were divided into two main categories that distinguished those pieces detached during biface reduction from the remainder of the sample. The latter group consisted of artifacts for which it was impossible to determine the exact nature of the reduction sequence. Once the two groups were identified, a three-tiered model of early-middle-late reduction was applied to the biface debitage. The unspecified reduction flakes were divided simply into early- and late-stage reduction, based on attributes such as the presence and amount of cortex, or natural surface, on the dorsal surface of each flake, as well as hard-hammer flaking mode. The debitage was examined to clarify the general character of lithic reduction as a technological process at this site. Each piece was inspected individually and, where possible, assigned to a particular class relating to a specific reduction sequence or portion of a reduction sequence (see table 9.4).

Current approaches to the analysis of lithic artifacts include a study of the step-by-step procedures utilized by prehistoric knappers to make tools. A concept introduced by French archaeologists, *la chaîne opératoire*, may be used to describe the process of technological organization at any prehistoric site. In behavioral terms, this process envelops not only an original project as a response to a need but also the means and by-products of the activities employed to achieve the desired goal. Thus, prehistoric lithic artifacts must not be viewed as static objects but rather as residual "events" reflecting a dynamic, interrelated system comprising needs, projects, and organized activities involving modification of materials to achieve specific goals. In examining technological organization as expressed through a flaked-stone tool assemblage, consideration is usually given to raw material selection as well as to tool manufacturing, use, breakage, sharpening, and discard trajectories (Bergman and Doershuk 1992). In as much as each component of this sequence refers to a specific project or projects, it signifies task-oriented prehistoric behavior.

Once a raw material is selected and an adequate source is located, the process of tool manufacture begins. Two different strategies can be used: one involves the reduction of material directly into a tool form, like a biface, while the other involves the production of a core. This second reduction process involves the preparation of raw material so that flakes of a suitable shape and size can be detached. These blanks are then flaked by percussion or pressure flaking into a variety of tool types, including scrapers, drills, knives, or projectile points. In addition, further reduction of the core may result in the piece being modified into a biface.

## Results of the Debitage Analysis

A total of 14,657 pieces of debitage were recovered from features and excavation units at the Allen 1 site (table 9.4). The most frequently occurring debitage type is the biface thinning flake (class 4), comprising 26.4% of the sample, followed by biface finishing flakes (class 5) at 24.7%. In total, debitage produced as a result of biface manufacture (classes 3 [biface initial-reduction flake], 4, and 5) accounts for 53% of the debitage sample. This indicates that the manufacture and maintenance of bifacial tools was an important lithic reduction activity conducted at the Allen site. Flakes detached during unspecifiable reduction sequences, which can be derived from core, unifacial, or bifacial reduction, constitute the remaining 47% of the debitage. These include initial-reduction flakes (class 1 = 3.8%), flakes from unspecifiable reduction sequences (class 2 = 17.5%), chips (class 6 = 3.5%),

Table 9.4. Debitage from the Allen Site

| Debitage | Class | Total | % |
|---|---|---|---|
| Initial-reduction flake | 1 | 552 | 3.8 |
| Flake, unspec. reduction sequence | 2 | 2,565 | 17.5 |
| Biface initial-reduction flake | 3 | 262 | 1.8 |
| Biface thinning flake | 4 | 3,872 | 26.4 |
| Biface finishing flake | 5 | 3,620 | 24.7 |
| Chip (5–10 mm max. dimension) | 6 | 513 | 3.5 |
| Shatter | 7 | 3,001 | 20.5 |
| Microdebitage | 8 | 119 | 0.8 |
| Janus flake | 9 | 134 | 0.9 |
| Core | | 19 | 0.1 |
| Total | | 14,657 | 100.0 |

shatter (class 7 = 20.5%), microdebitage (class 8 = 0.8%), and Janus flakes (class 9 = 0.9%).

Chips and microdebitage (classes 6 and 8) are poorly represented in the lithic sample, accounting for less than 5% of the debitage total (table 9. 4). This probably reflects both preservation and sampling bias. The smaller debitage classes are generally numerically dominant in any lithic reduction sequence. Since the majority of soil excavated at the Allen 1 area was screened through ¼ in mesh rather than floated, the sample of the smaller lithic artifacts is consequently diminished.

Analysis of the debitage from the Allen 1 site indicates that initial-reduction flakes (classes 1 and 3) are relatively rare, making up less than 6% of the total sample. There were 7,492 biface thinning and finishing flakes (classes 4 and 5); these categories of debitage outnumber the biface initial-reduction products by a ratio of about 29:1. This suggests that bifacial preforms were initially flaked outside the site and were later finished onsite and that the sharpening and repair of worn and broken bifacial tools was a frequent focus of lithic reduction onsite.

Nineteen cores were examined in the sample, all of them flake cores. Multiple striking platforms and multidirectional flake removals are characteristic of the core sample, suggesting a random, nonpatterned approach to reduction. No bladelet cores were identified, although a limited number of bladelet fragments exist in the collection.

Debitage recovered from excavation unit contexts accounts for 95% (n = 13,680) of the debitage, while feature debitage comprises only 5% (n = 778). The difference in sample size directly correlates to the dispro-

### Table 9.5. Tools from the Allen Site

| Tool Type | Total | % |
|---|---|---|
| Biface/biface fragment | 80 | 39 |
| Projectile point | 46 | 23 |
| Projectile point fragment | 49 | 24 |
| Retouched flake | 16 | 8 |
| End scraper | 6 | 3 |
| Drill | 6 | 3 |
| Total | 203 | 100 |

portionate number of excavation units investigated verses the number of features. However, debitage class/percentages from units and features are generally similar, suggesting a consistent pattern of lithic reduction and artifact deposition activities across the site. In addition, debitage reflecting the manufacturing of bifacial tools was recovered from features dating from A.D. 600 (feature 12) through A.D. 1260 (feature 86), indicating economic continuity in lithic manufacture spanning centuries.

In all, 501 pieces of debitage were recovered from feature 3, a large pit 20 m west of the main residential zone. This feature contained more debitage than any other. Biface thinning and finishing flakes account for 68% of the total debitage while other classes are poorly represented. The dominance of the later-stage biface reduction flakes indicates that discard into the pit coincided with a zone of manufacture or tool maintenance. Given the recurrent placement of houses and the abundance of lithic material west of the main residential zone, we suggest that this western area was at least one of the major areas for specialized lithic reduction (fig. 9.10).

## Analysis of the Retouched Tools

A total of 203 retouched tools were recovered from excavations at the Allen 1 area (table 9.5). Bifaces and biface fragments are the most frequently encountered retouched tool type. All stages of biface manufacture are represented; however, bifaces in the initial stages of reduction are rare and the majority of tools do not display significant areas of cortex. This suggests that preforms or partially finished tools were transported to the site, a finding consistent with the debitage analysis.

Sixteen retouched flakes, including two retouched bladelets, were recovered from Allen 1. The majority of these pieces have discontinuous retouch along one or both lateral edges that may be the result of use. Six bifacially flaked drills were recovered, all broken by torsion or flexion at the tip and displaying both Y- and T-type basal portions. In addition, six end scrapers, comprising 3% of the retouched tool sample, were recovered. Most are teardrop shaped with retouch along both lateral edges.

One unique artifact not included in the statistics of tool types is a Brush Creek chert biface tentatively identified as the blade of a hoe or adze (fig. 9.8i). It was collected from the surface of the Allen 1 area before the 1990 excavations. It measures 98.2 mm long, 58.5 mm wide, and 31.4 mm thick. It is decidedly tapered for cutting but no wear pattern analysis has yet been conducted to refine its functional identification.

## Projectile Points

The sample of 46 chronologically diagnostic projectile points illustrates the multicomponent nature of the site. They span the entirety of known occupation in the Hocking Valley, attesting to the significant reuse of prime space within the region. Table 9.6 identifies and quantifies the points from the Allen site, with identifications based on Justice (1987), and a sample of points is shown in figure 9.8 (e, f, g, h).

Point types predominate (46%) from those centuries during which the Allen site was occupied by a relatively sedentary agricultural community. According to Justice (1987, 208), the Lowe cluster includes the Steuben expanding stem, Bakers Creek, Lowe flared base, and Chesser notched types. Steuben Expanding Stem points date from the terminal Middle Woodland to the early Late Woodland cultural periods. Bakers Creek projectile points are diagnostic of middle and terminal Middle Woodland periods and appear in the southeast around A.D. 150 (211). Lowe flared-base points, which are closely related to the Bakers Creek type, are indicative of the terminal Middle Woodland (213). Chesser notched points date from the terminal Middle Woodland to the Late Woodland period and apparently fit chronologically between the Snyders cluster and other Late Woodland types such as the unnotched pentagonal cluster points (214). Projectile points attributed to the Lowe cluster recovered from the Allen 1 site are all classified as Chesser notched.

The most frequent projectile point type from the Allen 1 area is the fine triangular type. Recent research conducted by Henderson, Pollack, and Turnbow (1992) in northeastern, northern, and central Kentucky has shown that the once nondescript triangular projectile points, most commonly known as Madison and Hamilton, reveal diachronic trends in style and morphology. As a result of their research, and the excavation of numerous

| Table 9.6. Projectile Points from the Allen Site | | |
|---|---|---|
| *Period* | *Type of Point* | *Number* |
| Late Paleoindian/Early Archaic | Dalton cluster | 1 |
| | Kirk cluster | 1 |
| | Large side-notched cluster | 1 |
| Middle Archaic | Stanly cluster | 5 |
| Late Archaic | Lamoka cluster | 4 |
| | Matanzas cluster | 4 |
| | Merom cluster | 4 |
| | McWhinney heavy-stemmed | 1 |
| Early Woodland | Kramer | 1 |
| Middle Woodland | Snyders cluster | 3 |
| Late Woodland | Lowe cluster | 9 |
| | Jack's Reef cluster | 1 |
| Late Prehistoric | Fine triangulars | 11 |

Fort Ancient sites within the central Ohio River Valley which pre- and post-date their studies, seven types of fine triangulars have been identified (Henderson and Turnbow 1987; Railey 1992, 137). Of the recovered triangulars from the Allen 1 area, type 4 Fine Triangulars are the most frequently occurring type (n = 4). Henderson, Pollack, and Turnbow (1992) suggest that type 4 Fine Triangulars occur most frequently in contexts that date to the thirteenth century A.D. Type 3 Fine Triangulars (n = 3) are indicative of Middle Fort Ancient contexts (168). Finally type 1, 2, 5,and 6 Fine Triangulars are represented by one specimen each.

## Other Village Features

Twelve features at the Allen 1 area were sufficiently large in length and overall size to be classified as cooking units, divided into four categories (table 9.2). In addition to their size, the presence of charcoal and fire-cracked rocks indicates a cooking function. One cooking feature, however, stands apart from all others. Feature 93 is a cooking unit located some 40 m north of the residential core at the Allen 1 area (fig. 9.10). Its diameter of 1.38 m placed it statistically as a category unto itself. We mention this particular cooking unit since it is spatially separated from the area of greatest cooking activity. Hypothetically it represented the nondaily cooking of foods, as for aggregate feasting or other special purpose.

Finally, of all the units excavated, only one yielded evidence that it may have been the locus of intended community waste deposition. Unit 72, at N20/E24, contained soil with a high organic content. Given that almost no faunal remains were found at the site, the five fragments of white-tailed deer bone from level 1 are significant. Further, it is at the downward slope of the eastern edge of the cleared Allen 1 village site.

Local resource zones of clay, lithic material (predominantly of Brush Creek chert), and wood from the terrace and adjacent forests (Wymer, this volume) provided the raw materials for the manufacture of the bulk of artifacts produced by the inhabitants of this Late Prehistoric village. An analysis of our data imparts a picture of specialized areas within the site, used recurrently by members of the community, a pattern that began at least by the Middle Woodland period (Crowell et al., this volume; Dancey 1991). The village was centered around a residential core. Cooking, lithic reworking, and other tasks were conducted in this area. Larger-scale lithic reduction took place in the broad space to the west of the residential core, overlooking the creek. Pottery firing occurred to the east of the residential core, and recreational/ceremonial activities took place to the north of the center of the site. A refuse area northeast of the residential core sloped off the eastern "edge" of the village's living area.

This reconstruction of village organization compares favorably with intra- and extraregional patterns inferred from sites outside the Hocking Valley such as the South Park Village site (Brose 1994) and the Muir site (Turnbow and Sharp 1988b). The present village differs, however, in a lower population size and lack of a circular arrangement of the residential core, as evidenced from the Philo II site (Carskadden and Morton 2000) and the Sunwatch site (Nass and Yerkes 1995). This variability, as expressed by Griffin (1992), who coined the term Fort Ancient, sharpens our focus as to what archaeologists mean by that single cultural designation. It encourages an exploration as to the ecological, economic, and sociopolitical causes of such village variability.

# 10

# LATE PREHISTORIC AGRICULTURE AND LAND USE IN THE HOCKING VALLEY

Dee Anne Wymer

COMMUNITIES IN THE HOCKING VALLEY, OHIO, beginning ca. A.D. 700 were attracted to floodplain pockets of rich agricultural soil along the Hocking River and its tributaries (Abrams 1992b; Wakeman, this volume), a pattern evidenced in other portions of the mid–Ohio Valley (Maslowski 1985). Their village economy was based on a new introduced crop, maize (corn), which began to dominate and replace the Eastern Agricultural Complex (EAC). Of tropical origin, maize required many generations and perhaps several reintroductions until it was sufficiently acclimatized to the Midwestern temperate climate to become a viable food source and by A.D. 700 a staple crop influencing societal change.

## The Sample

Paleoethnobotanical samples from the Allen 1 area of the Allen site (33AT653; see figs. 1.2; 9.1, 9.2, 9.3) included both sediment subjected to flotation processing and macrobotanical materials hand-collected in the field during excavation (Abrams, Bergman, and Miller, this volume). The macrobotanical specimens were principally obtained for radiocarbon analysis. A total of 35 flotation samples from 33 separate features were analyzed. Samples ranged in volume from approximately 0.5 L to nearly 30 L; most were between 2 and 3 L. These 33 features represent 26.2% of the total 126 features encountered at the site. Of the 33 features, 14 (42.4%) were postholes, 17 (51.5%) were pits, and 2 (6.1%) were cooking features. Twenty-six macrobotanical samples, from as many features, were also examined and the materials identified.

## Laboratory Procedures

The light and heavy fractions from each flotation sample were sifted through nested geological sieves to produce three size classes: > 2.00 mm, 2.00–1.00 mm, and < 1.00 mm. These size fractions were then examined with the aid of a binocular microscope with magnifications ranging from 7× to 30×. Weights were taken with an electronic top-loading balance (Mettler P163).

The analysis consisted of examining the samples in two stages. All botanical debris was first sorted into identifiable categories, such as wood charcoal, nutshell, and carbonized seeds. Second, after the initial sorting, certain classes of plant material (e.g., wood charcoal) were reexamined and identified to generic, and where possible, specific taxonomic levels.

Material in the > 2.00 mm fraction was sorted and the number of fragments and total weight were recorded for all botanical classes except wood charcoal. Only the weight was noted for wood charcoal for this size class since wood fragments often number in the hundreds or thousands. This plant category was also recorded as present or absent for the fractions below 2.00 mm but was not separated into a discrete category from its sediment matrix. Seeds and any unusual items were removed from the sediment matrix for all size classes and examined. Acorn nutshell, due to the tendency for this material to fragment into small pieces, was also sorted out of the 2.00–1.00 mm fraction and counts and weights were duly registered. Modern debris (e.g., uncarbonized seeds, rootlets, insects) in the samples was noted as well.

Wood charcoal fragments in flotation samples that contained large amounts of this plant class were sampled for identification to tree taxa. Fragments in the > 2.00 mm class were inspected, and at least 20 specimens were analyzed from samples containing abundant amounts of wood charcoal. In samples with smaller quantities of this plant class, fragments were identified to genus and species whenever material size and condition permitted.

A number of samples hand-collected in the field (here termed macrobotanical specimens) were also submitted to Bloomsburg University's archaeology laboratory for analysis. Each sample was examined by first removing as much of the surrounding sediment as possible (while minimizing damage to the specimen); the material was then identified with the stereomicroscope and weighed. For those items identified as wood charcoal, the cross-sections were examined to identify the tree taxa. After analysis, the sample was placed in aluminum foil and then put in a sterile, labeled plastic specimen bag. Notes were also kept about the condition of the macrobotanical specimens.

Various standard identification manuals (Core, Côté, and Day 1979; Martin and Barkley 1973; Montgomery 1977; Panshin and de Zeeuw 1980; USDA 1974), as well as the modern comparative collection at the Bloomsburg laboratory, were consulted. Identifications were made to the genus level where possible. Identifications to the species level were made when only one species of a genus is native to the area (i.e., *Gymnocladus dioicus*—Kentucky coffeetree) or when it was possible to rule out all related species on the basis of comparative morphology (e.g., *Juglans nigra*—black walnut, as opposed to *Juglans cinerea*—butternut).

The major assumption underlying the sorting and identification of the botanical material was that only items that were charred (carbonized) or partially carbonized represented prehistoric material. Uncarbonized seeds, for example, are assumed to be the result of present-day seed rain. This caveat is followed by the majority of paleoethnobotanists, especially when dealing with open-air sites (see discussions by Ford 1979; Lopinot and Brussel 1982; Minnis 1981; Munson, Parmalee, and Yarnell 1971).

## Paleoethnobotanical Results

Two measurements, *ubiquity* and *density* of plant classes, were calculated for the Allen materials. An *index of ubiquity* reflects how often a particular botanical class appears in samples from a site or sites. Ubiquity indices are generated by dividing the number of samples containing a particular item by the total number of samples in the analysis and are expressed as percentages. Accordingly, ubiquity actually measures dispersion of an item, or rather, how material is distributed over a given site.

Density, a measurement of abundance, allows for comparison of sample to sample, feature to feature, and site to site. An *index of density* is produced by dividing the count or weight (or both) of a class of botanical material by the total volume (in liters) of sediment from which the material is derived (see also Miller 1988). The density figure thus represents the count or weight of a specific plant class per liter of soil. The following discussions will utilize both ubiquity and density measurements, as well as percentage calculations estimating the importance of specific taxa, such as wood types, in the paleoethnobotanical record of the site.

## Table 10.1 Paleoethnobotanical Materials from Flotation Samples from the Allen Site

| | Raw Data | | Density[a] | | Ubiquity[b] | |
|---|---|---|---|---|---|---|
| Material | No. | Weight (g) | No. | Weight (g) | No. features | % |
| Wood charcoal | — | 104.65 | — | 0.69062 | 33 | 100 |
| Nutshell | 156 | 1.61 | 1.029 | 0.01062 | 29 | 87.88 |
| Nutmeat | 2 | 0.01 | 0.013 | trace | 1 | 3.03 |
| Maize | 7 | 0.06 | 0.046 | trace | 5 | 15.15 |
| Seeds | 6 | — | 0.04 | — | 5 | 15.15 |

[a]Based on 151.53 liters of soil examined to date.
[b]Ubiquity is based on presence in 33 features.

## Flotation Samples

Five broad categories of carbonized botanical materials were recovered from the Allen site flotation samples: wood charcoal, nutshell, nutmeat, maize, and seeds (table 10.1). The most prevalent material in the samples, not surprisingly, is wood charcoal, with approximately 105 g sorted in the > 2mm size fraction. This quantity yields a total site density of 0.69 g/L. Wood charcoal was also identified in every sample from the site.

Nutshell was also fairly common, appearing in nearly 88% of the features (table 10.1). However, the quantity is quite low; less than 2 g were extracted in the > 2mm size fraction, producing a total site density of around 1 fragment at 0.01 g/L. In addition, two fragments of acorn nutmeat were identified in a single sample. Last, seven fragments of maize, including an entire intact kernel, were identified in the flotation samples, and six carbonized seeds were recovered. Both botanical classes have a low ubiquity, appearing in five features.

## Wood Charcoal Taxa

Seven distinct taxa were identified during examination of wood charcoal fragments (table 10.2). The taxa included oak (*Quercus* spp.), represented by both the white group and red group, hickory (*Carya* spp.), walnut (*Juglans* spp.), ash (*Fraxinus* spp.), beech (*Fagus grandifolia*), and buckeye (*Aesculus* spp.). Many of the specimens were highly distorted from intense burning, and this is reflected in the large number of fragments assigned to the ring-porous, diffuse-porous, and unidentifiable categories. Of the identified taxa, oak is clearly predominant, contributing approximately 59% of

## Table 10.2 Identification of Wood Taxa in Flotation Samples from the Allen Site

| Taxon | Raw Data | | | Ubiquity[a] | |
| --- | --- | --- | --- | --- | --- |
| | No. | Weight (g) | % of Ident. Wood Wt. | No. features | % |
| Oak-white group | 21 | 1.09 | 11.30 | 6 | 28.57 |
| Oak-red group | 85 | 3.77 | 39.07 | 12 | 57.14 |
| Unid. Oak spp. | 24 | 0.81 | 8.39 | | |
| Total oak | 130 | 5.67 | 58.76 | 18 | 85.71 |
| Hickory | 40 | 2.32 | 24.04 | 11 | 52.38 |
| Walnut | 15 | 0.83 | 8.60 | 1 | 4.76 |
| Ash | 13 | 0.53 | 5.49 | 8 | 38.10 |
| Beech | 7 | 0.24 | 2.49 | 3 | 14.29 |
| Buckeye | 2 | 0.06 | 0.62 | 2 | 9.52 |
| Ring-porous | 50 | 1.62 | | | |
| Diffuse-porous | 7 | 0.17 | | | |
| Unident | 61 | 11.39 | | | |

[a]Ubiquity is based on presence in 21 samples that contained identified taxa.

the identified fragment weight and found in nearly 86% of the features with examined wood charcoal. Hickory is also an important wood type, with over 2 g identified. In fact, when oak and hickory weights are combined the two taxa constitute almost 83% of the entire weight of identified wood for the site's flotation samples.

The remaining four taxa—walnut, ash, beech, and buckeye—were relatively rare in the samples. However, although only about 5% of the identified wood weight, ash reveals a fairly widespread occurrence across the samples (showing a ubiquity of 38%). This pattern may relate more to the carbonization and preservation factors of *Fraxinus* (the wood may fragment more heavily upon firing than oak or hickory) than to the degree of preference of this wood as a firewood resource by the prehistoric populations.

## Nutshell Taxa

Four distinct taxa were identified from the nutshell fragments recovered in the flotation samples (table 10.3): hickory, black walnut (*Juglans nigra*), butternut (*J. cinerea*), and acorn (*Quercus* sp.). In addition, a number of fragments that were clearly walnut, but that could not be definitely assigned to either black walnut or butternut, were placed in the general "Unid. walnut"

## Table 10.3 Nutshell Taxa from Flotation Samples from the Allen Site

| Taxon | No. | Ident. Taxa % by No. | Weight (g) | Ident. Taxa % by Wt. |
|---|---|---|---|---|
| Hickory | 33 | 39.76 | 0.53 | 51.96 |
| Black walnut | 7 | 8.43 | 0.08 | 7.84 |
| Butternut | 1 | 1.20 | 0.11 | 10.78 |
| Unid. walnut | 41 | 49.40 | 0.30 | 29.41 |
| Total walnut | 49 | 59.04 | 0.49 | 48.04 |
| Acorn | 1 | 1.20 | < 0.01 | |
| Juglandaceae | 73 | | 0.59 | |

category. The category Juglandaceae includes specimens that could represent any of the thick-shelled varieties of hickory or walnuts. (Juglandaceae is the family taxon for both hickory and walnut.)

Hickory appears to be the most common nut type by weight, although a greater number of walnut fragments were recovered in the samples (table 10.3). A single specimen of acorn nutshell was identified (feature 25), although, as noted above, acorn nutmeat was recovered in a separate feature (feature 17).

## Maize Specimens

Although only a few fragments of maize were recovered in the flotation samples (tables 10.1, 10.4), given the time period represented by the site, this constitutes an important botanical class. Both isolated kernel fragments and cupules were identified, as well as an entire intact corn kernel. This kernel from F17 was submitted for AMS radiocarbon dating and the calibrated intercept date was A.D. 689 (Abrams, Bergman, and Miller, this volume).

## Carbonized Seeds

Only three taxa were identified from the carbonized seeds recovered from the flotation samples. Two separate features (69, 72) each contained a single raspberry (*Rubus* sp.) seed. A bedstraw (*Galium* sp.) seed was identified in the sediment from feature 69, and a possible bedstraw seed was noted in the sample from feature 86. The same feature yielded a highly carbonized un-

| Table 10.4 Maize Specimens from Flotation Samples from the Allen Site | | |
|---|---|---|
| | *No.* | *Weight (g)* |
| *Kernels* | | |
| Entire | 1 | 0.03 |
| Fragments | 4 | 0.02 |
| *Cupules* | 2 | 0.01 |

known specimen that could not be identified to taxa. Lastly, a single probable Solanaceae seed (the nightshade family) was identified in sediment from feature 25.

## Macrobotanical Samples

As noted above, this group of samples represents larger specimens hand-collected during excavation with the intent of utilizing them for radiocarbon dating. In all, 26 samples, from as many features, were examined. In every case, wood charcoal was the primary, if not exclusive, material appearing in the samples (table 10.5). Wood charcoal ranged from less than 1 g to nearly 40 g (feature 61), with the majority around 2 to 3 g. In addition to the wood charcoal, one fragment of eroded possible nutshell was noted (feature 8). One fragment of unidentified nutmeat was also identified in the specimens collected from feature 51.

The taxa identified during analysis of the wood charcoal fragments mirror the genera noted for the specimens from the flotation samples, albeit with slightly greater diversity. Nine distinct taxa were identified, including the white and red group of oak, ash, hickory, walnut, elm (*Ulmus* spp.), maple (*Acer* spp.), possible black cherry *(Prunus serotina),* and chestnut *(Castanea).* Many of the fragments were heavily burned and thus the cell structure was too distorted to permit identification; consequently the "Unidentifiable" category represents the greatest quantity (over 41 g) of material. Of the fragments that could be identified to taxa, oak (nearly equally divided between the white and red group) forms roughly 66% of the weight. Oak, not surprisingly, was also the most ubiquitous of the wood taxa, appearing in approximately 65% of the macrobotanical samples. Ash was quite significant in these samples, with nearly 8 g identified, but was recovered in only five features. Hickory, although the total weighed less, had a slightly

Table 10.5 Identification of Wood Taxa in Radiocarbon Macrobotanical Samples from the Allen Site

| Taxon | Weight (g) | % of ident. wood weight | Ubiquity[a] No. samples | % |
|---|---|---|---|---|
| White group | 8.98 | 25.24 | 12 | 46.15 |
| Red group | 9.69 | 27.21 | 7 | 26.92 |
| Oak spp. | 4.67 | 13.13 | | |
| Total oak | 23.33 | 65.57 | 17 | 65.38 |
| Ash | 7.87 | 22.12 | 5 | 19.23 |
| Hickory | 2.51 | 7.05 | 6 | 23.08 |
| Walnut | 1.01 | 2.84 | 1 | 3.85 |
| Elm | 0.51 | 1.43 | 2 | 7.69 |
| Maple | 0.05 | 0.14 | 2 | 7.69 |
| (Hard maple) | 0.11 | 0.31 | | |
| Black cherry (?) | 0.14 | 0.39 | 1 | 3.85 |
| Chestnut | 0.05 | 0.14 | 1 | 3.85 |
| Ring-porous | 6.66 | | | |
| Diffuse-porous | 0.19 | | | |
| Unidentifiable | 41.13 | | | |

[a]Ubiquity is based on presence in 26 samples with identified wood taxa.

higher ubiquity. The remaining taxa were identified in only one or two samples. Thus, the main distinctions between the macrobotanical and flotation samples seems to be the decreased appearance of hickory and the greater quantity of ash (however, the ubiquity of this taxon was quite high in the flotation samples—38%).

## Environmental Parameters

Paleoethnobotanical samples contribute to the understanding of cultural dynamics in a number of ways. For example, this type of material gives direct (and often indirect) clues to the economic basis of prehistoric populations, environmental parameters, and cultural patterns of site usage (e.g., subsistence processing and storage practices, and ceremonial plant utilization). Most important, these data serve as the foundation for examining the evolution of subsistence practices for the region.

In order to place the paleoethnobotanical materials from the Allen site in perspective, it is necessary to first reconstruct the general character of the prehistoric environment for the site locality based on previous paleo-environmental reconstruction in the Hocking Valley (Wymer 1990) and forest composition surveys in Athens County (Boetticher 1929; Rypma 1961). Although each Late Prehistoric community was faced with its own microenvironment, the Allen site setting replicates the general forest and landform structure for many contemporary sites (Abrams, Bergman, and Miller, this volume).

The site sits on a terrace overlooking Margaret Creek to the west and a smaller run to the southwest, and it lies directly west of a series of uplands that overlook the site. Thus, the elevation ranges from around 900 fasl (274 masl) for the top of the adjacent ridge to around 665 fasl (203 masl) for the bottomlands below the site, a shift of some 235 feet (72 m) within less than a mile. Consequently, the forest composition and overall botanical community must have reflected considerable topographic and related soil changes.

The Allen site inhabitants had access to a wide diversity of resources in immediate proximity to the site's locality. At the outset the higher ridges to the east would have held a more xeric community, most likely dominated by chestnut oak, chestnut, and possibly some species of pine. A mixed meso-phytic community (which includes a wide variety of tree and herbaceous species) undoubtedly grew on the lower portions of the slopes, especially on the shadier north slopes. The site locality itself, given the lay of the land and the good drainage, would have been dominated by an oak-hickory forest (largely white oak and possibly shagbark hickory). Last, evidence from early surveys points to a rather dense bottomland forest throughout the county, and the creek bottoms were probably covered with a mixture of mesic species, including beech, maples, elms, ash, tulip tree, willows, syca-more, and cottonwood.

## Resource Utilization and Economic Factors

### Firewood Collection Patterns

There is an extremely close match between the wood taxa from the Allen site samples and the above environmental reconstruction. Oak and hickory are the most common taxa identified in the samples (composing around 85% of the wood weight), followed by fairly high quantities of ash and wal-nut. A few fragments of the mesic taxa of beech, buckeye, elm, and maple were also noted, as were fragments of black cherry and chestnut from the macrobotanical samples. Thus, the identified wood types indicate that the Allen population was utilizing the most easily accessible firewood resources on the terrace—oak and hickory. These two wood types are also the best firewood, burning for the greatest amount of time and at relatively high temperatures (Panshin and de Zeeuw 1980). The Allen villagers also gathered some firewood from the lower slopes and bottomlands surrounding the site.

## Utilization of Nuts and Other Resources

The nutshell taxa from the site, not surprisingly, also indicate that the prehistoric inhabitants were drawing on local mast-producing species from the immediate vicinity. Hickory undoubtedly came from the site's terrace and surrounding hillsides, and black walnut and butternut must have been fairly common on the lower northern slopes and bottomlands of the area (both species frequent moist, rich soils). The fall would have been a rather active season of nut collecting and processing. What is perhaps unexpected is the relative lack of acorn nutshell, although one nutshell fragment and a few nutmeat fragments were recovered. Although the more fragile acorn nutshell does reduce the preservation of this taxa in the archaeological record, other sites from the same time period indicate an increased use of this nut type (see discussion below).

The paucity of seeds in the Allen samples precludes an extensive discussion of the original genesis of the seeds (accidental inclusions or the remnants of past meals?). All the taxa identified are indicative of disturbed soils; bedstraw is typically found in low numbers in archaeological sediments and has been interpreted as representing noneconomic utilization. This genus produces seedheads that effectively cling to clothing, hair, fur—just about anything—and may merely represent weedy intrusions into campfires around occupation sites. The only possible economically utilized seed specimens are the raspberry seeds, and this genus also inhabits more weedy, disturbed, and open areas and could also represent accidental inclusions.

The most significant data from the Allen site is represented by maize directly dated at A.D. 689. This AMS date sets the general time frame when maize became part of the economy and diet. In addition to the seven fragments of maize, five fragments of maize were recovered from the Gabriel site (J. Murphy 1989, 271–72) and one small corncob was recovered from the Graham site (McKenzie 1967, 79). Murphy (1989, 355) states that "substantial remains of maize were recovered" from the later McCune site, but this is difficult to evaluate in the absence of specific figures.

# Maize Agriculture Outside the Hocking Valley

Botanical materials from only a few sites, including Woods and a number of features from Niebert (both in West Virginia), have been analyzed for the crucial period around A.D. 900, when a series of rather rapid and dramatic cultural changes occurred throughout the Ohio Valley. Of particularly great value were the nearly complete excavations of the Childers site (ca. A.D. 600–800) and the adjacent Woods site (A.D. 900; Shott et al. 1990; Shott and Jefferies 1992).

The analysis of botanical materials from these sites has produced a clear and distinctive pattern: (1) the early Late Woodland sites show a remarkable similarity that includes a high density and diversity of paleoethnobotanical remains, and (2) the late Late Woodland sites have produced a much lower density and diversity of botanical items, with a concomitant increase in the presence of maize (Wymer 1989, 1992).

However, maize is rare in sites of the early Late Woodland period. For example, the only site that produced maize was the West Virginia Childers site; 14 fragments were recovered in six features (a site ubiquity of 12.24%). The earliest feature that yielded maize at the Childers site was radiocarbon-dated to A.D. 425, although the majority of features that dated from A.D. 398 to A.D. 669 (calibrated) did not produce maize. Interestingly, the maize exhibited a distinctive spatial pattern. The only features that produced maize were located in the internal central core area—in pit features surrounding what had been the central residential area.

As noted above, little information exists for the period from A.D. 800 to A.D. 1000, a period noteworthy for the dramatic shift to the large nucleated Fort Ancient communities dependent on maize field agriculture. Information from the Woods site (based on 53 flotation samples from 41 features), augmented with data from other sites, suggests that fundamental patterns in both settlement configuration and plant use changed from earlier periods (Wymer 1990, 1992). Rather than the large nucleated communities of the Newtown phase, the late Late Woodland sites appear to represent small scattered household clusters devoid of formal boundaries (most Newtown sites are clearly delineated with earthwork and ditch constructions surrounding the villages). However, this pattern—of shifting from small scattered Hopewell hamlets, to large nucleated Newtown villages, back to small scattered household clusters, and finally, to the large nucleated Fort Ancient villages —seems *not* to have transpired in the Hocking Valley south of the Hocking Hills.

Wood taxa identified in the Childers samples reveal 30 distinct taxa, while the Woods site produced 19 wood types, including many second-growth genera (however, the floodplain in the vicinity of the site could have been so impacted by previous populations that second-growth forests may have been the norm). Nut utilization exhibited a striking transformation from a heavy use of acorn in the early Late Woodland Childers site to a use of selected high-oil species (especially black walnut) in the late Late Woodland Woods site samples.

In some ways the density and diversity of plant material from the Allen site parallel the indices calculated for other sites and, at the same time, are quite distinct. For example, the wood charcoal density for the Allen site closely matches density values for a number of early Late Woodland sites and, in fact, far surpasses the values calculated for the late Late Woodland. Identified wood taxa, unlike other sites, exhibits a lower diversity and little utilization of second-growth genera.

Nutshell and seed densities, however, are extremely low for the Allen site compared to Late Woodland sites. What is particularly puzzling is the lack of carbonized seeds in the samples; it is not uncommon for Late Woodland sites, especially sites early in this period, to produce thousands of seed specimens. The absence of any examples of the EAC is quite intriguing. Lastly, the amount and ubiquity of maize fragments at the Allen site more closely matches the indices for the early Late Woodland Childers site rather than the late Late Woodland Woods site.

# 11

# THE IMPACT OF MAIZE ON SETTLEMENT PATTERNS IN THE HOCKING VALLEY

Joseph E. Wakeman

No DOMESTICATED GRAIN HAD as profound an impact on preconquest societies in the Americas as maize, or corn (Johannessen and Hastorf 1994). Archaeobotanical research has established that maize was central to the agricultural economy in the Midwest United States (Munson 1973; Wagner 1994; Wymer 1994; Church and Nass 2002) and specifically in the Hocking Valley, Ohio (Wymer, this volume), beginning ca. A.D. 700, with its significance expanding until the conquest. This acceptance and subsequent increase in dependence on maize as a staple food influenced many facets of life for community members during the Late Woodland and Late Prehistoric periods.

The commitment to maize agriculture had a major impact on settlement patterns, since maize does not grow equally well in all environments. Floodplains, with their deeper soils seasonally replenished through flooding, were primary zones for planting maize. Presumably, as maize production was increased through time, landforms conducive to maize growth assumed greater economic significance. This basic relationship between maize agriculture and floodplain preference is confirmed for small portions of the Hocking Valley (Skinner and Norris 1981; Black 1979; J. Murphy 1989; Abrams 1992b).

# Environmental Setting

This research is guided by the theoretical perspective of ecological anthropology, which views human culture in a systemic and dynamic relationship with the natural ecological system. In this approach, society is seen as interdependent with elements of the natural world (Moran 2000). Several environmental aspects of the Hocking River watershed influenced decision making by Late Woodland and Late Prehistoric agricultural communities. The Hocking Valley is situated on three major physiological divisions. The upper reaches of the valley—in the vicinity of Lancaster in Fairfield County —entails the flat, glaciated Central Lowland till plain (figs.1.1, 1.2). The southeastern portion of Fairfield County and a small portion of northwestern Hocking County are located on the glaciated Allegheny Plateau. Finally, the central and lower portions of the valley in most of Hocking, Athens, and parts of Meigs Counties are on the unglaciated Allegheny Plateau. This makes the Hocking Valley unique in Ohio; no other major drainage system traverses such a diverse geological landscape.

The current topography of the valley was sculpted throughout the last 1.8 million years, during the Pleistocene epoch. In the early part of the Pleistocene, the drainage patterns in southeastern Ohio were quite different from today. The ancient Teays River once flowed northwest through the region but was stopped by glacial ice near Lancaster in pre-Illinoian times. This created the huge Lake Tight (Sturgeon et al. 1958; J. Murphy 1989), whose overflow eventually breached adjacent small ridges and reversed the flow of the system to a southeasterly direction. At this point, the Teays system and most of its tributaries either became dry or were redirected as glacial outwash (Merrill 1953). The subsequent Illinoian glaciation was significant to valley soil formation, depositing several outwash terraces still visible today between Rockbridge and Logan as well as in the modern community of The Plains. These smooth-topped, elevated terraces are typically 60 to 90 ft (18–27 m) above the modern floodplain (Kempton and Goldthwait 1959; J. Murphy 1989).

The boundary of the last continental glacial ice sheet, the Wisconsin, can still be seen just south of Lancaster. The effects of the glacial outwash of the Wisconsin deepened and widened the channel of the Hocking River, creating the lowest terraces in the valley today. Many of these terraces blocked small tributaries from the newly formed Hocking River. These tributaries in turn flooded, eventually forming small glacial lakes whose lacustrine deposits are currently found throughout the periphery of the valley. For example, the Margaret Creek watershed (fig. 1.4) is laden with such deposits and, as such, has an unusually high agricultural productivity.

In sum, the Hocking Valley soils and, thus, agricultural potential, are heterogeneous. The upper valley, composed of thick ground moraine deposits and relatively broad expanses of bottomland, is best suited for large-scale agriculture. However, as the valley narrows to the southeast, the floodplain zone and especially the terraces become increasingly restricted. An analysis of the southern central valley showed that the floodplain comprised 7% and terraces comprised 3% of the total landscape (Abrams and Freter, chapter 1, this volume). This pattern of narrowing is offset to varying degrees by alluvial soils in tributaries, especially in Margaret Creek.

## Methodology

The data in this settlement analysis come from all sites recorded on OAI forms identified chronologically as only Late Woodland, only Late Prehistoric, or multicomponent sites representing occupation through both the Late Woodland and Late Prehistoric periods in the Hocking Valley. This massive amount of data has been coded, digitized, and entered into a mapping database by the Ohio Historic Preservation Office in Columbus. The data were compiled per county using a GIS technology, resulting in a flexible database that can be queried according to any of the attributes on the OAI forms. These data for the Hocking Valley were made available by the Ohio Historic Preservation Office.

There are two primary flaws in the use of any large database compiled by numerous researchers over several decades. First, there are gaps and a lack of clarity in the data recorded on the OAI forms. The distinction between Late Woodland and Late Prehistoric sites, generally based on point types and ceramic affiliations, is often blurred. Omissions of specific data (such as the landform on which the site is located) exist that reduce the value of that entry.

Second, portions of the Hocking Valley have not been systematically investigated with standardized archaeological field methods. Since most survey research is conducted in the context of cultural resource management projects, those areas of the Hocking that have not been subject to major highway construction or development since the 1970s remain undersurveyed. Despite these acknowledged flaws, the pattern that links sites with agricultural soils and landforms is strong; future inquiries of an expanded and improved database may further detail or modify the preliminary findings reported here.

## Querying Criteria

The OAI form contains 76 broad categories of information for each site. There are also specific fine-grained criteria within many of the broad categories. As mentioned, these criteria have been coded for each site and entered into an ArcView GIS platform, enabling researchers to access and query any criteria of coded data.

Since it is empirically confirmed that maize agriculture began in the valley in the Late Woodland period and continued through the Late Prehistoric (Wymer, this volume; J. Murphy 1989), sites with these two temporal affiliations were the first criteria queried in this study. Of the total of 2,562 sites from *all* time periods in the watershed, this initial query resulted in 96 Late Woodland sites and 77 Late Prehistoric sites. However, the majority of sites within each category actually belong to *both* time periods. Since many artifact types in the Hocking Valley do not clearly distinguish between these two temporal categories, they are often coded as multicomponent. To avoid confusion, I separated these sites into three distinct analytic categories: Late Woodland single-component sites, Late Prehistoric single-component sites, and multicomponent sites. This procedure resulted in a clarified visualization of the site distribution in the valley, with 37 Late Woodland single-component sites (fig. 11.1), 18 Late Prehistoric single-component sites (fig. 11.2), and 114 multicomponent sites (fig. 11.3).

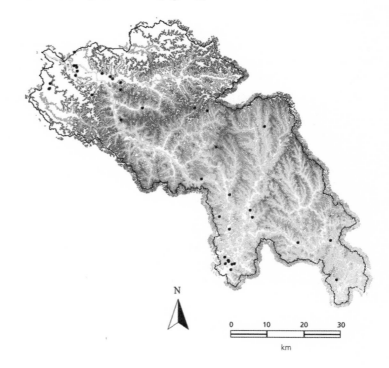

FIG. 11.1. Distribution of Late Woodland sites in the Hocking Valley

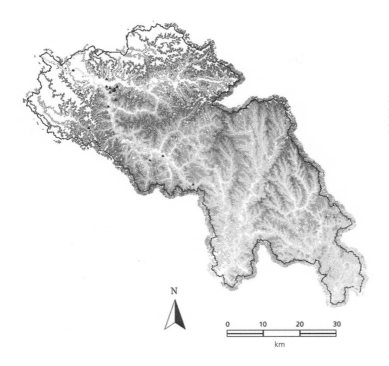

FIG. 11.2. Distribution of
Late Prehistoric sites in the
Hocking Valley

N

0    10    20    30
km

FIG. 11.3. Distribution of
multicomponent sites in the
Hocking Valley

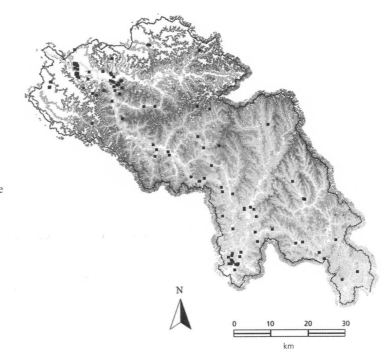

N

0    10    20    30
km

### Table 11.1. Landform Criteria

|  | Moraine | Floodplain | Terrace | Bluff/Ridgetop | Unknown | Total |
|---|---|---|---|---|---|---|
| Late Woodland | 5 | 8 | 7 | 9 | 8 | 37 |
| Late Prehistoric | 1 | 3 | 0 | 0 | 14 | 18 |
| Multicomponent | 20 | 22 | 22 | 18 | 32 | 114 |
| Total | 26 | 33 | 29 | 27 | 54 | 169 |

### Table 11.2. Site Types

|  | Camp | Habitation | Mortuary | Unknown | Total |
|---|---|---|---|---|---|
| Late Woodland | 1 | 5 | 1 | 30 | 37 |
| Late Prehistoric | 0 | 4 | 4 | 10 | 18 |
| Multicomponent | 2 | 19 | 9 | 84 | 114 |
| Total | 3 | 28 | 14 | 124 | 169 |

These three site categories were then queried by landform. Since the OAI form contains an extensive list of local environmental settings, these settings were condensed into five broader categories: moraine, floodplain, terrace, bluff/ridgetop, and unknown (table 11.1). The moraine of the upper valley and the floodplain throughout the valley are prime agricultural lands. The terraces are adjacent to these lands and are also considered prime locales, whereas the bluff/ridgetops are situated on poorer soils, generally away from the steady flow of water.

The database was further queried by site types for each time period (table 11.2). As with landforms, OAI categories were combined into the following categories: camps, habitation, mortuary, and unknown. The fact that 73% of all sites from these periods are unknown in terms of function speaks to the need for greater archaeological testing in the valley. The final criterion used to analyze the late settlement pattern was preference by specific watershed within the entire valley (fig.1.4; table 11.3). The watersheds considered are only those with recorded archaeological sites within their boundaries. Collectively, these categories and queries were condensed and selected based on the research design of the project and my assessment of the quality of data from the individual OAI forms.

## Table 11.3. Drainage Preference

| Minor Watershed | LW | LP | MC | Total |
|---|---|---|---|---|
| Amney Run | 1 | 0 | 2 | 3 |
| Baldwin Run | 1 | 1 | 3 | 5 |
| Center Branch Creek | 0 | 0 | 1 | 1 |
| Clear Creek | 3 | 1 | 4 | 8 |
| Factory Creek | 1 | 0 | 1 | 2 |
| Four Mile Creek | 1 | 0 | 1 | 2 |
| Hocking River | 13 | 5 | 40 | 58 |
| Hunters Run | 0 | 1 | 14 | 15 |
| Hyde Fork | 0 | 0 | 1 | 1 |
| Lindscott Run | 0 | 0 | 2 | 2 |
| Little Monday Creek | 1 | 0 | 2 | 3 |
| Little Rush Creek | 0 | 0 | 2 | 2 |
| Margaret Creek | 7 | 0 | 15 | 22 |
| Monday Creek | 3 | 0 | 4 | 7 |
| Pleasant Run | 4 | 9 | 13 | 26 |
| Raccoon Run | 0 | 0 | 3 | 3 |
| Rush Creek | 1 | 0 | 2 | 3 |
| Scott Creek | 0 | 1 | 2 | 3 |
| Sunday Creek | 1 | 0 | 1 | 2 |
| Willow Creek | 0 | 0 | 1 | 1 |
| Total | 37 | 18 | 114 | 169 |

## Results

Analyses began with a data set of 37 Late Woodland sites, 18 Late Prehistoric sites, and 114 multicomponent sites. When "unknown" sites are removed from each of the three temporal categories, 82 multicomponent sites, 29 Late Woodland sites, and only 4 Late Prehistoric sites remain. The unrepresentative nature of this sample clearly has an impact on the differential confidence of suggested patterns per period; however, this settlement database is the best currently available and consequently is still useful for generating future research questions. Accordingly, the several patterns that emerge from the present analysis are viewed as preliminary, and it is hoped that as the OAI database matures, greater detail and testing of the patterns seen here will become possible.

The primary inquiry concerning settlement is whether there was a preference to live on or near agricultural land with the advent of maize agriculture. The database for best addressing that question comes from the 114 multicomponent sites by individual landform (table 11.1). Initial scrutiny of their location reveals a balance among landforms. However, when the 32 multicomponent sites in the unknown category are removed and areas of prime agricultural land are collapsed as one category, the data indicate a clear preference for agricultural land. The combination of moraine, floodplain, and terrace settings comprise 78% of all multicomponent sites, indicating a solid preference for lower elevations on or adjacent to richer agricultural soils. This confirms that there was a preference for agricultural soils during these late periods and further that this pattern was valleywide rather than specific to any limited portion of the valley.

A second issue concerns the timing of this settlement focus on prime agricultural land. To address this question, it is necessary to observe the Late Woodland patterns (table 11.1). Again, eliminating the unknown category and collapsing landforms of richer agricultural soils indicates that 69% (20 of 29) of Late Woodland sites are associated with soils of high agricultural potential. This confirms that a movement toward such soils existed ca. A.D. 600–700.

It is important to recognize, however, that the attraction to floodplain soils among past Hocking societies did not begin in the Late Woodland period but rather was part of a trend toward such soils that began ca. 1500 B.C. Based on the identical survey sample in the valley, Stump et al. (this volume) conclude that 38% of the Late Archaic sites in the valley were on either floodplains or terrace zones, a figure that increased to 47% by the combined Early/Middle Woodland period. Thus the increase to 69% by the Late Woodland period reflects a gradual continuation of settlement preference rather than a new settlement pattern. In that sense, the settlement pattern of the Late Woodland period is predictable in the context of targeting resources of prime economic potential; in this case, lands suitable for agricultural intensification as outlined by Boserup (1965).

This pattern of diminished upland zone usage by the late population is supported further by research at the Walker site (33AT960; Abrams and DeAloia, this volume). Point types from this upland hunting and gathering site indicate use by Archaic as well as by Early and Middle Woodland populations, but not by Late Woodland or Late Prehistoric groups, despite the presence of such late communities in the vicinity. Further, the analysis of activity areas at the Allen site (Abrams, Bergman, and Miller, this volume) indicate that the processing of a wide range of raw materials took place at the habitation site. These two observations strengthen the conclusion that the settlement trend toward the floodplain and the concomitant reduction of use of other areas was a real phenomenon.

This settlement trend continued through the Late Prehistoric period. Although the sample of Late Prehistoric sites is very small, only 4, it was shown that 78% of multicomponent sites are on or adjacent to prime agricultural soils. This is further observed by comparing Late Woodland and multicomponent site location (table 11.1). The moraine soils of the upper valley contained 13.5% Late Woodland sites and 17.5% multicomponent sites. The floodplain contained 21.6% Late Woodland sites and 19.2% multi-component sites. The terraces contained 18.9% Late Woodland sites and 19.2% multicomponent sites. Thus far, these are quite comparable in settlement by landform. However, the bluff/ridgetop category drops from 24.3% Late Woodland sites to 15.8% multicomponent sites. This represents the continued shift from upland settings to lower-elevation zones during the Late Prehistoric period. Again, this shift occurred as the contribution of maize agriculture increased in the economy of these communities, placing a premium on larger areas of deeper, nutrient-rich soils.

Given the absence of representative survey coverage in the valley and a lack of knowledge of the amount of area surveyed, no statistical analyses of distance between sites has yet been conducted. However, as a consequence primarily of the Route 33 archaeological survey (Skinner and Norris 1981) and other surveys surrounding the Athens area, the distribution of multi-component sites in this section of the floodplain of the Hocking River can be considered representative (fig. 11.3). Based solely on visual observation of these sites, it appears that their site distribution is linear and dispersed; that is, there is no conspicuous clustering of sites along the main Hocking floodplain. If this dispersed settlement is confirmed, it would best fit Boserup's description of the forest-fallow system of crop production, in which farmers "need a large area of land per family—including of course the land lying in fallow at any given time—and they must therefore be thinly spread over the territory, grouped in relatively small communities" (1965, 70). On a site-specific level, this description fits the community settlement pattern of the Allen site (Abrams, Bergman, and Miller, this volume), where a small multicomponent community of roughly 40 to 60 people living on a terrace of over 3 ha had access to several hectares of floodplain soil along Margaret Creek.

As with the above inference, several other observations are suggested by the current database but ultimately require additional data and testing. One question concerns the relationship between settlement in the tributaries compared to the main stem of the Hocking. From table 11.3 we see that 40 multicomponent sites are located along the Hocking River proper, or roughly one site every 2 miles (3.2 km) along this zone of greatest agricultural potential. Only three tributaries contain significant settlements. Pleasant Run, with 13 multicomponent sites, and Hunters Run, with 14 multicomponent sites, are both in the upper valley in proximity to the broader and flatter moraine soils that characterize the Hocking till plain. Margaret Creek, with 15 multicomponent sites, rests in the remnants of the Albany River and is uncharacteristically broad with rich soils. These tributaries of high agricultural potential contained comparable numbers of sites per area relative to the Hocking River. These tributaries however are areas well surveyed through cultural resource management projects and thus settlement statements derived exclusively from these areas may be unrepresentative of the valley as a whole.

However, Monday Creek, a narrower, V-shaped tributary of the valley, has been professionally surveyed as part of research on Wayne National Forest (Ann Cramer, pers. comm., 2004). The four multicomponent sites in this approximately 15-mile tributary represent approximately one site every 4 miles (6.5 km). These sites are roughly proportionate to the amount of floodplain soils and consistent flow of water within this tributary. The presence of some communities in even the narrow tributaries indicates that these areas could sustain late populations. Thus, hypothetically, while these tributaries increasingly served as reservoirs of natural resources housing lower numbers of late communities, they did remain areas of occupation.

A final observation from the data that is suggestive rather than definitive concerns the pattern of community fissioning. From table 11.3 and figures 11.1 and 11.2, we observe that the upper valley is the only portion of the Hocking with Late Prehistoric sites. That is, communities which were newly created ca. A.D. 1000 were restricted to the upper valley, whereas other portions of the valley see Late Prehistoric communities emerge from existent Late Woodland ones. The data are far too scant to offer any conclusions concerning patterns of fissioning. Rather this observation is offered simply to introduce into settlement research the question of site formation and fissioning in the context of absolute amounts of productive land for later settlements.

## Comparisons to Adjacent Watersheds

Although this pattern of continued movement into the floodplain zones with the acceptance of maize agriculture is evidenced elsewhere (Maslowski

Table 11.4. Distribution of Fort Ancient Communities in the Central Ohio Valley

| Stream Order | Floodplain | Terrace | Bluff | Upland | Total |
|---|---|---|---|---|---|
| 1 | 0 | 1 | 1 | 0 | 2 |
| 2 | 0 | 1 | 3 | 1 | 5 |
| 3 | 8 | 14 | 6 | 0 | 28 |
| 4 | 1 | 6 | 0 | 0 | 7 |
| Total | 9 | 22 | 10 | 1 | 42 |

Source: Nass 1988.

1985), the best regional comparison for the Hocking Valley settlement models is with the neighboring tributaries of the Ohio, Great Miami, Little Miami, and Scioto rivers. These valleys have received greater systematic survey than has the Hocking Valley and provide the basis for comparison of the selection of landforms.

Table 11.4, compiled by Nass (1988), indicates settlement preference for Late Prehistoric (or Fort Ancient) sites by landform and stream order. In this latter hierarchy, the larger the stream the higher the stream order number. Translated to the Hocking Valley, an ephemeral stream (1) flowing into Sunday Creek (2) would feed the Hocking River (3) and eventually enter the Ohio River (4). Several patterns suggested for the Hocking Valley are paralleled in the Central Ohio Valley. Late Prehistoric sites on the floodplain and terrace zones represent 74% (31 of 42) of the total, nearly identical to the selection of land in the Hocking. Although not measured for the Hocking, a full 83% of Late Prehistoric sites (35 of 42) in the Central Ohio Valley are along third- or fourth-order streams.

The high frequency of third-order stream settlements on terraces in the Central Ohio Valley accentuates the distinction in geomorphology between these regions. The terraces of both the Miami drainages, and especially the Scioto drainage, are considerably larger than any terraces in the Hocking Valley (also Abrams and Freter, chapter 1, this volume). This places a premium on the terraces in the Hocking and reminds us of the distinctions among valley systems in the Ohio River drainage.

Clearly, the intensified planting of maize in these zones of highest agricultural productivity should be explored further in terms of varying agricultural strategies and altered political relations among these increasingly settled communities. Only then will we have a fuller appreciation of community life during these last centuries of indigenous control over the Hocking Valley.

# 12

# TRIBAL SOCIETIES IN
# THE HOCKING VALLEY

Elliot M. Abrams and AnnCorinne Freter

THE GOALS AND ETHOS OF ARCHAEOLOGICAL RESEARCH in the Hocking Valley, southeastern Ohio, have changed considerably over the last hundred years. Initial efforts in the late nineteenth century addressed the identity of the moundbuilders (Squier and Davis 1848; Andrews 1877). The first half of the twentieth century saw research aimed at defining the archaeological cultures of the Adena and the Fort Ancient societies based on artifactual indices (Greenman 1932; Griffin 1966). In the 1960s research designs began to articulate models from comparative ethnology, cultural process, and ecology with expanded field methods and technologies (Prufer 1967; McKenzie 1967; Skinner and Norris 1981; J. Murphy 1989; Abrams 1992a, 1992b).

Today archaeological research in the valley continues to expand our database through both survey and field excavation to refine cultural evolutionary and ecological models from an anthropological perspective (Gillespie and Nichols 2003). The primary goal of this volume was to present our most current data analyzed through modern technologies to better understand the ecological contexts and processual patterns that characterized the formation and expansion of indigenous tribes in the Hocking Valley. This topic is significant on a global scale and the reconstruction of those societies whose history over four millennia reveal this broader process of tribal organization adds to the growing inventory of societies who similarly created tribal institutions.

## Redefining the Tribe

Two core institutional elements of tribes identified by Service (1962) and Sahlins (1961, 1968) remain. The first focuses on *local communities* that shared a unifying identity on the basis of kinship or sodalities or both, the resulting alliances altering the ways in which these communities interacted. Research in the Hocking Valley illustrates the significance of the local community as a primary societal unit of analysis, adding the homestead spatial concept as its material representation. Although a wide range of archaeological site types were created by local communities and fully deserve research attention, the residential site/homestead area offers the greatest potential for understanding past societies in the valley, and archaeologists should redouble their efforts toward the excavation of these types of sites.

A second principle, based on ethnological models, is that the alliances created by these communities made possible the capacity for *expanding scales of inclusiveness,* in effect situationally or historically reshaping the scope of regional tribal membership. This structural relationship is the core of an archaeological definition of tribal society. That is, when small, somewhat sedentary communities sharing a material inventory (especially in the realm of ideology) are defined archaeologically, they are classified as tribal, in contrast to an ethnographic definition of tribes, which often is based more on cognitive rather than material criteria. This notion of expanding inclusiveness has been modified to some extent (Ehrenreich, Crumley, and Levy 1995), but it too remains an enduring aspect of the definition of tribal societies.

Although Elman Service's (1962) goal of creating the categories of bands and tribes succeeded in organizing a complex diversity of data, recent research has modified, refined, and even replaced some of basic concepts defining tribes. First, although scholars note the typological significance of Service's classification into bands and tribes as a means of ordering and organizing a diverse set of ethnographic data, they similarly note the inherently nonevolutionary nature of such typologies (Price and Feinman 1995; Price and Brown 1985). This is perhaps the greatest inherent flaw of typologies. As Hayden (1995, 18) specifies, these foundational categories are monolithic and thus logically nonexplanatory. For example, if bands categorically are leaderless but tribes have leadership positions, then the mechanisms for the formation of leadership must logically exist in some band societies, a condition precluded by the normative typology. Archaeologists imbued with the diachronic perspective often seek transitional elements that serve as preconditions to new forms of institutional structure.

This point is supported by research in the Hocking Valley. For example, by archaeologically defining feasting among hunting-gathering communities related to the formation of aggregate, macroband communities on a seasonal basis (Heyman, Abrams, and Freter, this volume), the societal precondition for the emergence of leadership circumstances is met well before such positions are formalized on a continual basis. From an evolutionary perspective, this observation argues that it is not the normative conditions that often lead to change but rather the episodic circumstances that are the source of societal reorganization.

Second, many of the composite traits that categorize bands and tribes are viewed as potentially independent from any unilineal evolutionary model. That is, horticulture and sedentism, cultural elements that normatively define tribes, may or may not be historically instituted simultaneously (Brown 1985, 1992). Feinman (1995, 258), for example, specifically argues for the "decoupling" of such categories as agriculture and inequality. In effect, the units of analysis should be specific composite behaviors such as sedentism and horticulture that are not a priori simultaneously instituted.

Several cases of such temporal separation of tribal elements are evident in the Hocking Valley. Hunting and gathering societies, for example, began manufacturing ceramics for the processing of wild nuts and plants well before formal horticulture was instituted (Pecora and Burks, this volume), thus separating these "markers" of tribes. In fact, one could argue that the early presence of ceramics bolstered the nutritional contribution of wild plants such as chenopods in the diet, delaying in a sense the economic trend toward gardening.

Another example of the decoupling of tribal traits in the Hocking Valley is full sedentism and food production. Horticultural, and even later, agricultural communities in the valley, as reflected by the Allen site (Abrams, Bergman, and Miller, this volume) moved seasonally, never establishing the degree of sedentism associated with fixed permanence of place, as is the case for tribes elsewhere (e.g., Flannery 1976, 2002; Redman 1978).

Third, the process which leads to the formation of tribes from bands is no longer viewed as uniformly gradual. No community evolves independent of the changes or circumstances effecting other communities. When a local group outside the Hocking Valley began growing chenopods in prepared gardens, they in effect were experimenters and the results became known to others through such mechanisms as familial visitations and larger communal aggregations. This diffusion of successes (as well as of failed experiments) led to their eventual adoption by other communities, resulting in a variant of punctuated equilibria. Historically, then, transitions may have occurred over relatively short periods of time. The fact that archaeological periods reflecting the regional acceptance of shared behaviors can even be observed suggests the *interdependence* of decision making by politically autonomous communities. For example, in the Hocking Valley the earthen mounds built ca. 500 B.C. were shown to be visible from adjacent mounds (Waldron and Abrams 1999). Although subject to further chronological testing, this may reflect the designed placement of mounds and perhaps a relatively short time frame within which many were built.

Fourth, scholars today recognize the considerable *variability* that exists within these categories. This observation is the logical outcome of recognizing the chronological separation of major institutions within single categories and the articulated but not necessarily synchronized continua of change in social behaviors. Thus, fully sedentary tribal communities subsisting on hunted and gathered food resources, such as Natufian society in the Near East (Henry 1989), are not only possible but predictable and even expected.

There are numerous examples of this type of categoric variability in the Hocking Valley. Small communities involved in gardening ca. 500 B.C. were part of very localized political units whereas these same types of communities ca. A.D. 1 were members of broad regional political units. Similarly, communities ca. A.D. 500 in the upper reaches of the valley lived in larger, enclosed villages (Schweikart, this volume), whereas coeval villages in the narrower southern and central valley were not protected by embankments, reflecting varying political pressures within the same valley.

This observation of variability relates to a fifth refinement, that of discarding the subtle unilineality inherent in simple evolutionary models. Population growth, for example, is often modeled as increasing with the advent of agriculture (Boserup 1965). While this tends to be correct from a very long temporal perspective, population size within the valley does not always increase and rates of growth (or decline) may fluctuate through time. In the Hocking Valley, population growth during the Late Archaic period may have been higher than that of the Early Woodland period (Stump et al., this volume) and as we suggest below, there was a two-hundred-year period of population decline in the valley. This same pattern of nonlinear fluctuation is reflected in regional scales of political unification, or political complexity. It could certainly be argued that political leadership reached its height of complexity ca. A.D. 200 with the construction of mounds and circles in The Plains rather than in later periods.

A sixth refinement in defining tribes involves the archaeological consideration of tribal society from the macrolevel to the microlevel as a scale of historical modeling and analysis. This refocusing of the societal scale of one's archaeological imagination is often subsumed under the very diverse paradigmatic heading of postprocessualism. Hayden (1995, 20), for example, hypothesizes that societal inequality emerged under conditions of differential control of or access to predictable surplus production. This general correlation is a macrolevel observation within the traditional processual paradigm. The refinement in scale lies in his suggestion that the variable that drove surplus production was the greed of insidious "aggrandizers," thus placing ultimate causality in the realm of psychology (see also Stothers, Abel, and Schneider 2001). By placing people as the agents of decision making, this perspective is seen as both humanizing and balanced, forcing the archaeologist to view the past society from a more personalized vantage point of historical sociology. In effect, this microlevel perspective urges the analysis of a subject often ignored in anthropological archaeology—the diversity of personalities within a society. The difficulty with this perspective is its measurability—the archaeological data often are not conducive to such types of investigations, yet narratives can be created that augment a more empirical approach to archaeological studies. For example, one could speculate that earthen mounds built on ridgetops took that specific form in an effort to mimic the natural landscape, thus cognitively associating the interred and the community with the land itself. This perspective is just now emerging in research in the Hocking Valley.

## Redefining the Periodization of Hocking Valley Processual History

Collectively, our conceptual refinements of the tribe category are supported by the archaeological data from the Hocking Valley. Based on the expanded data obtained over the past two decades and guided by these refined models, we offer a descriptive and explanatory template of societal change as occurred in the Hocking Valley.

### The Period of Intensive Hunting and Gathering (3000–1500 B.C.)

This period of fifteen hundred years, corresponding to the Late Archaic, experienced gradually rising rainfall levels. This relatively high rainfall was conducive to the natural productivity of a wide range of plant and animal

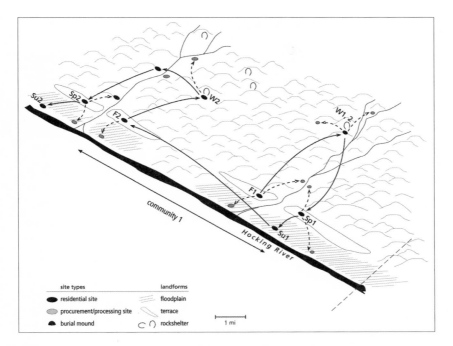

species. Although specific rates of population increase are unknown, the significantly larger number of sites during these centuries suggests a marked increase in population size throughout the Hocking (Stump et al., this volume), paralleled by increased population size elsewhere in the Ohio Valley (Adovasio et al. 2001; Muller 1986; Meindl, Mensforth, and York 2001).

FIG. 12.1. Late Archaic settlement patterns in the Hocking Valley

Community size varied seasonally, with relatively larger communities housing 12 to 15 people during the fall, when abundance of food resources brought concomitant labor demands. Residential locales were occupied for as long as two to three months during the fall and the spring. These were complemented by communities of five to eight people—as small as a single family—dispersing during the winter to occupy rockshelters or warmer locales.

The space available to any community is unknown but relatively unrestricted. Thus communities could move their residence some distance along the main river and up tributaries (fig. 12.1). Further, while residential sites were created in all environmental zones in the valley, there was a clear preference for prime locations (Smith 1992), or protected areas with relatively easy access to floodplain resources. The Late Archaic focus on terraces and floodplain locales supports this general trend in settlement selection (Stump et al., this volume), as do the Late Archaic data from the County Home site (Heyman, Abrams, and Freter, this volume), which indicate recurrent occupation of a desired floodplain site.

This reconstruction of Late Archaic settlement conforms to the model offered by Binford (1980), which identified residential mobility, or community resettlement toward seasonally productive resource zones, balanced by a diverse set of satellite extraction sites (also termed bivouac sites; Adovasio et al. 2001). Foods were diverse and abundant. A great number of large and small animals and fish, as well as nuts and other botanical species, were hunted and gathered. There is no evidence that local seed-bearing plants were included in the inventory of plants selected for consumption. The small size and high cost of processing relative to alternatives made these species less inviting. The high rainfall, however, may have exacerbated the number of floods, encouraging food collection from the terrace and upland zones during the spring. In some respects, this period parallels that of the Mesolithic in Europe and the Natufian in the Near East, where a greater sedentism, or restriction of movement by hunters and gatherers, corresponds with a heightened natural abundance of food resources.

## The Period of Protohorticultural Communities (1500–500 B.C.)

Beginning ca. 1500 B.C., the climate in southern Ohio became markedly drier and warmer. The rate of change of this climatic trend is unknown, but the reduction in rainfall was severe. The pollen data for Ohio indicate that rainfall levels may have dropped by 50% (Ogden 1966; Shane, Snyder, and Anderson 2001). This scale of reduction affected the dispersed local communities in various ways. Population size within the valley continued to increase but, based solely on the comparative number of sites, the rate of increase was lower than the previous period of optimal rainfall (Stump et al., this volume). The local community was typified by a maximum seasonal population of 15 to 20.

Nomadic patterns were increasingly restricted across the year, with local communities residing in the same locales for several months each year (fig. 12.2). Floodplain and terrace zones, especially at the confluence of waterways, were preferred landscapes for occupation and use; if for no other reason, the reduction in rainfall lowered the availability of potable water, more severely experienced in the tributaries of the Hocking. The territorial concept of a homestead, or spatial territory designed for recurrent occupation by a specific local community (Crowell et al., this volume), emerged during this period and small communities seasonally aggregated into larger cooperative groups, as evidenced by feasting, beginning ca. 1500 B.C. (Heyman, Abrams, and Freter, this volume).

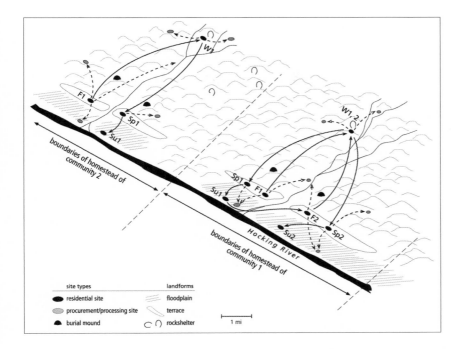

The steady increase in population density and gradual restriction in settlement movement is associated with the concept of *circumscription* (Carneiro 1970). This concept of societal containment is caused by both physical and social barriers, as well as by economic attraction to localized environmental zones. The reduced resource availability and documented preference for spaces near the main river represent a form of circumscription in the Hocking Valley that invariably affected economic and settlement patterns by these hunting and gathering communities.

FIG. 12.2. Early Woodland settlement patterns in the Hocking Valley

As a consequence of the diminished space or homestead area from which each local community could hunt and collect foods, the decline in nuts available in the fall owing to the reduced rainfall, and the attractiveness of floodplain resources (Brown 1985), wild seed-bearing plants collected from the floodplain in the fall were added to the inventory of botanical food resources. Various nut species continued to be significant sources of proteins and fats as seeds were being reconceived as foods rather than as the by-products of weeds or as some other nonfood item.

However, it is not the unavailability of nuts that prompted this shift to augment or supplement the diet with seeds, for there are literally millions of nuts available each fall and spring in the Hocking Valley. Rather, it appears to be the episodic *inaccessibility* of these nuts that prompted the addition of seed plants as dietary supplements. With homesteads and greater sedentism emerging, the effort needed to travel greater distances to obtain these nuts may have been precluded or simply discarded in favor of more locally and readily available foods. Given the variability of rainfall during any single year in the Hocking Valley (Abrams and Freter, this volume) and the differential response of trees to rainfall (McCarthy and Quinn 1989, 1992), we suggest a general trend through time of increased wild-seed collection, but also an opportunistic gathering pattern of both nuts and seeds based on availability. That is, years of higher rainfall may have seen a reduction of seed collection, whereas a lower rainfall year may have prompted higher seed collection. Nonetheless, the first "stage" toward horticulture—simply including those eventual EAC domesticates into the diet—is evidenced (Ford 1985).

Pottery as a cooking technology is added to the artifact inventory ca. 1500 B.C., if not earlier (Pecora and Burks, this volume). The nutritional value of nuts and seeds is greatly expanded when they are boiled (Talalay, Keller, and Munson 1984). The timing of the first pottery corresponds with this downward trend in rainfall, with ceramic technology a response to diminished resources. Significantly, small group aggregation is also evidenced at this time (Heyman et al., this volume). What emerges is a general picture of economic stress ca. 1500 B.C. caused by various factors which was responded to by the local population through a series of decisions to change economic behaviors, add or develop new technologies, and increase political dialogue between local communities via an increasingly shared ideology mediated through communal feasting.

## The Period of Horticultural Tribal Communities (500–50 B.C.)

During this period, many of the new ways of life, as well as general trends initiated in the prior period, were crystallized. It is this set of centuries that sees the archaeological evidence for the Adena in the Hocking Valley, or those communities associated with the first tribes in the Ohio Valley. The climatic patterns for these years were more or less stable, bearing in mind the normal range of variation. Population size in the valley continued to gradually increase, with local communities having 20 to 25 members at most. The base residential locale was increasingly focused on a terrace or flood-plain space, which served as an anchor for the homestead, or residential domain, within a local community's territory. In terms of settlement patterns, we found evidence of a growing logistical pattern of residence (Binford

1980); that is, there is reduced residential movement and greater sedentism in general within the homestead. Many of the extractive satellite sites created during the Late Archaic, such as the Walker site (Abrams and DeAloia, this volume) continue to be exploited during this period of greater residential fixedness. In some regions, the number of satellite sites decreases relative to the number of residential sites (Adovasio et al. 2001, 155).

The concept of territoriality is more fully established, and members of these communities share some form of social identity with people from other communities through recognized kinship ties or sodality membership. The smallest supracommunity segment of tribal identity is established, linking lineage members from local communities within watersheds of the Hocking Valley. Many of these communities were formed through the process of fissioning from earlier communities, thus maintaining small community size and spreading kin into different microenvironmental zones. This pattern of dispersed kin offsets to some degree the risks that jeopardize economic security by providing social access to more dispersed resources.

The intentional sowing of wild seed plants is added to the array of economic activities involving seed plant procurement. Areas within the homestead that are no longer used as habitation spaces were converted to gardens. Following Edgar Anderson's "dump heap" model of plant domestication (1956), the simple abandonment and perhaps burning of cleared house space produced an "accidental garden." The collected local species such as chenopods and other members of the Eastern Agricultural Complex grow particularly well in cleared areas. With a stable climate moderately conducive to the growing of crops, horticultural gardening was established as an important economic supplement to the largely hunting and gathering economy. In addition, experiments with ceramic technology continued as a means of improving the nutritional value of nuts and seeds.

Smith notes that "explanatory frameworks for domestication need to be tailored to the environments, plants and animal species, and developmental sequences of the particular areas under study" (1995, 208). The pattern of changes resulting in plant domestication that we derive specifically from the Hocking data involves a lengthy Late Archaic population increase that correlates with protracted periods of seasonal sedentism in what Smith (1992, 1995) terms "domestilocalities"—residential locales in proximity to high-yield natural resources. These two general trends are followed by a decrease in food resources—especially nuts, the staple plant—and by the addition of seed plants as collected foods. This is followed by increased territorial identity and homesteads and by an expansion of environmental management relating to seed-bearing plants such that gardens are established.

Several scholars have cautioned against the use of population pressure and economic stress as causal factors in culture change. Drennan (1987) argues that population growth was less a causal agent of change and more a "condition" of change. Similarly, Smith (1995, 212) minimizes the notion of stress as a causal component in the explanation of plant domestication in the eastern riverine zones. Although we agree that stress and pressure are psychological and culture-specific concepts, and thus difficult to measure, they are far too powerful to discard completely within the equation of variables leading to plant domestication (Braun and Plog 1982).

During this period, small mounds were first built as burial features, often overlooking the residential homestead or individual hamlet. These features are interpreted as representing the ancestral ties to that particular homestead, reflecting the significance of territory as an increasingly concrete part of community ideology. It is beyond our access to specify exactly *how* these mounds served to establish horizontal or vertical linkages among and within local communities. However, the burial of a community member and the return of related people to that nearby burial locale, as documented by the archaeological record, is consistent with multigenerational identity and the presence of descent groups (Saxe 1970; Charles and Buikstra 1983). The geographic modeling of a sample of ridgetop burial mounds indicated that each could be viewed from the adjacent mound, assuming that these ridgetop areas near the mounds were cleared of forest (Waldron and Abrams 1999). This is interpreted as a display of conspicuous presentation of one's ancestral ties to the land, reinforcing our inference of increasing territoriality with greater sedentism and gardening.

Burial mound construction began prior to 500 B.C. outside the Hocking Valley (Dragoo 1963). As tribal formation began taking place outside of the Hocking, presumably there was a competitive advantage to establishing such institutions in a spreading sociopolitical environment of tribal formation. In that sense, regional alliances within the Hocking may be seen as responses to external competition, with the threat of loss of land and other resources by expanding tribal groups prompting communities in the valley to form larger unions. This would account for variability among specific forms of burial in distinct riverine systems while simultaneously revealing a generalized comparable material record; i.e., burial mounds.

We suggest that the threat of loss of land and vital resources on that land or the difficulties of obtaining foods given declining productivity of land were conditions which encouraged the population to create burial mounds with their inferred significance as tribal unifiers. The burial itself places the deceased in a fixed space bearing ancestral connectivity and clear territorial definition. Further, the shared ceremonial behaviors across the social landscape are interpreted as evidence of shared ritualism. That is, the religious affiliation of some or all members of society through a culture-specific form of animism may have strengthened the alliance of communities established through kinship ties, these being the cornerstones for defining tribal society. Since these mounds are inextricably linked to the concept of the Adena, a discussion of that term is necessary.

The concept of Adena has had a long and intriguing history in Ohio Valley archaeological research. Created by William Mills to describe the Adena burial mound and associated artifacts on Governor Worthington's estate in Chillicothe, Ohio, the term came to identify any society that built small conical burial mounds. By adding to the traits that defined the people who built such mounds, archaeologists reified this archaeological culture as a unified political organization extending throughout and beyond the Ohio Valley. By the 1950s, the term Adena represented a single archaeological culture in the manner used by V. Gordon Childe.

Since then, the term has assumed various meanings, including a period synonymous with the Early Woodland, as well as sociopolitical organizations ranging from nomadic bands (Clay 1998) to tribes (Mainfort 1989) to chiefdoms (Webb 1941; Shryock 1987). Given this set of contradictory meanings, it is not surprising that some have argued that the best approach to untangling the quagmire is to simply drop the term Adena, since it has confused more than it has added to intellectual growth over the last hundred years (Brown 1992). In our opinion, the only circumstance for maintaining the term Adena is when archaeologists use it exclusively and explicitly as a heuristic rather than an analytic device to represent those diverse *tribal* communities that built burial mounds at some time during the Early Woodland period. In essence, Adena simply connotes colloquially the first tribes in the Ohio Valley. This removes the term from any significant archaeological research effort but at the same time allows it to be used in the most general sense in communication and education, especially in conveying the archaeological past to the lay public, a major goal of contemporary archaeology.

The Hocking Valley has literally hundreds of small ridgetop burial mounds, which, according to the available chronology, were first built ca. 500 B.C. (J. Murphy 1989; Crowell et al., this volume). The Muskingum River Valley in southeastern Ohio similarly has numerous ridgetop mounds (Carskadden and Morton 1996). However, riverine systems such as the Scioto Valley do not seem to have this pattern of homesteaded communities associated with local mounds. One possible reason for this variability is the relative narrowness of the Hocking floodplain and limited terrace zones. As described by Abrams and Freter (this volume), the central and southern Hocking Valley is relatively steep, with terrace zones comprising a maximum of 5% of the total area. The terrace as a severely limited resource may have accentuated the need to identify one's homestead, especially in a heavily dissected topographic setting such as the Hocking Valley.

## The Period of Regional Tribal Integration (50 B.C.–A.D. 250)

During this period, climate was relatively stable and suitable to the growing of domesticates in gardens. Local community size increased to 25 to 35 people (Crowell et al., this volume), with a continued focus on terraces and floodplain areas (Stump et al., this volume). Sedentism intensifies, but movement away from the primary terrace or upper floodplain habitation within the homestead remained an option, especially in the winter and summer (fig. 12.3). The economy was increasingly horticultural but hunting and gathering represented the major set of procurement activities for community members. Maize, as part of the long-distance trade network that spanned much of the continent, may have been first introduced at this time but was ineffective as a crop, given the temperate climate and specific agricultural limitations of the Hocking Valley.

By ca. 50 B.C. tribal identity, linking local communities within watersheds, had been expanded. This mosaic of horizontal integration across the sociopolitical landscape of communities reached its peak of segmentary inclusiveness. People from multiple lineages (or tribal segments) now congregated at centralized mounds for many reasons, all of which reenforced a broader tribal affiliation. Local communities within distinct watersheds minimally constituted the extent of tribal affiliation, although the scale of regional inclusiveness may have expanded along the Hocking River from the Hocking Hills to the Ohio River. Those Hocking Valley communities north of the Hocking Hills, and especially in the till plain of the upper valley, appear to be part of a distinct tribal alliance, evidenced by the presence of the "Hopewellian" Rock Mill earthworks (J. Murphy 1989, 219).

Although the specific (and fluctuating) boundaries of political affiliation on this tribal level are beyond our database, the increased scale of inclusiveness and alliance is evidenced through mound construction. The mounds in The Plains required significantly greater labor participation than did the earlier, much smaller ridgetop mounds (Abrams and LeRouge 2004), an empirical measure of participation and thus inclusiveness. The Plains represented a true ceremonial center, a place where lineages assembled, reaffirming their shared ancestry, as well as partaking of other activities

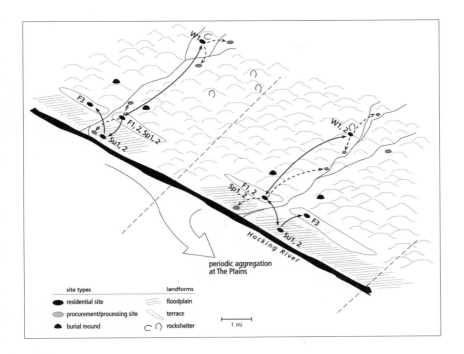

site types
- ● residential site
- ● procurement/processing site
- ▲ burial mound

landforms
- floodplain
- terrace
- ⌒ ∩ rockshelter

1 mi

periodic aggregation
at The Plains

Hocking River

spanning from the economic, such as sharing gifts, to the psychological, such as discussing interpersonal stresses with sympathetic listeners. The responsibilities of leadership intensified during those short-term episodes of community aggregation, but receded in significance following each specific event. The lack of permanence of this level of authority or influence supports the concept of a heterarchic rather than hierarchic relationship among communities and their leaders (Ehrenreich, Crumley, and Levy 1995).

FIG. 12.3. Middle Woodland settlement patterns in the Hocking Valley

Leadership is further solidified and expressed through religion, as shamans are evidenced archaeologically. The positions of community leader and shaman may have overlapped at times. Animism, with an ancestry as old as the first people in the Americas, may have evolved as a consequence of the broader evolution of tribalism. That is, following a cultural ecological model, religious views should be modified probabilistically to accommodate other changes within the broader structure of life. Thus, as regionalism expanded, an ideology of greater inclusiveness generated through animistic religion similarly was created.

This period is coeval with societies in other portions of the Ohio Valley and central Ohio termed the Hopewell. Although this term, like Adena, has caused some confusion, it generally connotes those local communities that formed regional ties on a large tribal scale, identified by the huge earthwork

centers, the architectural result of repeated aggregations of these communities (Brose and Greber 1979). Excavations of the local communities (Dancey
1991), settlement surveys of broader riverine areas (Pacheco 1996a, 1997), and
comparative analyses of the Hopewell (Braun 1986; Yerkes 1994, 2002, n.d.)
have brought us closer to understanding the political structure of those regional tribes near the Hocking Valley.

There are several general similarities in cultural pattern between the
Hocking communities and those designated as Hopewell. First, The Plains
as a vacant ceremonial center was built and used at the same time as those
larger centers constructed by the Hopewell. The primary difference is the
*scale* of construction, a function of the larger numbers of people and thus
participants in the construction process by the Hopewell. Second, communities in the Hocking participated in the Hopewell Interaction Sphere, evidenced minimally by the presence of copper and obsidian in the valley. The
amounts are far lower than found elsewhere but their presence links the
valley with other participants in this long-distance network of exchange.
Third, there is considerable variability in the contents of the mounds in
The Plains, as is typical of Hopewell mounds. This variability is not solely
a function of chronology since mound 435 (the Coon Mound; Greenman
1932) and mound 434 (the Armitage Mound; Abrams 1992a) overlap in time.
Fourth, the size of the local community, the settlement pattern, and the establishment of a homestead for each community are similar when sites
such as the Boudinot 4 and the Murphy sites are compared. Ultimately, the
Hocking Valley community political organization represents a variation on
the theme of tribal regionalism, reflecting a distinctive expression of parallel cultural practices evidenced elsewhere in the Ohio Valley. The regional
divisions between tribal units reflect the cultural pluralism that typifies
tribal societies (Clay 2002).

Finally, there is no evidence that political organization evolved to the
complexity associated ethnologically with chiefdoms (Earle 1991). Chiefdoms as political organizations are marked by an instituted hierarchy of
decision making, differential access to land and other vital resources, and a
redistributive economy. Economic, social, and religious leverage of some
type is essential for the emergence of chiefdoms. Chiefdoms generally evolve
in the context of predictable but differential surplus production. Currently
there are no data that indicate that such institutions or conditions existed
in the Hocking Valley, even during the peak of political complexity.

Hypothetically, if one lineage or unified set of lineages were to have differential control over floodplain resources and assume a more central role
in amassing resources from other communities for later redistribution, we

might expect that set of communities to spatially expand by assuming occupation of The Plains, thus seizing the ideological center of the region to bolster its claims to economic and political centrality. Although chiefdoms did not evolve in the valley, that pattern of vertical economic integration, with each community having access to resources spanning the riverine and upland zones, is typical of more complex political organizations, serving as a prelude to potential political change.

## The Period of Regional Tribal Fragmentation (A.D. 250–500)

Beginning ca. A.D. 250 the construction of burial mounds and other earthworks ceased as a cultural practice throughout the Ohio Valley. The Hocking Valley is no exception, as the latest reliable radiocarbon dates from The Plains are mid-third century A.D. (Skinner and Norris 1984; J. Murphy 1989; Blazier, Freter, and Abrams, this volume). If we correlate the construction of large earthworks with regional alliances, then logically the cessation of such construction efforts reflects their fragmentation. Data are sparse for this 250-year period; there are currently no radiocarbon dates from any sites for these years. The latest date from The Plains is A.D. 240; the latest from the County Home site is A.D. 236. Many sites, such as the Allen site, have artifact types reflecting the Late Archaic through Late Prehistoric, yet are devoid of artifacts and radiocarbon dates for this period of fragmentation.

There are two approaches to this issue. The first is that we simply lack sufficiently detailed data and adequate radiocarbon dates to have identified the continued presence of people and that there is in fact no occupation gap. Point typologies often extend beyond their presumed ending date in the Hocking Valley; thus Robbins points or bladelets, which elsewhere are viewed as Middle Woodland (i.e., ending ca. A.D. 250; Justice 1987), may have been used at A.D. 400 in the Hocking Valley.

The alternative approach is that the gap in dates is real, reflecting some extent of valley abandonment. If such occurred, it was far from uniform. Different portions of the valley may have been effected differently; further, as one community left, greater resources were available to those remaining. A longer-term residual population, especially in the upper valley, is probable since populations in the Scioto and the Licking Valleys, while small, did remain (Dancey 1991). If future research confirms that abandonment characterized to some degree the fourth and fifth centuries A.D., then the possible ecological and economic underpinnings of such a process must be further considered (Vickery 1994), as well as the role of lineages in mobilizing local communities in the process of out-migration.

## The Period of Agricultural Tribal Communities (A.D. 500–1450?)

The sixth and seventh centuries A.D. in the Hocking Valley are relatively unknown, in part a consequence of the ambiguity of the preceding period of regional fragmentation. However, by the eighth century the climate was conducive to crop growth and the first maize was evidenced in the valley ca. A.D. 700 (Wymer, this volume). Until its final abandonment, the valley was occupied by local communities increasingly dependent on maize.

Community size ranged from a low of 35 to 40 in the smaller tributaries to a maximum of perhaps 80 along or abutting the floodplain of the main stem of the Hocking. According to the settlement data (Wakeman, this volume), the vast majority of communities resided along the main stem of the Hocking, with only sporadic settlement along tributaries (fig. 12.4). As Wakeman notes, only the broader expanses and high soil fertility of the floodplain zones could meet the economic needs of maize agriculturalists.

The concept of a territorial homestead is maintained during this late period. Within that homestead, a new village could be reestablished a short distance away if land was available; thus the village site was not absolutely permanent. Several factors were responsible for the movement of a community. The growing of maize leads to a serious depletion of soil nutrients if fallow is insufficient. Deforestation can produce a shortage of trees necessary for nuts, fuelwood, and other associated resources. The use of the same house for several years can lead to lowered hygiene as a result of insect infestation. These and other factors may have prompted the ritual burning of residential sites, resulting in their transformation into fields, fallow lands, or forests, all of which are distinct resource reservoirs of the greater landscape mosaic.

These agricultural villagers also had the option to move during severe winters. Rockshelters, such as Chesser rockshelter (Prufer 1967), used by hunting and gathering parties were also used by members of the agricultural village seeking shelter from bitter winter weather. The rockshelters within the Hocking Valley provided a natural respite for populations from initial colonization until the end of indigenous occupation.

These late agricultural villages combined the growing of maize, which replaced the Eastern Agricultural Complex based on the Allen site data (Wymer, this volume), with hunting and gathering. Murphy's statement that maize became "a major component in the Late Prehistoric diet" (1989, 354) is confirmed, although the specific contribution of maize to the diet varied among Hocking communities. Although chemical analyses of skeletal material from Hocking populations has not yet been conducted, such

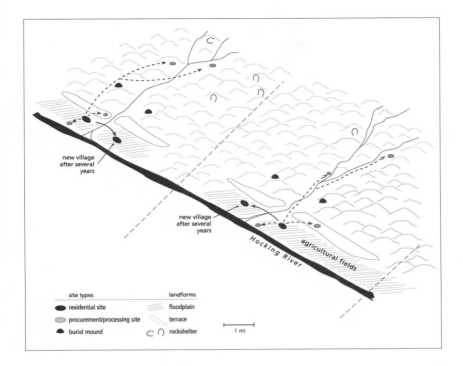

FIG. 12.4. Late Prehistoric settlement
patterns in the Hocking Valley

analyses from late communities in southwestern Ohio concluded that maize represented as much as 65% of the diet
(summarized in Nass 1988, 331). This commitment to maize
agriculture required extensive amounts of land for each
community, resulting in the linear, dispersed settlement pattern evidenced
along the entire Hocking River (Wakeman, this volume).

Socially and politically, lineage membership still defined many social
roles and leaders of limited influence orchestrated trade and ritual. The political relations among villages, however, is not well known. The data do
not exist, for example, that would clarify the political and economic relationship of those communities along the Hocking with those in the smaller
tributaries.

This period apparently ends ca. A.D. 1450. Like other riverine systems in
the Ohio Valley (Drooker and Cowen 2001), the Hocking Valley seems to
have been abandoned at this time, the population moving to the larger Ohio
River. The most accepted explanation for this large-scale process of abandonment is that people chose to leave the region as declining rainfall produced conditions unsuitable for the predictable growing of maize relative
to the appeal of the larger-river setting (Graybill 1981). In the context of the
highest population levels and density ever in the valley, several hundred
years of soil nutrient depletion from maize agriculture, the environmental

vulnerability of the valley, and other factors, these communities out-migrated, representing the last indigenous occupation of the valley before historic colonization.

Based on the data from the Hocking Valley, the above historical narrative of tribal formation strongly supports our current models of the complex nature of tribal society. Many of the elements of tribes described in the anthropological literature (e.g., Price and Feinman 1995; Price and Gebauer 1995) and specific to past Ohio societies (e.g., Brose 1994; Yerkes 2002, n.d.) are evident in the Hocking. Effectively the models and expanded data presented in this volume have moved our scale of analysis closer to a social history of tribes in the Hocking River Valley.

In summarizing tribal formation in the Hocking Valley, several keystone characteristics are observed. First, the tribe is typified by *organizational flexibility.* People living in small groups reconfigured their behavioral patterns as was needed to adjust or adapt to the stochastic challenges of their expected vision of life. For example, when particularly severe winters encouraged the dispersal of the community, the group possessed the organizational ability to fission, temporarily occupying rockshelters. Again, when droughts reduced the availability of nuts as a staple food, seed plants were targeted as dietary supplements and the organizational shifts in labor were readily made.

Second, there is a great degree of *variability* in tribal organization. Communities ca. A.D. 600 in the upper valley built defensive earthworks reflecting the threat of attack from neighboring communities (Schweikart, this volume). Those coeval communities in the central Hocking did not build such embankments. Although we lack comparable data, hypothetically villages at the confluence of the Hocking and Ohio Rivers varied from both these types of community organizations.

Third, there is, however, a *conservatism* or *resilience* evidenced by these tribal societies. Despite the adjustments that communities made, the core structure of society remained relatively unchanged over long periods. The combination of lineages ca. 500 B.C. with an animistic religion produced the social structure and ideological justification for rules of social behavior that remained unchanged for many generations. Thus seasonal dispersal to rockshelters was mitigated by the return to settled communities. The broad scale of tribal inclusiveness ca. 50 B.C. was replaced with a lesser and prior scale of organization ca. A.D. 250. Although long-term structural changes did occur, the relative stability of cultural behaviors complemented the flexibility of instituted behaviors; that is, the core of society—the local community—could remain relatively stable for many generations in part owing to its flexibility.

There are several factors that contextualize this conservatism. Certainly from a social psychological level one could cite religion, sanctions against deviant behavior that are more powerful in small groups, and the small size of domestic groups as encouraging the strong reproduction of culture through generations. From a broader processual level, one could cite low population growth and density as a collective factor that encouraged relative stability.

From a more direct ecological perspective, the inability of these past communities to produce a consistent and abundant food surplus was a factor that limited societal change. When we view patterns and rates of societal change in other regions of the world, we see that *differential surplus accumulation* underlies the process. In the Hocking Valley, local communities of horticulturalists and maize agriculturalists *could not* consistently produce a surplus, given the climatic and seasonal variability and risks of food production; neither could any one set of communities produce a significantly higher amount of food relative to other communities to create the economic leverage associated with hierarchic political organizations.

However, qualitative changes of a structural scale did occur; nomadic hunting and gathering communities did evolve into more sedentary gardening communities. The pattern and rate of change is slow and incremental. The long-term changes we observe archaeologically may have had little impact on the pattern of daily life for most generations, since such changes are often too gradual to be emically noticed.

In this regard, we see many innovations that eventually led to change as being instituted *in order to maintain rather than alter* social behaviors. Ceramics predating horticulture were manufactured to conserve the established hunting and gathering lifeway. This follows Romer's Rule (1960) from paleontology, which sees innovation as arising first to maintain the organism and only later contributing to new adaptations of the organism.

Although the rate of societal change was generally gradual, there were episodes of relatively rapid historical change that reflect punctuated equilibria. This accelerated rate of acceptance of new instituted behaviors characterized stages in sedentism, gardening of local crops, membership in regional tribal alliances, and the adoption of maize as an economic staple. For example, as local communities experimented and succeeded at gardening, that knowledge spread through kinship and other lines to neighboring communities. The decision to intentionally grow crops in gardens may have been prompted by any combination of economic, sociometric, or social psychological factors by any community, but once gardening began, it was accepted as an economic option by dispersed Hocking communities within a relatively short period of time. Collectively, we see both incremental and accelerated rates of change typifying the process of societal evolution.

Finally, in summarizing trends of tribal formation in the Hocking Valley it is difficult to ignore the role played by environmental variability on many levels in influencing cultural decisions. Many scholars have recently distanced themselves from ecological anthropology based on the specter of environmental determinism. However, such a stance is premature; as Hegmon (2003) states, we are now in a period of theory that might be termed "processual plus," which in the context of Hocking research recognizes an empowered and evolving society responsive to the influences of climate, seasonality, and the myriad of other external factors that challenge these and all societies.

## Future Research

The overarching goal of the archaeological research presented in this volume was to contribute to a better understanding the indigenous societies who once occupied the Hocking Valley. Several categories of future research would move us even closer to that goal.

Many of the reconstructions of societies in the Hocking Valley are based on a very limited sample of intensively excavated sites. This contributes to a somewhat normative picture of community life and reduces the real scope of variation that once existed. Far more habitation sites from all time periods must be excavated to corroborate or modify the present picture of village organization.

In addition to residential sites, there has been only one well-excavated and -documented rockshelter (Prufer 1967) in the valley. Since rockshelters were used by virtually all societies throughout the entire occupation of the valley, these sites warrant systematic and intensive attention. Similarly, there was a dynamic use of extraction sites of various types as residential sedentism increased, and detailed excavation of these sites is required. All these sites must be placed in a total settlement system anchored by the residential site(s) if they are to approach their full significance.

In addition to increased excavation, large-scale systematic surveys must be conducted. Most survey data are recovered from cultural resource management (CRM) efforts that provide valuable data but are limited to those areas of mitigation. Broad portions of the Hocking Valley, such as Federal Creek, have not been surveyed, and this certainly remains a gap in our ability to move our reconstructions into the realm of local and regional demography, a topic central to the study of social process.

The chronology of these sites, and thus the study of social change in the valley, must be refined. The best means of achieving a more detailed chronology is by targeting large numbers of features and ecofacts from excavated contexts for regular radiocarbon dating or accelerator mass spectroscopy dating. We currently have perhaps two dozen or so such dates from the entire valley. When we possess hundreds of such dates, far more historical detail will emerge from the archaeological record, leading to an improved division of the broad categories of time or cultural periods and producing a synergy of analyses with a wide range of databases.

Although all periods require further chronological refinement, the period between A.D. 250–500 is by far the most enigmatic in the valley. Research specifically directed to test the abandonment hypothesis previously cited must be conducted. In this same vein, the chronology of final abandonment ca. A.D. 1450 must be tested. Given the documented variability among riverine societies, the pattern observed elsewhere cannot a priori be accepted for the Hocking.

Further, continued application of technology must be pursued in Hocking Valley research. The use of GIS technology and genetic research, to name just two prominent analyses, hold great promise for advancing our understanding of social patterns practiced by the past population.

Finally, future research in the Hocking Valley should continue the present overarching effort of contributing toward Native American issues. For example, it is a convenient myth in American popular culture that Native Americans did not "own" land as defined by European standards, a myth often used to justify the historic theft of indigenous territory (Patterson 1995). However, the analysis of archaeological data in this volume demonstrates that indigenous societies not only created their own culture-specific concept of territoriality but did so by at least 500 B.C. Continued analyses may address the issues of health status and demography before the conquest.

The collective efforts of archaeologists in academia, cultural resource management, museums, and government, combined with input from Native Americans and other informed and concerned citizens, will continue to add substance to these archaeological societies. As there is no viable alternative to reconstructing the diverse and distant past other than archaeology, we hope that continued efforts will illuminate the array of indigenous societies who first occupied, modified, and established a pride of place in what we today call the Hocking River Valley.

# REFERENCES

Abrams, E.

1989a    Architecture and Energy: An Evolutionary Perspective. In *Archaeologi-cal Method and Theory,* ed. M. Schiffer, 1:47–87. Tucson: University of Arizona Press.

1989b    The Boudinot #4 Site (33AT521): An Early Woodland Habitation Site in Athens County, Ohio. *West Virginia Archaeologist* 41:16–26.

1992a    Archaeological Investigation of the Armitage Mound (33-AT-434), The Plains, Ohio. *Midcontinental Journal of Archaeology* 17:80–111.

1992b    Woodland Settlement Patterns in the Southern Hocking River Valley, Southeastern Ohio. In *Cultural Variability in Context: Woodland Settle-ments of the Mid-Ohio Valley,* ed. M. Seeman, 19–23. MCJA Special Paper no. 7. Kent, Ohio: Kent State University Press.

Abrams, E., and M. LeRouge

2004    Political Complexity and Mound Construction among the Early and Late Adena of the Hocking Valley, Ohio. In *The Early Woodland and Adena Prehistory in the Ohio Area,* ed. M. Otto. Columbus: Ohio Ar-chaeological Council.

Adovasio, J., R. Fryman, A. Quinn, D. Dirkmaat, and D. Pedler

2001    The Archaic of the Upper Ohio Valley: A View from Meadowcroft Rock-shelter. In *Archaic Transitions in Ohio and Kentucky Prehistory,* ed. O. Prufer, S. Pedde, and R. Meindl, 141–82. Kent, Ohio: Kent State Univer-sity Press.

Anderson, D.

2002    The Evolution of Tribal Social Organization in the Southeastern United States. In *The Archaeology of Tribal Societies,* ed. W. Parkinson, 246–77. International Monographs in Prehistory, Archaeological Series 15, Ann Arbor.

Anderson, E.

1956    Man as a Maker of New Plants and New Plant Communities. In *Man's Role in Changing the Face of the Earth,* ed. W. Thomas, 763–77. Chicago: University of Chicago Press.

Andrews, E. B.

1877    Report of Explorations of Mounds in Southeastern Ohio. *Tenth Annual Report of the Trustees of the Peabody Museum of American Archaeology and Ethnology* 2 (1): 51–74.

Andrefsky, W.

1994    Raw Material Availability and the Organization of Technology. *American Antiquity* 59:21–34.

Appadurai, A.

1986    *The Social Life of Things: Commodities in Cultural Perspective.* Cambridge: Cambridge University Press.

Atwater, C.

1820    *Description of the Antiquities Discovered in the State of Ohio and Other Western States.* Transactions and Collections of the American Antiquarian Society, vol. 1. Worcester, Mass.

Baby, R., and M. Potter

1965    *The Cole Complex: A Preliminary Analysis of the Late Woodland Ceramics in Ohio and Their Relationships to the Ohio Hopewell Phase.* Ohio Historical Society Papers in Archaeology, no. 2. Columbus.

Bamforth, D.

1986    Technological Efficiency and Tool Curation. *American Antiquity* 51:38–50.

Beck, C.

1981    X-Ray Diffraction Analysis and Petrography as Useful Methods for Ceramic Typology. *Journal of Field Archaeology* 8:511–13.

Bergman, C. A., and J. F. Doershuk

1992    How the Data Come Together: Refitting in Lithic Analysis. *Journal of Middle Atlantic Archaeology* 8:139–60.

Binford, L.

1980    Willow Smoke and Dogs' Tails: Hunter-Gatherer Settlement Systems and Archaeological Site Formation. *American Antiquity* 45:4–21.

Black, D.

1979    Adena and Hopewell Relations in the Lower Hocking Valley. In *Hopewell Archaeology: The Chillicothe Conference,* ed. D. S. Brose and N. Greber, 19–26. Kent, Ohio: Kent State University Press.

Blazier, J.

2002    A Re-Examination of Mound 24, The Plains, Ohio. Master's thesis, Department of Environmental Studies, Ohio University.

Blazier, J., and A. Freter

2002    A Re-Examination of Mound 24, The Plains, Ohio, Utilizing Harris Matrix Stratigraphic Profiling. Paper presented at the 48th Annual Midwest Archaeological Conference, Columbus, Ohio.

Boetticher, A. W.

1929    A Study of Type Forest Associations of Athens County, Ohio. Master's thesis, Department of Botany, Ohio State University.

Bordes, F.

1961    *Typologie du paléolithique ancien et moyen.* Institut de Préhistoire de l'Université de Bordeaux, Memoire 1. Bordeaux: Delmas.

Boserup, E.

1965    *The Conditions of Agricultural Growth.* Chicago: Aldine.

Bradley, B., and C. G. Sampson

1986    Artifacts from the Cottages Site. In *Palaeoecology and Archaeology of an Acheulian Site at Caddington, England,* ed. C. G. Sampson, 83–137. Dallas: Southern Methodist University Press.

Braun, D.

1986   Midwestern Hopewellian Exchange and Supralocal Interaction. In *Peer Polity Interaction and Socio-Political Change,* ed. C. Renfrew and J. Cherry, 117–26. Cambridge: Cambridge University Press.

Braun, D., and S. Plog

1982   Evolution of "Tribal" Social Networks: Theory and Prehistoric North American Evidence. *American Antiquity* 47:504–25.

Brose, D.

1994   *The South Park Village Site and the Late Prehistoric Whittlesey Tradition in Northeast Ohio.* Monographs in World Archaeology 20. Madison, Wis.: Prehistory Press.

Brose, D., and N. Greber, eds.

1979   *Hopewell Archaeology.* Kent, Ohio: Kent State University Press.

Brown, J.

1985   Long-Term Trends to Sedentism and the Emergence of Complexity in the American Midwest. In *Prehistoric Hunter-Gatherers,* ed. T. D. Price and J. Brown, 201–31. Orlando: Academic Press.

1986   Early Ceramics and Culture: A Review of Interpretations. In *Early Woodland Archeology,* ed. K. Farnsworth and T. Emerson, 598–608. Kampsville Seminars in Archeology, no. 2. Kampsville, Ill.: Center for American Archeology Press.

1992   Closing Commentary. In *Cultural Variability in Context: Woodland Settlements in the Mid-Ohio Valley,* ed. M. Seeman, 81–82. MCJA Special Paper no. 7. Kent, Ohio: Kent State University Press.

Burks, J., and W. Dancey

1999   The Strait Site: A Middle to Late Woodland Settlement in Central Ohio. *Ohio Archaeological Council Newsletter* 11 (2): 6–11.

2000   Terminal Middle Woodland Period Settlement Aggregation in the Middle Ohio River Valley: Recent Findings from the Strait Site in Central Ohio. Paper presented at the 65th annual meeting of the Society for American Archaeology, Philadelphia.

Burrough, P., and R. McDonnell

1998   *Principles of Geographic Information Systems.* New York: Oxford University Press.

Callahan, E.

1979   The Basics of Biface Knapping in the Eastern Fluted Point Tradition: A Manual for Flintknappers and Lithic Analysts. *Archaeology of Eastern North America* 7:1–180.

Callender, C.

1978   Great Lakes–Riverine Sociopolitical Organization. In *Handbook of North American Indians,* vol. 15, *Northeast,* ed. B. Trigger, 610–21. Washington, D.C.: Smithsonian Institution Press.

Carneiro, R.

1970   A Theory of the Origin of the State. *Science* 21:733–38.

Carskadden, J., and T. Gregg

1974   Excavation of an Adena Open Site, Duncan Falls, Ohio. *Ohio Archaeologist* 24:4–7.

Carskadden, J., and J. Morton

1996    The Middle Woodland–Late Woodland Transition in the Central Musk-
        ingum Valley of Eastern Ohio: A View from the Philo Archaeological
        District. In *A View from the Core: A Synthesis of Ohio Hopewell Archae-
        ology,* ed. P. Pacheco, 316–38. Columbus: Ohio Archaeological Council.

1997    Living on the Edge: A Comparison of Adena and Hopewell Communi-
        ties in the Central Muskingum Valley in Eastern Ohio. In *Ohio Hopewell
        Community Organization,* ed. W. Dancey and P. Pacheco, 365–401. Kent,
        Ohio: Kent State University Press.

2000    Fort Ancient in the Central Muskingum Valley of Eastern Ohio: A View
        from the Philo II Site. In *Cultures before Contact: The Late Prehistory of
        Ohio and Surrounding Regions,* ed. R. Genheimer, 158–93. Columbus:
        Ohio Archaeological Council.

Chagnon, N.

1997    *Yanomamö.* 5th ed. Fort Worth: Harcourt Brace College Publishers.

Charles, D., and J. Buikstra

1983    Archaic Mortuary Sites in the Central Mississippi Drainage: Distribu-
        tion, Structure, and Behavioral Implications. In *Archaic Hunters and
        Gatherers in the American Midwest,* ed. J. Phillips and J. Brown, 117–45.
        New York: Academic Press.

Church, F., and J. Nass Jr.

2002    Central Ohio Valley during the Late Prehistoric Period: Subsistence-
        Settlement Systems Responses to Risk. In *Northeast Subsistence-Settlement
        Change, A.D. 700–1300,* ed. J. Hart and C. Rieth, 11–42. New York State
        Museum Bulletin 496. Albany.

Chute, E. H.

1951    An Analysis of Early Surveyor's Line Descriptions as a Basis for Map-
        ping Primeval Vegetation. Master's thesis, Departmet of Botany, Ohio
        State University.

Clay, R. B.

1986    Adena Ritual Spaces. In *Early Woodland Archaeology,* ed. K. Farnsworth
        and T. Emerson, 581–95. Kampsville, Ill.: Center for American Archeol-
        ogy Press.

1991    Adena Ritual Development: An Organizational Type in a Temporal Per-
        spective. In *The Human Landscape in Kentucky's Past,* ed. C. Stout and
        C. Hensley, 30–39. Lexington: Kentucky Heritage Council.

1992    Chiefs, Big Men, or What? Economy, Settlement Patterns, and Their
        Bearing on Adena Political Models. In *Cultural Variability in Context:
        Woodland Settlements in the Mid-Ohio Valley,* ed. M. Seeman, 77–80.
        MCJA Special Paper no. 7. Kent, Ohio: Kent State University Press.

1998    The Essential Features of Adena Ritual and Their Implications. *South-
        eastern Archaeology* 17:1–21.

2002    Deconstructing the Woodland Sequence from the Heartland: A Review
        of Recent Research Direction in the Upper Ohio Valley. In *The Wood-
        land Southeast,* ed. D. Anderson and R. Mainfort Jr., 162–84. Tuscaloosa:
        University of Alabama Press.

Clay, R. B., and S. Creasman

    1999    Middle Ohio Valley Late Woodland Nucleated Settlements: "Where's the Beef?" *West Virginia Archaeologist* 51:1–10.

Clay, R. B., and C. Niquette, eds.

    1989    *Phase III Excavations at the Niebert Site (46MS103) in the Gallipolis Locks and Dam Replacement Project, Mason County, West Virginia.* Contract Publication Series 89–06. Lexington, Ky.: Cultural Resource Analysts.

Collins, M.

    1975    Lithic Technology as a Means of Processual Inference. In *Lithic Technology, Making and Using Stone Tools,* ed. E. Swanson, 15–34. The Hague: Mouton.

Converse, Robert N.

    1978    *Ohio Slate Types.* Columbus: Archaeological Society of Ohio.

    1993    The Troyer Site: A Hopewell Habitation Site, and a Secular View of Ohio Hopewell Villages. *Ohio Archaeologist* 43 (3): 4–12.

Core, H. A., W. A. Côté, and A. C. Day

    1979    *Wood: Structure and Identification.* Syracuse: Syracuse University Press.

Cowan, C. W., H. E. Jackson, K. Moore, A. Nickelhoff, and T. Smart

    1981    The Cloudsplitter Rockshelter, Menifee County, Kentucky: A Preliminary Report. *Southeastern Archaeological Conference Bulletin* 24:60–76.

Cowan, F.

    1999    Making Sense of Flake Scatters: Lithic Technological Strategies and Mobility. *American Antiquity* 64 (4): 593–607.

Crowell, D.

    2002    Architectural Feature Analysis at a Late Archaic-Early Woodland Habitation Site: A View From the County Home Site (33AT40) in Athens County, Ohio. Master's thesis, Department of Environmental Studies, Ohio University.

Crabtree, D.

    1966    A Stone-Workers' Approach to Analyzing and Replicating the Lindenmeier Folsom. *Tebiwa* 10:60–73.

    1967    Notes on Experimental Flintknapping: Tools Used for Making Stone Artifacts. *Tebiwa* 10:8–24.

    1972    *An Introduction to Flintworking.* Idaho State University Museum, Occasional Papers, no. 128.

Dancey, W.

    1988    The Community Plan of an Early Late Woodland Village in the Middle Scioto River Valley. *Midcontinental Journal of Archaeology* 13:233–58.

    1991    A Middle Woodland Settlement in Central Ohio: A Preliminary Report on the Murphy Site (33LI212). *Pennsylvania Archaeologist* 61:37–72.

    1992    Village Origins in Central Ohio: The Results and Implications of Recent Middle and Late Woodland Research. In *Cultural Variability in Context: Woodland Settlements of the Mid-Ohio Valley,* ed. M. Seeman, 24–29. MCJA Special Paper no. 7. Kent, Ohio: Kent State University Press.

    1998    The Value of Surface Archaeological Data in Exploring the Dynamics of Community Evolution in the Middle Ohio Valley. In *Surface Archaeology,* ed. A. Sullivan III, 3–20. Albuquerque: University of New Mexico Press.

Dancey, W., and P. Pacheco, eds.

1997　*Ohio Hopewell Community Organization.* Kent, Ohio: Kent State University Press.

DeRegnacourt, T., and J. Geogiady

1998　*Prehistoric Chert Types of the Midwest.* Occasional Monographs Series of the Upper Miami Valley Archaeological Research Museum, no. 7. Arcanum, Ohio.

DeWert, J., J. Kime, and J. Gardner

1981　*A Preliminary Archaeological Survey of the Proposed Widening of U.S. 50 between Albany and Athens, Athens County, Ohio.* CRM Report submitted to the Ohio Department of Transportation.

Dietler, M., and B. Hayden, eds.

2001　*Feasts: Archaeological and Ethnographic Perspectives on Food, Politics, and Power.* Washington, D.C.: Smithsonian Institution Press.

Dincauze, D.

2000　*Environmental Archaeology.* Cambridge: Cambridge University Press.

Douglass, A., and D. Schaller

1993　Sourcing Little Colorado White Ware: A Regional Approach to the Compositional Analysis of Prehistoric Ceramic. *Georchaeology* 8:177–201.

Dragoo, D.

1963　*Mounds for the Dead: An Analysis of the Adena Culture.* Annals of the Carnegie Museum, vol. 37. Pittsburgh.

Drennan, R.

1987　Regional Demography in Chiefdoms. In *Chiefdoms in the Americas,* ed. R. Drennan and C. Uribe, 307–24. Lanham, Md.: University Press of America.

Drooker, P., and C. W. Cowan

2001　Transformation of the Fort Ancient Cultures of the Central Ohio Valley. In *Societies in Eclipse,* ed. D. Brose, C. W. Cowan, and R. Mainfort Jr., 83–106. Smithsonian Institution Press, Washington, D.C.

Dunne, M., and W. Green

1998　Terminal Archaic and Early Woodland Plant Use at the Gast Spring Site (13LA152), Southeast Iowa. *Midcontinental Journal of Archaeology* 23:45–88.

Earle, T., ed.

1991　*Chiefdoms: Power, Economy, and Ideology.* Cambridge: Cambridge University Press.

Ehrenreich, R., C. Crumley, and J. Levy, eds.

1995　*Heterarchy and the Analysis of Complex Societies.* Archaeological Papers of the American Anthropological Association, no. 6. Arlington, Va.

Emerson, T., D. McElrath, and A. Fortier, eds.

2000　*Late Woodland Societies.* Lincoln: University of Nebraska Press.

Erasmus, C.

1965　Monument Building: Some Field Experiments. *Southwestern Journal of Anthropology* 21:277–301.

Ericksen, A., R. Norris Sprague, and A. Almstedt

2000　*Results of Data Recovery and Public Archaeology Program at 33DL27 for the Proposed I–71 Maxtown Road Extension in Orange Township, City of*

*Westerville, Delaware County, Ohio.* Submitted to the City of Westerville City Manager's Office. ASC Group.

Essenpreis, P.
1978    Fort Ancient Settlement: Differential Response at a Mississippian–Late Woodland Interface. In *Mississippian Settlement Patterns,* ed. B. Smith, 141–67. New York: Academic Press.

Fagan, B.
2000    *Ancient North America.* London: Thames and Hudson.

Farnsworth, K., and T. Emerson, eds.
1986    *Early Woodland Archeology.* Kampsville, Ill.: Center for American Archeology.

Feinman, G.
1995    The Emergence of Inequality: A Focus on Strategies and Processes. In *Foundations of Social Inequality,* ed. T. D. Price and G. Feinman, 255–79. New York: Plenum Press.

Flannery, K.
1976    *The Early Mesoamerican Village.* New York: Academic Press.
2002    The Origins of the Village Revisited: From Nuclear to Extended House-holds. *American Antiquity* 67:417–33.

Flenniken, J.
1981    *Replicative Systems Analysis: A Model Applied to the Vein Quartz Artifacts from the Hoko River Site.* Washington State University Laboratory of Anthropology Reports of Investigation, no. 59. Pullman.

Ford, R.
1979    Paleoethnobotany in American Archaeology. In *Advances in Archaeological Theory,* ed. M. Schiffer, 285–336. New York: Academic Press.
1985    Patterns of Prehistoric Food Production in North America. In *Prehistoric Food Production in North America,* ed. R. Ford, 341–64. Museum of Anthropology, Anthropological Paper no. 75. Ann Arbor: University of Michigan.

Freter, A.
1996    Rural Utilitarian Ceramic Production in the Late Classic Period Copan Maya State. In *Arqueología mesoamericana: Homenaje a William T. Sanders,* ed. A. Guadalupe, J. Parsons, R. Santley, and M. Carmen, 2:209–29. Mexico City: Instituto Nacional de Antropología e Historia.

Fried, M.
1967    *The Evolution of Political Society.* New York: Random House.
1975    *The Notion of Tribe.* Menlo Park, Calif.: Cummings.

Frison, G.
1974    *The Casper Site: A Hell Gap Bison Kill on the High Plains.* New York: Academic Press.

Geiger, R.
1959    *The Climate Near the Ground.* Trans. M. N. Stewart et al. Cambridge, Mass.: Harvard University Press.

Genheimer, R., ed.
2000    *Cultures before Contact: The Late Prehistory of Ohio and Surrounding Regions.* Columbus: Ohio Archaeological Council.

Gillespie, S., and D. Nichols, eds.

2003    *Archaeology Is Anthropology.* Archeological Papers of the American Anthropological Association, no. 13. Washington, D.C.

Gilman, P.

1987    Architecture as Artifact: Pit Structures and Pueblos in the American Southwest. *American Antiquity* 52:538–564.

Graybill, J.

1981    The Eastern Periphery of Fort Ancient (A.D. 1050–1650): A Diachronic Approach to Settlement Variability. Ph.D. diss., Department of Anthropology, University of Washington.

Greber, N.

1991    A Study of Continuity and Contrast between Central Scioto Adena and Hopewell Sites. *West Virginia Archaeologist* 43:1–26.

Green, W., and J. Doershuk

1998    Cultural Resource Management and American Archaeology. *Journal of Archaeological Research* 6:121–167.

Greenman, E.

1932    Excavation of the Coon Mound and an Analysis of the Adena Culture. *Ohio State Archaeological and Historical Quarterly* 41:366–523.

Gremillion, K., and C. Ison

1989    Terminal Archaic and Early Woodland Plant Utilization along the Cumberland Plateau. Paper presented at the 54th Annual Meeting of the Society for American Archaeology, Atlanta.

Griffin, J.

1966    [1943]. *The Fort Ancient Aspect.* University of Michigan Museum of Anthropology Anthropological Papers, no. 28. Ann Arbor.

Grumet, R.

1995    *Historic Contact.* Norman: University of Oklahoma Press.

Hall, R.

1997    *An Archaeology of the Soul.* Urbana: University of Illinois Press.

Harlan, J.

1995    *Living Fields: Our Agricultural Heritage.* Cambridge: Cambridge University Press.

Harris, E.

1989    *Principles of Archaeological Stratigraphy.* London: Academic Press.

Hayden, B.

1990    Nimrods, Piscators, Pluckers, and Planters: The Emergence of Food Production. *Journal of Anthropological Archaeology* 9:31–69.

1995    Pathways to Power: Principles for Creating Socioeconomic Inequalities. In *Foundation for Social Inequality,* ed. T. D. Price and G. Feinman, 15–86. New York: Plenum.

2001    Fabulous Feasts: A Prolegomenon to the Importance of Feasting. In *Feasts: Archaeological and Ethnographic Perspectives on Food, Politics, and Power,* ed. M. Dietler and B. Hayden, 23–64. Washington, D.C.: Smithsonian Institution Press.

Hays, C.

1994    Adena Mortuary Patterns and Ritual Cycles in the Upper Scioto Valley, Ohio. Ph.D. diss., Department of Anthropology, SUNY Binghamton.

Hegmon, M.

2003    Setting Theoretical Egos Aside: Issues and Theory in North American Archaeology. *American Antiquity* 68:213–43.

Henderson, A. G., ed.

1992    *Fort Ancient Cultural Dynamics in the Middle Ohio Valley.* Monographs in World Archaeology, no. 8. Madison, Wis.: Prehistory Press.

Henderson, A. G., D. Pollack, and C. Turnbow

1992    Chronology and Cultural Patterns. In *Fort Ancient Cultural Dynamics in the Middle Ohio Valley,* ed. A. G. Henderson, 253–79. Monographs in World Archaeology, no. 8. Madison, Wis.: Prehistory Press.

Henderson, A. G., and C. Turnbow

1987    Fort Ancient Developments in Northeastern Kentucky. In *Current Archaeological Research in Kentucky: Volume One,* ed. D. Pollack, 205–32. Frankfort: Kentucky Heritage Council.

Henry, D.

1989    *From Foraging to Agriculture.* Philadelphia: University of Pennsylvania Press.

Heyman, M.

2000    Communal Feasting and the Formation of Prehistoric Tribal Societies in Southeastern Ohio. Master's thesis, Department of Anthropology, Ohio University.

Howard, J.

1981    *Shawnee.* Athens: Ohio University Press.

Hudnell, D.

1994    The Allen Site #2—Points. Manuscript on file at Ohio University.

Ison, C.

1988    The Cold Oak Shelter: Providing a Better Understanding of the Terminal Archaic. In *Paleoindian and Archaic Research in Kentucky,* ed. C. D. Hockensmith, D. Pollack, and T. N. Sanders, 205–20. Frankfort: Kentucky Heritage Council.

Jakle, J.

1969    Salt on the Ohio Valley Frontier, 1770–1820. *Annals of the Association of American Geographers* 59:687–709.

Jefferies, R., E. Breitburg, J. Flood, and C. Scarry

1996    Mississippian Adaptations of the Northern Periphery: Settlement, Subsistence, and Interaction in the Cumberland Valley of Southeastern Kentucky. *Southeastern Archaeology* 15:1–28.

Johannessen, S., and C. Hastorf, eds.

1994    *Corn and Culture in the Prehistoric New World.* Boulder: Westview Press.

Joyce, R.

2002    *The Languages of Archaeology.* Oxford: Blackwell.

Justice, N.

1987    *Stone Age Spear and Arrow Points of the Midcontinent and Eastern United States.* Bloomington: Indiana University Press.

Keene, A.

1981    *Prehistoric Foraging in a Temperate Forest: A Linear Programming Model.* New York: Academic Press.

Keener, C. S., and A. M. Pecora

2003    *Phase II Archaeological Assessment of Site 33MS29 Located at the Proposed Ohio River Boat Access in Racine, Sutton Township, Meigs County, Ohio, with contributions by Jarrod Burks and Norm Haywood.* Professional Archaeological Servies Team Contract Report 235. Plain City, Ohio.

Keesing, R.

1975    *Kin Groups and Social Structure.* New York: Holt, Rinehart and Winston.

Kempton, J., and R. Goldthwait

1959    Glacial Outwash Terraces of the Hocking and Scioto River Valleys, Ohio. *Ohio Journal of Science* 59:135–51.

Kent, S., and H. Vierich

1989    The Myth of Ecological Determinism—Anticipated Mobility and Site Spatial Organization. In *Farmers as Hunters: The Implications of Sedentism,* ed. S. Kent, 96–130. Cambridge: Cambridge University Press.

Kintz, E.

1990    *Life under the Tropical Canopy: Tradition and Change among the Yucatec Maya.* Chicago: Holt, Rinehart and Winston.

Knapp, A., and W. Ashmore

1999    *Archaeologies of Landscape.* Malden, Mass.: Blackwell.

Kurlansky, M.

2002    *Salt: A World History.* New York: Walker.

Ledbetter, R. J., and L. O'Steen

1992    The Grayson Site: Late Archaic and Late Woodland Occupations in the Little Sandy Drainage. In *Current Archaeological Research in Kentucky,* ed. D. Pollack and A. G. Henderson, 2:13–42. Frankfort: Kentucky Heritage Council.

Lopinot, N. H., and D. E. Brussel

1982    Assessing Uncarbonized Seeds from Open-Air Sites in Mesic Environments: An Example from Southern Illinois. *Journal of Archaeological Science* 9:95–108.

Lucht, T. E., D. L. Brown, and N. H. Martin

1985    *Soil Survey of Athens County Ohio.* Washington, D. C.: U.S. Department of Agriculture.

MacNeish, R.

1981    Tehuacan's Accomplishments. In *Handbook of Middle American Indians, Supplement 1,* ed. J. Sabloff, 31–47. Austin: University of Texas Press.

Mainfort, R., Jr.

1989    Adena Chiefdoms? Evidence from the Wright Mound. *Midcontinental Journal of Archaeology* 14:164–78.

Martin, A. C., and W. D. Barkley

1973    *Seed Identification Manual.* Berkeley: University of California Press.

Maslowski, R.

1985    Woodland Settlement Patterns in the Mid and Upper Ohio Valley. *West Virginia Archaeologist* 37:23–34.

Maslowski, R., and M. Seeman

1992    Woodland Archaeology in the Mid-Ohio Valley: Setting Parameters for Ohio Main Stem/Tributary Comparisons. In *Cultural Variability in Con-*

*text: Woodland Settlements in the Mid-Ohio Valley,* ed. M. Seeman, 10–14. MCJA Special Paper no. 7. Kent, Ohio: Kent State University Press.

McCarthy, B., and J. Quinn

1989      Within—and Among—Tree Variation in Flower and Fruit Production in Two Species of Carya (Juglandaceae). *American Journal of Botany* 76:1015–23.

1992      Fruit Maturation Patterns of *Carya* spp. (Juglandaceae): An Intra-Crown Analysis of Growth and Reproduction. *Oecologia* 91:30–38.

McKenzie, D.

1967      The Graham Village Site: A Fort Ancient Settlement in the Hocking Valley, Ohio. In *Studies in Ohio Archaeology,* ed. O. Prufer, 63–97. Cleveland: Case Western University Press.

McMichael, E. V.

1984      Type Description for Newtown Series Ceramics. In *The Pyles Site (15MS28): A Newtown Village in Mason County, Kentucky,* ed. J. A. Railey, 132–35. Occasional Paper no. 1. Lexington: William S. Webb Archaeological Society.

Means, B.

1999      Sites on the Margins Are Not Marginal Archaeology: Small, Upland Sites in the Vicinity of Meyersdale, Pennsylvania. *North American Archaeologist* 20:135–61.

Meeker, R. L., J. Petro, and S. Bone

1960      *Soil Survey of Fairfield County, Ohio.* Washington, D.C.: U.S. Soil Conservation Service.

Meindl, R., R. Mensforth, and H. York

2001      Mortality, Fertility, and Growth in the Kentucky Late Archaic: The Paleo-demography of the Ward Site. In *Archaic Transitions in Ohio and Kentucky Prehistory,* ed. O. Prufer, S. Pedde, and R. Meindl, 87–109. Kent, Ohio: Kent State University Press.

Meltzer, D.

1998      Ephraim Squier, Edwin Davis, and the Making of an American Archaeological Classic. Introduction to *Ancient Monuments of the Mississippi Valley,* by E. Squier and E. Davis, 1–98. Washington, D.C.: Smithsonian Institution Press.

Mensforth, R.

2001      Warfare and Trophy Taking in the Archaic Period. In *Archaic Transitions in Ohio and Kentucky Prehistory,* ed. O. Prufer, S. Pedde, and R. Meindl, 110–38. Kent, Ohio: Kent State University Press.

Merrill, W.

1953      Pleistocene History of a Part of the Hocking River Valley, Ohio. *Ohio Journal of Science* 53:143–58.

Miller, N. F.

1988      Ratios in Paleoethnobotanical Analysis. In *Current Paleoethnobotany,* ed. C. A. Hastorf and V. S. Popper, 72–85. Chicago: University of Chicago Press.

Mills, W.

1914      *Archaeological Atlas of Ohio.* Columbus: Ohio State Archaeological and Historical Society.

Milner, G., and R. Jefferies

1987    A Re-Examination of the W.P.A. Excavation of the Robbins Mound of Boone County, Kentucky. In *Current Archaeological Research in Kentucky,* ed. D. Pollack, 1:33–42. Frankfort: Kentucky Heritage Council.

Minnis, P. E.

1981    Seeds in Archaeological Sites: Sources and Some Interpretive Problems. *American Antiquity* 46:143–52.

Montgomery, F. H.

1977    *Seeds and Fruits of Plants of Eastern Canada and Northeastern United States.* Toronto: University of Toronto Press.

Moran, E.

2000    *Human Adaptability.* Boulder: Westview Press.

Muller, J.

1986    *Archaeology of the Lower Ohio River Valley.* Orlando: Academic Press.

Munson, P. J.

1973    The Origins and Antiquity of Maize-Beans-Squash Agriculture in Eastern North America: Some Linguistic Implications. In *Variation in Anthropology: Essays in Honor of John C. McGregor,* ed. D. Lathrap and J. Douglas, 107–35. Urbana: Illinois Archaeological Survey.

Munson, P. J., P. W. Parmalee, and R. A. Yarnell

1971    Subsistence Ecology of Scovill, a Terminal Middle Woodland Village. *American Antiquity* 36:410–31.

Murphy, H.

1986    *Further Investigations along the Proposed ATH-50–4.95 Project Corridor (P.F. 464 and 1065).* CRM Report submitted to the Ohio Department of Transportation.

Murphy, J.

1989    *An Archaeological History of the Hocking Valley.* 2d ed. Athens: Ohio University Press.

Nass, J.

1988    Fort Ancient Agricultural Systems and Settlement: A View from Southwestern Ohio. *North American Archaeologist* 9:319–47.

Nass, J., and R. Yerkes

1995    Social Differentiation in Mississippian and Fort Ancient Societies. In *Mississippian Communities and Households,* ed. J. Rogers and B. Smith, 58–80. Tuscaloosa: University of Alabama Press.

Newcomer, M.

1971    Some Quantitative Experiments in Handaxe Manufacture. *World Archaeology* 3:85–93.

Newcomer, M., and C. Karlin

1987    Flint Chips from Pincevent. In *The Human Uses of Chert,* ed. G. deG. Sieveking and M. Newcomer, 42–52. Cambridge: Cambridge University Press.

Ogden, J.

1966    Forest History of Ohio. I. Radiocarbon Dates and Pollen Stratigraphy of Silver Lake, Logan County, Ohio. *Ohio Journal of Science* 66:387–403.

Olmstead, E.

    1991    *Blackcoats among the Delaware: David Zeisberger on the Ohio Frontier.*
              Kent, Ohio: Kent State University Press.

Otto, M.

    1979    Hopewell Antecedents in the Adena Heartland. In *Hopewell Archaeol-
              ogy,* ed. D. Brose and N. Greber, 9–14. MCJA Special Paper no. 3. Kent,
              Ohio: Kent State University Press.

Ozker, D.

    1982    *An Early Woodland Community at the Schultz Site 20SA2 in the Saginaw
              Valley and the Nature of the Early Woodland Adaptation in the Great
              Lakes Region.* University of Michigan Museum of Anthropology Papers,
              no. 70. Ann Arbor.

Pacheco, P.

    1991    Woodland Period Archaeology in Central Ohio: LCALS Contributions.
              *Ohio Archaeological Council Newsletter* 3 (3): 4–7.

Pacheco, P.

    1996a   Ohio Hopewell Regional Settlement Patterns. In *A View From the Core:
              A Synthesis of Ohio Hopewell Archaeology,* ed. P. Pacheco, 16–35. Colum-
              bus: Ohio Archaeological Council.

    1997    Ohio Middle Woodland Intracommunity Settlement Variability: A Case
              Study from Licking Valley. In *Ohio Hopewell Community Organization,*
              ed. W. Dancey and P. Pacheco, 41–84. Kent, Ohio: Kent State University.

Pacheco, P., ed.

    1996b   *A View from the Core: A Synthesis of Ohio Hopewell Archaeology.* Colum-
              bus: Ohio Archaeological Council.

Panshin, A. J., and C. de Zeeuw

    1980    *Textbook of Wood Technology.* New York: McGraw-Hill.

Parkinson, W.

    2002a   Integration, Interaction, and Tribal "Cycling": The Transition to the
              Copper Age on the Great Hungarian Plain. In *The Archaeology of Tribal
              Societies,* ed. W. Parkinson, 391–438. International Monographs in Pre-
              history, Archaeological Series 15. Ann Arbor.

Parkinson, W., ed.

    2002b   *The Archaeology of Tribal Societies.* International Monographs in Pre-
              history, Archaeological Series 15. Ann Arbor.

Patterson, T.

    1995    *Toward a Social History of Archaeology in the United States.* Fort Worth:
              Harcourt Brace.

Pecora, A. M.

    2000    *Phase I Archaeological Survey of the Proposed Wireless Telephone Tower
              Location in Rush Creek Township (Section 22), Fairfield County, Ohio.*
              OVAC Contract Report 2000–06. Columbus: Ohio Valley Archaeologi-
              cal Consultants.

    2002    The Organization of Chipped-Stone Tool Manufacture and the Forma-
              tion of Lithic Assemblages. Ph.D. diss., Department of Anthropology,
              Ohio State University.

Pecora, A. M., and J. Burks

2000    *Phase II Archaeological Assessment of Site 33FA1460, Rush Creek Township, Fairfield County, Ohio.* Columbus: Ohio Valley Archaeological Consultants.

Pedde, S., and O. Prufer

2001    The Kentucky Green River Archaic as Seen from the Ward Site. In *Archaic Transitions in Ohio and Kentucky Prehistory,* ed. O. Prufer, S. Pedde, and R. Meindl, 59–86. Kent, Ohio: Kent State University Press.

Peters, W.

1947    *Athens County, Ohio.* Vol. 1. Athens: by author.

Phillips, P. and J. Brown, eds.

1983    *Archaic Hunters and Gatherers in the American Midwest.* Orlando: Academic Press.

Pillay, A., C. Punyadeera, L. Jacobson, and J. Eriksen

2000    Analysis of Ancient Pottery and Ceramic Objects Using X-Ray Fluorescence Spectrometry. *X-Ray Spectrometry* 29:53–62.

Pitts, E.

2001    An Analysis of Hocking Valley Pottery Using X-Ray Diffraction, X-Ray Fluorescence and Optical Petrography. Honors thesis, Department of Geology, Ohio University.

Pollack, D., and A. G. Henderson

1992    Toward a Model of Fort Ancient Society. In *Fort Ancient Cultural Dynamics in the Middle Ohio Valley,* ed. A. G. Henderson, 281–94. Monographs in World Archaeology, no. 8. Madison, Wis.: Prehistory Press.

Potter, M.

1971    Adena Culture Content and Settlement. In *Adena: The Seeking of an Identity,* ed. B. Swartz Jr., 4–11. Muncie, Ind.: Ball State University Press.

Price, T. D., and J. Brown, eds.

1985    *Prehistoric Hunter-Gatherers.* Orlando: Academic Press.

Price, T. D., and G. Feinman, eds.

1995    *Foundations of Social Inequality.* New York: Plenum Press.

Price, T. D., and A. Gebauer, eds.

1995    *Last Hunters, First Farmers.* Santa Fe: School of American Research Press.

Prufer, O.

1965    *The McGraw Site: A Study in Hopewellian Dynamics.* Cleveland Museum of Natural History, Scientific Publication 4 (1).

1967    Chesser Cave: A Late Woodland Phase in Southeastern Ohio. In *Studies in Ohio Archaeology,* ed. O. Prufer, 1–62. Cleveland: Case Western Reserve Press.

Prufer, O., and D. McKenzie

1966    Peters Cave: Two Woodland Occupations in Ross County, Ohio. *Ohio Journal of Science* 66:233–53.

Prufer, O., S. Pedde, and R. Meindl, eds.

2001    *Archaic Transitions in Ohio and Kentucky Prehistory.* Kent, Ohio: Kent State University Press.

Prufer, O., and O. Shane III

1970    *Blain Village and the Fort Ancient Tradition in Ohio.* Kent, Ohio: Kent State University Press.

Purdue, J.

1986   The Size of White-Tailed Deer (*Ordocoileus virginianus*) during the Archaic Period in Central Illinois. In *Foraging, Collecting, and Harvesting: Archaic Period Subsistence and Settlement in the Eastern Woodlands,* ed. S. Neusius, 5–95. Center for Archaeological Investigations Occasional Papers, no. 6. Carbondale: Southern Illinois University.

Raab, L., R. Cande, and D. Stahle

1979   Debitage Graphs and Archaic Settlement Patterns. *Midcontinental Journal of Archaeology* 4 (2): 167–82.

Railey, J.

1992   Chipped Stone Artifacts. In *Fort Ancient Cultural Dynamics in the Middle Ohio Valley,* ed. A. G. Henderson, 137–169. Monographs in World Archaeology, no. 8. Madison, Wis.: Prehistory Press.

Redman, C.

1978   *The Rise of Civilization.* San Francisco: W. H. Freeman.

Reidhead, V.

1984   A Reconstruction of the Presettlement Vegetation of the Middle Ohio Valley Region. In *Experiments and Observations on Aboriginal Wild Plant Food Utilization in Eastern North America,* ed. P. Munson, 386–426. Prehistoric Research Series, vol. 6, no. 2. Indianapolis: Indiana Historical Society.

Rolingson, M., and M. Rodeffer

1968   The Zilpo Site, 15BH37: Preliminary Excavations in the Cave Run Reservoir, Kentucky: 1968. Report on file, Museum of Anthropology, University of Kentucky.

Romer, A.

1960   *Man and the Vertebrates, Vol. 1.* Harmondsworth: Penguin.

Rypma, R. B.

1961   The Structure and Pattern of the Primary Forests of Athens and Washington Counties, Ohio. Ph.D. diss., Department of Botany, Ohio State University.

Sahlins, M.

1961   The Segmentary Lineage: An Organization of Predatory Expansion. *American Anthropologist* 63:322–43.

1968   *Tribesmen.* Englewood Cliffs, N.J.: Prentice-Hall.

Saxe, A.

1970   Social Dimensions of Mortuary Practices. Ph.D. diss., Department of Anthropology, University of Michigan.

Schumm, S.

1977   *The Fluvial System.* New York: Wiley.

Scott, S.

1991   Problems with the Use of Flake Size in Inferring Stages of Lithic Reduction. *Journal of California and Great Basin Anthropology* 13 (2): 172–79.

Seeman, M.

1979   *The Hopewell Interaction Sphere: The Evidence for Interregional Trade and Structural Complexity.* Prehistory Research Series 5 (2). Indianapolis: Indiana Historical Society.

1986    Adena "Houses" and Their Implications for Early Woodland Settlement Models in the Ohio Valley. In *Early Woodland Archeology,* ed. K. Farnsworth and T. Emerson, 564–80. Kampsville, Ill.: Center for American Archeology Press.

1992a.    Woodland Traditions in the Midcontinent: A Comparison of Three Regional Sequences. *Research in Economic Anthropology Supplement 6,* ed. B. Isaac, 3–46. Greenwich, Conn.: JAI Press.

Seeman, M., ed.

1992b    *Cultural Variability in Context: Woodland Settlements of the Mid-Ohio Valley.* MCJA Special Paper no. 7. Kent, Ohio: Kent State University Press.

Seeman, M., and W. Dancey

2000    The Late Woodland Period in Southern Ohio: Basic Issues and Prospects. In *Late Woodland Societies: Tradition and Transformation across the Midcontinent,* ed. T. Emerson, D. McElrath, and A. Fortier, 583–611. Lincoln: University of Nebraska Press.

Service, E.

1962    *Primitive Social Organization.* New York: Random House.

Shane, L., G. Snyder, and K. Anderson

2001    Holocene Vegetation and Climate Changes in the Ohio Region. In *Archaic Transitions in Ohio and Kentucky Prehistory,* ed. O. Prufer, S. Pedde, and R. Meindl, 11–55. Kent, Ohio: Kent State University Press.

Shane, O., III, and J. Murphy

1967    A Survey of the Hocking Valley, Ohio. In *Studies in Ohio Archaeology,* ed. O. Prufer, 329–56. Cleveland: Case Western Reserve University Press.

Shanks, M., and C. Tilley

1992    *Re-Constructing Archaeology: Theory and Practice.* London: Routledge.

Shott, M., and R. Jefferies

1992    Late Woodland Economy and Settlement in the Mid-Ohio Valley: Recent Results from the Childers/Woods Project. In *Cultural Variability in Context: Woodland Settlements of the Mid-Ohio Valley,* ed. M. Seeman, 52–64. MCJA Special Paper no. 7. Kent, Ohio: Kent University Press.

Shott, M., R. Mandel, G. Oetelaar, N. O'Malley, M. Powell, and D. Wymer

1990    *Childers and Woods: Two Late Woodland Sites in the Upper Ohio Valley, Mason County, West Virginia.* University of Kentucky Program for Cultural Resource Assessment, Report 200.

Shryock, A.

1987    The Wright Mound Reexamined: Generative Structures and the Political Economy of a Simple Chiefdom. *Midcontinental Journal of Archaeology* 12:243–68.

Silverberg, R.

1986    *The Moundbuilders.* Athens: Ohio University Press.

Simon, M.

2000    Regional Variations in Plant Use Strategies in the Midwest during the Late Woodland. In *Late Woodland Societies: Tradition and Transformation across the Midcontinent,* ed. T. E. Emerson, D. L. McElrath, and A. C. Fortier, 37–76. Lincoln: University of Nebraska Press.

Sinopoli, C.

1991    *Approaches to Archaeological Ceramics.* New York: Plenum Press.

Skinner, S., and R. Norris

1981    *Archaeological Assessment of Six Sites in the Central Hocking River Valley for the Proposed Relocation of Route 33 through Athens and Hocking Counties, Ohio (HOC/ATH 33–14.87/16.82/0.00/2.00/3.80).* 2 vols. CRM Report submitted to the Ohio Department of Transportation.

1984    *Archaeological Investigation in the Adena Park Subdivision, Including Excavations of the Connett Mounds 3 and 4, the Wolf Plains National Register District, The Plains, Ohio.* Submitted to the Ohio Historical Preservation Office.

Smith, B.

1992    *Rivers of Change.* Washington, D.C.: Smithsonian Institution Press.

1995    Seed Plant Domestication in Eastern North America. In *Last Hunters, First Farmers,* ed. T. D. Price and A. Gebauer, 193–213. Santa Fe: School of American Research Press.

2001    The Transition to Food Production. In *Archaeology at the Millennium: A Sourcebook,* ed. G. Feinman and T. Price, 199–229. New York: Kluwer Academic.

Sonneville-Bordes, D. de

1960    *La paléolithique supérieur en Perigord.* Bordeaux: Delmas.

Squier, E. G., and E. H. Davis

1848    *Ancient Monuments of the Mississippi Valley. Smithsonian Contribution to Knowledge 1.* Washington, D.C.: Smithsonian Institution.

Stealey, J., III

1993    *The Antebellum Kanawha Salt Business and Western Markets.* Lexington: University Press of Kentucky.

Steward, J.

1938    *Basin-Plateau Aboriginal Sociopolitical Groups.* Bureau of American Ethnology, Smithsonian Institution Bulletin 120, Washington, D.C.

Stothers, D., T. Abel, and A. Schneider

2001    Archaic Perspectives in the Western Lake Erie Basin. In *Archaic Transitions in Ohio and Kentucky Prehistory,* ed. O. Prufer, S. Pedde, and R. Meindl, 233–89. Kent, Ohio: Kent State University Press.

Stout, A., and A. Hurst

1985    X-Ray Diffraction of Early Iron Age Pottery from Western Norway. *Archaeometry* 27:225–30.

Stout, W., and R. Schoenlaub.

1945    *The Occurrence of Flint in Ohio.* Ohio Geological Survey Bulletin 46, Columbus.

Striker, M., K. Gibbs, R. Rahe, and A. Tonetti

2001    *Report of Phase 2 of a Phase 1 Cultural Resources Survey for the Proposed University Estates Planned Unit Development in Athens Township, Athens County, Ohio.* Submitted to University Estates, Athens.

Stuiver, M., P. Reimer, E. Bard, J. W. Beck, G. S. Burr, K. Hughen, B. Kromer, G. McCormac, J. van der Plicht, and M. Spurk

1998    INTCAL98 Radiocarbon Age Calibration, 24,000–0 ca. B.P. *Radiocarbon* 40:1041–83.

Sturgeon, M. T., et al.

    1958    *The Geology and Mineral Resources of Athens County, Ohio.* Ohio Geological Survey Bulletin 46. Columbus.

Styles, B.

    2000    Late Woodland Faunal Exploitation in the Midwestern United States. In *Late Woodland Societies: Tradition and Transformation across the Midcontinent,* ed. T. Emerson, D. McElrath, and A. Fortier, 77–96. Lincoln: University of Nebraska Press.

Sutton, M., and B. Arkush

    1998    *Archaeological Laboratory Methods: An Introduction.* Dubuque: Kendall/Hunt.

Sutton, A., and M. Sutton

    1985    *Eastern Forests.* New York: Knopf.

Talalay, L., D. Keller, and P. Munson

    1984    Hickory Nuts, Walnuts, Butternuts, and Hazelnuts: Observations and Experiments Relevant to their Aboriginal Exploitation in Eastern North America. In *Experiments and Observations on Aboriginal Wild Plant Food Utilization in Eastern North America,* ed. P. Munson. Prehistory Research Series, 6 (2). Indianapolis: Indiana Historical Society.

Taxman, S.

    1994    Nonmetric Trait Variation in the Adena Peoples of the Ohio River Drainage. *Midcontinental Journal of Archaeology* 19:71–98.

Thompson, J. E.

    1954    *The Rise and Fall of Maya Civilization.* Norman: University of Oklahoma Press.

Tixier, J., M. Inizan, and H. Roche

    1980    *Préhistoire de la pierre taillée.* Vol. 1, *Terminologie et technologie.* Valbonne, France: Cedex.

Turnbow, C.

    1988    The Muir Site Ceramics. In *Muir: An Early Fort Ancient Site in the Inner Bluegrass,* ed. C. Turnbow and W. Sharp, 97–177. Archaeological Report No. 165, Program for Cultural Resource Assessment, University of Kentucky.

Turnbow, C., and W. Sharp

    1988a    Site Interpretations. In *Muir: An Early Fort Ancient Site in the Inner Bluegrass,* ed. C. Turnbow and W. Sharp, 265–77. Archaeological Report no. 165, Program for Cultural Resource Assessment, University of Kentucky, Lexington.

Turnbow, C., and W. Sharp, eds.

    1988b    *Muir: An Early Fort Ancient Site in the Inner Bluegrass.* Archaeological Report no. 165, Program for Cultural Resource Assessment, University of Kentucky, Lexington.

U.S. Department of Agriculture. Forest Service

    1974    *Seeds of Woody Plants in the United States.* Agricultural Handbook 450. Washington, D.C.: Government Printing Office.

U.S. Department of Agriculture. Soil Conservation Service

    1960    Soil Survey of Fairfield County, Ohio. U.S. In cooperation with ODNR, Division of Lands and Soil, and the Ohio Agricultural Research and Development Center.

Vickery, K.

1980 Preliminary Definition of Archaic Study Units in Southwestern Ohio. Ms. on file, Ohio Historical Society, Columbus.

1994 Evidence Supporting the Theory of Climatic Change and the Decline of Hopewell. *Wisconsin Archeologist* 75:142–63.

Wagner, G.

1994 Corn in Eastern Woodlands Late Prehistory. In *Corn and Culture in the Prehistoric New World,* ed. S. Johannessen and C. Hastorf, 335–46. Boulder: Westview Press.

Waldron, J., and E. Abrams

1999 Adena Burial Mounds and Inter-Hamlet Visibility: A GIS Approach. *Midcontinental Journal of Archaeology* 24:97–111.

Wallace, A.

1990 *King of the Delawares: Teedyuscung, 1700–1763.* Syracuse: Syracuse University Press.

Wandsnider, L.

1997 The Roasted and the Boiled: Food Composition and Heat Treatment with Special Emphasis on Pit-Hearth Cooking. *Journal of Anthropological Archaeology* 16:1–48.

Watson, P. J.

1986 Archaeological Interpretation, 1985. In *American Archaeology, Past and Future,* ed. D. Meltzer, D. Fowler, and J. Sabloff, 439–57. Washington, D.C.: Smithsonian Institution Press.

Webb, W.

1941 *The Morgan Stone Mound, Site 15, Bath County, Kentucky.* Reports in Anthropology and Archaeology 5 (3), University of Kentucky, Lexington.

Webster, D., and A. Freter

1990 The Demography of Late Classic Copan. In *Precolumbian Population History in the Maya Lowlands,* ed. T. P. Culbert and D. Rice, 37–61. Albuquerque: University of New Mexico Press.

Werner, D.

1990 *Amazon Journey: An Anthropologist's Year among Brazil's Mekranoti Indians.* Englewood Cliffs, N.J.: Prentice-Hall.

Westcott, K., and R. Brandon

2000 *Practical Applications of GIS for Archaeologists: A Predictive Modeling Kit.* Philadelphia: Taylor and Francis.

Wheat, J. B.

1972 *The Olsen-Chubbuck Site: A Paleo-Indian Bison Kill.* Society for American Archaeology Memoir no. 26. Washington, D.C.

White, R.

1991 *The Middle Ground: Indians, Empires, and Republics in the Great Lakes Region, 1650–1815.* New York: Cambridge University Press.

Willey, G., and J. Sabloff

1980 *A History of American Archaeology.* San Francisco: Freeman.

Winters, H.

1969 *The Riverton Culture.* Illinois State Museum, Reports of Investigations 13, Springfield.

Wolfe, E. W., J. L. Forsyth, and G. D. Dove

1962      *Geology of Fairfield County.* Division of Geological Survey, Ohio Department of Natural Resources, Bulletin 60, Columbus.

Wymer, D.

1984      *The Archaeobotanical Assemblage from the Connett Mounds #3 and #4, the Wolf Plains Project, Athens County, Ohio.* Report submitted to the Ohio Historical Society, Department of Contract Archaeology.

1989      The Paleoethnobotanical Record of the Niebert Site. In *Phase III Excavations at the Niebert Site (46MS103) in the Gallipolis Locks and Dam Replacement Project, Mason County, West Virginia,* ed. R. Berle Clay and C. M. Niquette, 130–58. Cultural Resource Analysts, Inc., Contract Publication Series 89–06, Lexington.

1990      The Paleoethnobotanical Record of the Boudinot Site (33AT521), Athens County, Ohio. In possession of the author.

1992      Trends and Disparities: The Woodland Paleoethnobotanical Record of the Mid-Ohio Valley. In *Cultural Variability in Context: Woodland Settlements of the Mid-Ohio Valley,* ed. M. Seeman, 65–76. MCJA Special Paper no. 7. Kent, Ohio: Kent State University Press.

1994      The Social Context of Early Maize in the Mid-Ohio Valley. In *Corn and Culture in the Prehistoric New World,* ed. S. Johannessen and C. Hastorf, 411–26. Boulder: Westview Press.

1996      The Ohio Hopewell Econiche: Human-Land Interaction in the Core Area. In *A View from the Core: A Synthesis of Ohio Hopewell Archaeology,* ed. P. Pacheco, 36–53. Columbus: Ohio Archaeological Council.

1997      Paleoethnobotany in the Licking River Valley, Ohio. In *Ohio Hopewell Community Organization,* ed. W. Dancey, 153–71. Kent, Ohio: Kent State University.

Wymer, D., and E. Abrams, forthcoming

     Early Woodland Plant Use and Gardening: Evidence from an Adena Hamlet in Southeastern Ohio. *Midcontinental Journal of Archaeology.*

Yerkes, R.

1994      A Consideration of the Function of Ohio Hopewell Bladelets. *Lithic Technology* 19:109–27.

2002      Hopewell Tribes: A Study of Middle Woodland Social Organization in the Ohio Valley. In *The Archaeology of Tribal Societies,* ed. W. Parkinson, 227–45. International Monographs in Prehistory, Archaeological Series 15, Ann Arbor.

n.d.      Ideology and Social Organization in Ohio Hopewell Societies. In *A Deep-Time Perspective: Studies in Symbols, Meaning, and the Archaeological Record,* ed. J. Richards and M. Fowler. Tuscaloosa: University of Alabama Press.

Yerkes, R., ed.

1988      *Interpretations of Culture Change in the Eastern Woodlands during the Late Woodland Period.* Occasional Papers in Anthropology, no. 3, Ohio State University, Columbus.

# INDEX

Page numbers in *italics* refer to figures, tables, and maps.

Armitage Mound, 188; burial pattern from, 113; excavated by OU field school, 6; radiocarbon dates from, 110–11; subfloor in, 107
arrowwood, 17
art, 82
artifact analysis: from Bremen site, 47–56; from Walker site, 62–64
artifact counts: at Allen site, *128*
artifact density: at Allen site, 129, 137–38; at Bremen site, 42–44; at Walker site, 65
artifacts: at burial sites, 113; localized, 136; lost, 3–4; wooden, 12. *See also under individual sites and types*
ash: at Allen site, *141;* during Late Archaic, 23
ash pits, 119
ash (tree): at Allen site, 154, *155,* 157, *158,* 159. *See also under specific types*
Athens, Ohio: average rainfall, 19–20; average temperature, 19; botanical research in, 16; earthworks in, 3; killing frosts in, 22
Athens County, Ohio, 164; forest composition surveys from, 159; mounds in, 93; rockshelters in, 138; Walker site, 59–66
atomic mass spectroscopy dating, 9
Atwater, Caleb, 99
axes, 96

Bailey Run, 143
Bakers Creek projectile points: at Allen site, 148
Baldwin Run, *169*
Baldwin site, 4, *5*
bands: contrasted with tribes, 175–77
bark, 112; radiocarbon dating of, 110–11
bark blankets, 112, 113
base camps. *See* residential base camps
basswood, 17
beans, 1
bear, black, *18;* remains, 112
bear claws, 111
beaver, 15, *18*
bedstraw seeds, 156
beech, *14,* 17; at Allen site, 154, *155,* 159; during Late Archaic, 23; pollen profile for, 23, *24*
beech-maple forest: near Bremen site, 40
beech–sugar maple mesic association, 17
Beta Analytic, Inc., 47, 129
bidirectional cores, 50
biface blanks, 52; at Bremen site, 53, 54, *55*
biface finishing flakes: from Allen site, 145, *146*
biface margin removal flakes, 50–51
biface preforms, 52; at Allen site, 143, 144; at Bremen site, 53, 54
biface reduction, 144. *See also* early biface reduction; late biface reduction
biface thinning flakes, 50–52; from Allen site, 145, *146*
biface tools: from Allen site, 143–48; from Swinehart Village site, *118;* from Walker site, 63

Big Walnut Creek, 117
Binford, L., 64, 180
bipolar core, *55*
bird bone, 75
bison: cooking methods for, 76–77; hunting, 68
bitternut hickory, 16–17
black bear, *18;* remains, 112
black cherry, 17; at Allen site, 157, *158,* 160
black gum, 17
black huckleberry, 17
black oak, 17
black walnut, 17, *18, 19,* 95; at Allen site, 155–56, *156,* 160; at Bremen site, 56
blades/bladelets, 50; from Allen site, 146, 147, 148; biface, 54; dating of, 189; from Swinehart Village site, 116–17, *118;* from Walker site, 63
Blain Village site: houses at, 137
Bloomburg University: archaeological lab, 152–53
blue beech, 17
blueberry, 18
bobcat, 18
Bob Evans Mound: radiocarbon dating of, 93
Boetticher, A. W., 16
bone, 72; at Allen site, 150; calcined, 75; at County Home site, 72, *73,* 75, 86
Boserup, E., 170, 171
botanicals: at Boudinot 4 site, 95–96; at County Home site, 72, *73,* 75. *See also* floral resources *and under individual species*
Boudinot 4 site, *5,* 6, 188; chronology of, 83–84; cooking units in, 76; as demographic model, 84–85; excavation map for, *86;* excavation of, 85, 90; map of OAI designations, *91;* during Middle Woodland, 83–97 passim; mounds near, *69;* radiocarbon dating at, 83–84, *84;* residential settlement patterns at, 90–93; salt licks near, 16, 92; seasonal habitation at, 94
Boudinot Mound, 92–93, *93*
Boudinot 2 site, *91*
boundaries. *See* site boundaries
BoxCar® software, 121
boxelder, 16
Bremen site, *5,* 39–58; artifact analysis from, 47–56; artifact distribution, *45;* artifact density, 42–44; base camps at, 40–42; botanical remains from, 56; chert outcrops near, *41;* excavation of, 42–44, *43;* features, 44–47, *45;* formed artifacts from, *55;* lithic analysis from, 48–56; pottery analysis from, 47–48; radiocarbon dates from, 47, *47–56,* 57; reconstruction of function, 56–57; relative reduction stages at, *51;* shovel tests at, *43;* technological analysis from, 50–52; thermally altered rock from, *56;* tool diversity analysis for, 52–56; trenches, *43*
brine, 16
Bruce Chapman Mound, *5*

Connett Mound 3: eagle beak from, 112; skeletons from, 109
Connett Mound 4, 107
Continental Construction site, 48
contingency, 81
contour data, 123
cooking features: at Allen site, *133*, 142, 149, 152; at Boudinot 4 site, 85; at County Home site, *71, 72–79, 79, 86, 90*
cooking units. *See* cooking features
Coon Mound, 99, 188; excavation of, 4, 6; labor expenditure for, 110; skeleton at, 109
copper: artifacts, 111; at The Plains, *107*
cordmarking: at Allen site, 138–40, *139*
cores: from Allen site, 144, *146*; from Bremen site, 50, *55*; from Walker site, *63*
corn. *See* maize
Cottingham 1 site, 102
cottonwood, *14*, 16; at Allen site, 159
County Home site, *5, 69*; aggregation and feasting at, 67–81; architectural clusters at, 88–90, *89*; artifact inventory from, *73*; chenopodium from, 96; chert debitage from, *72*; chipped-stone inventory from, *74*; chronology of, 83–84; cooking features at, *71, 72–76, 78–79, 79*; domestic architecture at, 87–90; excavation by OU field school, 6, 68–81; excavation methods, 70–71, 86; feature chronology, 78; feature dimensions, *76*; features mapped, *87*; features profile, *73*; features volumes, *76*; during Late Archaic, 67–81; during Middle Woodland, 82–97 passim; population density at, 84–90; postmolds at, 87–88, *88*; radiocarbon dating from, *79*, 83–84, *84*, 189; reconstruction of food prep, 76–78; recurring floodplain occupation, 179; residential settlement at, 91; salt licks near, 16
Courtney Circle, 109–10; labor expenditure for, 110
Creasman, S., 94
cremation: at The Plains, 112–13
CRM. *See* cultural resource management
Cross Creek drainage (Pennsylvania), 29
cross-dating, 8–9; defined, 111; at The Plains, *107*; of projectile points, at Walker site, 64
cultigens, 124
cultural resource management (CRM), 6, 7, 194
Cumberland Plateau, 42
curvilinear house form, 137

Daines Mound, 5
Daines Mound II: radiocarbon dating of, 93; subfloor 107
Daines Mound III: subfloor, 107
Dalton cluster projectile points: from Allen site, *149*
Dancey, William, 119
dating. *See* accelerator mass spectroscopy dating; atomic mass spectroscopy dating; cross-dating; radiocarbon dating; relative dating

Davis, E. H.: *Ancient Monuments of the Mississippi Valley* (with Squier), 3, 99
debitage: at Allen site, 143–47, *146*; at Bremen site, 49–50, 53; at County Home site, 72, *74*; at Peters Cave site, 138; at The Plains, 102
debt relations: community aggregation and, 80
decoupling: of tribal traits, 176
deer, white-tailed, *18*, 75; at Allen site, 150; preparation of meat, 77–78, 80–81; and salt licks, 92
defense: community aggregation for, 120–21, 123–24
Delaware tribe, 2
density, index of, 153, *154*
De Regnaucourt, T., 49
Diamond site, *5*
differential surplus accumulation, 193
ditch features: at Swinehart Village site, 117
DNA analysis, 97
dogwood, 17, *18*
domestic architecture: at County Home site, 87–90
domestication of plant species, 82, 95–96
domestilocalities: defined, 183
Dorr Mound 1 and 2, 102
drainage basins. *See* watersheds *and under specific river names*
Drennan, R., 184
drill fragments: from Allen site, 143, *147*, 148; from Walker site, *63*
drum, 18
ducks, 18
Duncan Falls site, 94
dwarf sumac, 17

EAC. *See* Eastern Agricultural Complex
eagle: remains found at mounds, 112
Early Archaic period, *9*; Swinehart Village site, 116; Walker site, 64
early biface reduction, 50–51, *51*; at Bremen site, 53
early biface thinning flakes, 50–51
Early Paleoindian period, *9*
Early Woodland period, *9*, 82–97 passim; burial mounds, 68; cooking methods for meat, 76–78; and emergence of horticulture, 24; floral decline during, 24; and GIS analysis, 25–38 passim; marital patterns for, 97; population growth during, 177; Schultz site, 77; settlement patterns from, *181*; settlement studies on, 5; site clustering during, *35*; site distribution in, *31*; Walker site, 64
earthworks: circular, 1, 98, 99, 109–10; defined by Squier and Davis, 3; at The Plains, 98–114 passim, *100, 103, 107*; Rock Mill, 3, 186. *See also* mounds
Eastern Agricultural Complex (EAC), *14*, 17, 95, 182, 183; and introduction of maize, 151, 190
ecological anthropology, 12, 164, 194
ecological variability: mesoterm, 20–22
economic stress: as factor in culture change, 184
elk, *18*

elm, *14,* 17; at Allen site, 157, *158,* 159; during Late Archaic, 23. *See also under individual names*
el Niño effect, 121
environmental determinism, 194
Environmental Systems Research Institute (ESRI), 27
environmental variability, 12–24
erect knotweed, 17, *18,* 95
ericaceous taxa, 18
ESRI. *See* Environmental Systems Research Institute
ethnographic definition, 175
ethnohistoric record, 12
Ety site, *116,* 117
excarnation, 112
excavation units: at Walker site, *60*
expanding scales of inclusiveness: as core tribal element, 175
extraction camps, 40; satellite, 180, 183

Factory Creek, *169*
Fairfield County, Ohio, 115, 164; Bremen site in, 39–58; present-day growing season, 121, *122*
farming, 40
faunal assemblages, 121
faunal resources, 18–19
FCR. *See* fire-cracked rock
feasting, 68–70; competitive, 80; defining, 176; in Late Archaic, 67–81, 113; and seasonal aggregation, 180, 182; sociopolitical context of, 80; and tribal evolutionary process, 81
features. *See under specific types*
Federal Creek, 15, 194
Feinman, G., 176
Feurt pottery, 130, 139, 140; incised, 139
field school. *See* Ohio University field school
fine triangular projectile points: at Allen site, 148–49, *149. See also* triangular projectile points
fire-cracked rock (FCR), 72; at Allen site, 131, *141,* 149; at Bremen site, 54, 56; at County Home site, 72, *73,* 75, 76, 77, 86; at The Plains, 105, 106, 107–8; at Walker site, 63–64
firewood collection: at Allen site, 159–60
fish, *18;* bone, 75; salt curing of, 92
fissioning. *See* community fissioning
flake blanks, 50, 51, 52
flake cores, 52; at Allen site, 146, *146*
flakes: from Allen site, 143, 144; from Bremen site, *49,* 49–54; from County Home site, *74, 83, 85;* from The Plains, 107. *See also under individual types*
flake spalls, 50, 51
flint, 16; at Allen site, *141;* flake sizes, from Bremen site, *49;* microtools, at Bremen site, 41; as tempering material, 138. *See also* chert; Vanport chert
flint knapping: at Bremen site, 49, 50–52, 53
Flint Ridge/Vanport chert. *See* Vanport chert
flooding, 20

floodplain zones, 13, 164–65, *168;* botanical food resources of, 181; of Boudinot 4 site, 90; Fort Ancient communities in, *173;* habitation sites in, 57, 79, 91, 94; importance in Late Archaic, 179; lacustrine, 116; narrowness of, 185–86; as percent of Hocking Valley, 92; permanent settlement in, 19; preference for, 182; residential base camps in, 82; settlement patterns in, 170–73, 180; soils, 170; vegetation, *14,* 16–17; Walker site near, 59
floral resources, 16–18, 19; at Bremen site, 39; pollen profiles for, 22–24
flotation processing of paleoethnobotanical samples, 151–58, *154*
food extraction site: Walker site as, 65
food preparation: at County Home site, 70, 76–78; at Walker site, 65
food resources, *18;* and Late Archaic settlements, 91; in riverine zone, 37; seasonal variability of, 67–68
foraging societies. *See* hunting and gathering cultures
Fort Ancient culture, 5, 6, 174; dependence on maize agriculture, 161; distribution of communities, *173;* Feurt sherd, 130; fine triangular projectile points from, 149; Griffin's ceramic typology of, 4; house size, 137; named by Griffin, 150; village composition of, 136
Four Mile Creek, *169*
Fourth Street site, 102
foxglove, 17, 19
Fried, Morton, 8
frogs, 18
frost, 20; killing, *22;* plant cover and, 121; variability of, 22
functional reconstruction. *See* reconstructions
funerary rites: as collective act, 113; at The Plains, 106, 107, 108–9, 111–14

Gabriel site, *5,* 102, 126; maize from, 160
gardening, 1, 18, 40; accidental, 183; development of, 82; rate of acceptance of, 193–94; in sedentary communities, 95–96, 98, 184
geese, 18
genealogy, shared, 113
genetic research, 195
Geographical Information System (GIS), 25–38, 165; analysis of Athens County mounds, 93; for future research, 195
Geoprocessing wizard in ArcMap, 28
Georgiady, J., 49
geospatial data, 27
GIS. *See* Geographical Information System
goosefoot, 42
gorgets, 105, 117, *118*
Goslin, Robert, 119, 124
Graham Village site, *5,* 126; excavation of, 4, *5;* localized artifacts at, 136; maize from, 160; population estimate for, 136; sherds at, 138, 139

granitic cobbles: at County Home site, 72

grass, 17, 24, 72

Grayson site: pit features, 41, 42

Great Kanawha salt lick, 16

Great Miami River, 173

greenbrier, 17

Greenman, Emerson: and Adena culture, 4, 99; and skeletons, 109

Green River Valley (Kentucky), 29, 80

Griffin, J., 150; potsherds described by, 4, 139

grinding stones: at County Home site, 72

grit-tempered pottery: at Bremen site, 46, 48

groundhog, 19

groundstone artifacts: from County Home site, 72, 73; from The Plains, 105, 107; from Walker site, 62–63, 65

gum, black, 17

habitation: sedentism and, 94

habitation sites, 168; Allen site as, 126–50 passim; Bremen as short-term, 56–58; County Home site as, 78–81, 86; localized artifacts indicative of, 136; Walker as short-term, 64–66

Hamilton incurvate points, 130, 139

Hamilton triangular projectile points, 148

Hamlin Garden site, 102

Harris Matrix analysis: at The Plains, 105, 108

Hartman campsite, 102

Hartman Mound, 100

Hayden, B., 70, 175, 178

hazelnuts, 95

hearth firing: at Allen site, 141

hearths, 41; at Allen site, 132; at County Home site, 86

heating rock elements: at County Home site, 72, 76

Hegmon, M., 194

hematite celt fragments: from Walker site, 63, 64

Henderson, A. G., 135, 137, 148

herbs, 24

hickory, 14, 17, 18, 19, 79; at Allen site, 154, 155, 157, 158, 160; nut charcoal, 56, 75; pollen profile for, 23, 23, 23–24. See also under individual types

hickory nuts, 79, 95

hickory nutshell: from Allen site, 155–56, 156

hierarchical cluster analysis, 133

Hildreth, S. P., 3, 109; map of The Plains, 99, 100

hills. See uplands

Historic period, 9

HOBO® Temp data loggers: data from Swinehart Village site, 121, 122

Hocking County, 164

Hocking Hills, 186

Hocking River, 169; confluence with Sunday Creek, 68, 79; drainage, 115, 116, 118; physiographic zone of, 15; watershed, 26–28, 27

Hocking River Valley, 2; environmental variability of, 12–24; geological background of, 13–16; GIS analy-

sis of settlement trends in, 25–38; history of archaeological research in, 3; topography, 164–65; upper, 115–25

Hocking Valley. See Hocking River Valley

hoe, chert, 139, 148

Holocene, 40

homesteads, 174–95 passim; defined, 90–91; related to mounds, 92–93, 111; and social organization, 96; territorial, 190

Hope site: residential settlement at, 91

Hopewell Interaction Sphere, 84, 111, 188

Hopewell sites, 94, 187, 188

hop hornbeam, 17

horizontal linkages: and local communities, 184

horticulture, 8; as defining element, 176, 183; emergence of, 24, 38, 79; house form and, 137; in sedentary communities, 95–96

household: clusters, 119; in segmentary system, 7

houses: rectilinear vs. curvilinear forms, 137

HRAF, 119

huckleberry, black, 17

Hudnell, David L., 126, 130

Hudnell sherd, 139, 140

Human Relations Area Files (HRAF), 119

Humpf, Dorothy, 109

Hunters Run, 169, 172

hunting, communal, 80–81

hunting and gathering cultures, 1, 25, 40; and ceramic manufacture, 176, 193; evolution to sedentism, 193; in Late Archaic period, 78; residential camps for, 56–58; transition to horticulture, 38; Walker site and, 64–66

Hyde Fork, 169

hydrology, dendritic, 13

identity, shared, 113, 183

IDRISI software, 88, 89

igneous rock: at Bremen site, 54; at Walker site, 62

Illinoian glacier, 13, 164

Illinoian terrace of The Plains, 15, 99

inclusiveness, expanding scales of, 175

Indian Creek, 124

initial reduction, 50, 51; at Allen site, 145–46, 146; at Bremen site, 53

innovation: paleontological view of, 193

INTCAL 98, 9

interdependence among communities, 177

interior flakes, 50

interment, 111–12

Jackson County, Ohio, 48

Jacksonville quadrangle, 61

Jack's Reef cluster projectile points, 130; from Allen site, 139, 149

Janus flakes: at Allen site, 146

John Baker Foundation, 83, 129

maple: at Allen site, 157, *158*, 159. *See also under individual types*

Maple Creek phase, 40–42

Margaret Creek, 165, *169*, 172; Allen site near, 126, 159, 171; beech–sugar maple flat near, 17; clay from, 140; site density shift in, 33

Margaret Creek watershed: lacustrine deposits in, 164

marital patterns: for Early Woodland, 97

markers. *See* territorial markers

marriage: to expand kinship, 81; limitation of partners, 120, 124

marsh elder, 17, *18*

Maslowski, R., 15, 20, 22

Matanzas projectile points: from Allen site, *139*, 144, *149*

mate seeking during communal gatherings, 80, 81

maygrass, 17, *18*, 42, 95

McCune site, *5*, 126, 139; Feurt sherds from, 139; maize from, 160

McKenzie, D., 138

McWhinney heavy-stemmed projectile points: from Allen site, *149*

meat: bison, 76–77; deer, 77–78, 80–81; preparation for cooking, 76–78; salt-curing of, 92

Meigs County, Ohio, 48, 164

Meindl, R., 29

Mensforth, R., 29, 80

Merom cluster projectile points, 41, 48; from Allen site, 144, *149*

Merom expanding-stem projectile points: at Bremen site, 41

mesic species, 16

Mesolithic period, 180

mesoterm ecological variability, 20–22

Mexico: Tehuacan Valley of, 68, 70

mica, 111

micaceous sandstone: at County Home site, 72

Michaels 1 site, 102

microbands, 70; and communal hunting, 80–81

microdebitage: at Allen site, *146*

middens: at Allen site, *142;* at Bremen site, 44; at County Home site, 86

Middle Archaic period, *9*, 40; ceramics in, 37; and GIS analysis, 25–38 passim; site clustering, *34;* site distribution, *30*

Middle Woodland/Late Adena period: Walker site, 64

Middle Woodland period, 6, *9*, 82–97 passim; artifacts from, 110–11; and GIS analysis, 25–38 passim; and peer polity model, 113–14; projectile points from, 78; site clustering, *35;* site distribution, *31;* Swinehart Village site, 116–17

Midwest projectile point typology: used at Walker site, 63

migratory fowl, 18

Millfield flats, 17

Mills, William: and Adena concept, 185; *Archaeological Atlas of Ohio*, 4

mixed oak association, 17

mockernut hickory, 17

Monday Creek, *169*, 172

moraine, *168*, 171; soils, 171, 172

Moran, Ralph, 104

mortuary sites, *168;* at The Plains, 102

mound 33AT441, 102, 104–9, *105*, *106;* Harris Matrix analysis of, 105, *108*, 108–9. *See also* Plains, The

moundbuilders: early notions of, 3

mound construction, 82; cessation of, 189; development of, 79, 184; earliest, 184; labor expenditures for, 92, 109

mounds, 1; in Athens County, 93; at Boudinot sites, 92–93, *93;* conical, 99; early study of, 3–4; Hartman, 100; at The Plains, 3–4, 68, *69*, 104–9, *107*, 186, 188; and quest for artifacts, 3–4; related to homesteads, 92–93; as religious features, 93; skeletons from, 109; subfloors in, 106–7

Muir site, 150; houses at, 137; population estimate for, 136; sherds from, 138

multicomponent sites: distribution of, *167;* landform criteria, *168;* settlement patterns at, 169–73; site types, *168*

multidirectional cores, 50; at Bremen site, *55*

Murphy, James: *An Archaeological History of the Hocking Valley*, *5*, 6; on circular earthworks at The Plains, 109–10; on dated mounds, 93; on flint at Bremen site, 53; on maize, 190; on tempering at Carpenter Shelter, 138

Murphy site, 188; sherds from, 138

Muskingum River, 116; drainage, 115, *116*

Muskingum River Valley, 92, 185

muskrat, 15

mussel, *18*

Nass, J., 173

National Elevation Datasets (NED), 27

Native Americans: funeral rites of, 111–14; future research and, 195; spirituality, 112

Natufian society, 177, 180

NED. *See* National Elevation Datasets

Niebert site (West Virginia), 161

nomadic populations, 25

nonmound sites: at The Plains, 102

nucleated sites: characteristics of, 120

nut charcoal: at Bremen site, 44, 46, 47, 56, 57; at County Home site, 75; hickory, 56, 75

nutmeat: at Allen site, *154*, 157

nuts: effects of inaccessibility, 181–82, 183. *See also under individual types*

nutshell, burned: at Allen site, *154*, 156, 157; at Bremen site, 39; at County Home site, 75

nutting stone: at Bremen site, 56

OAI. *See* Ohio Archaeological Inventory

oak, *14*, 17; at Allen site, 154–55, *155*, 160; pollen profile for, *23*, 23–24. *See also under individual types*

oak-hickory forest: Allen site in, 159; in terrace zones, 17; Walker site in, 61

oak-maple forest: near Bremen site, 40

obsidian, 111; at County Home site, 84, *85*

Ohio Archaeological Inventory (OAI), 83, 90, 102; coding, 29; database, 37; forms, 27, 28, 90, 166; records for The Plains, 102, 104, 109

Ohio Department of Natural Resources, 27

Ohio Historic Preservation Office, 27, 165

Ohio River, 13, 173; physiographic zone of, 15

Ohio State University: Center for Mapping at, 123

Ohio University: Cartographic Center, 27; John Baker Foundation, 83, 129

Ohio University field school, 6–7; excavation of Allen site, 126–50; excavation of Boudinot 4 site, 90; excavation of County Home site, 68–81; excavation of Walker site, 59–66; remapping of Courtney Circle, 109

Ohio Valley, 29; tribes in, 2

Ohio Valley Archaeological Consultants, 39

Ohio Woodland Project, 4

Olsen-Chubbuck site (Colorado), 68

opossum, 19

optical petrography, 140

O'Steen, L., 42

otter, 15, 18

Ozker, D., 77

paleoclimatic reconstructions, 22–24

paleoethnobotanical materials, 121; from Allen site, 151–62 passim

Paleoindian/Early Archaic period: points from, 130–31

Parke silt loam, 40

Parks site, *5*, 136

pawpaw, 17

Peabody Museum of Harvard University, 99, 104

peer polity model, 113–14

Pennsylvania, 29

perch, 18

percussion thinning, 53

periodization of Hocking Valley processual history, 178–94

Period of Agricultural Tribal Communities, 190–94

Period of Horticultural Tribal Communities, 182–86

Period of Intensive Hunting and Gathering, 178–80

Period of Protohorticultural Communities, 180–82

Period of Regional Tribal Fragmentation, 189

Period of Regional Tribal Integration, 186–89

Peters, William, 4, 99

Peters Cave: cordmarked pottery in, 138

Philo II site, 137, 150

physiographic zones, 13–15, *14*

pignut hickory, 17

pine, 96

pin oak, 17

pit features: at Allen site, 129, 131, *132*, 152; at Bremen site, 39, 48, 56; at County Home site, *71*, 76–78, 86; at Graham site, 136; at Grayson site, 41, 42; at Walker site, absence of, 65

pits: ash, 119; communal roasting, 71; storage, 94; trash-filled, 41

Pitts, E., 140

Plains, The, 13, 15, *100*, 164, 189; Andrews's map of, 99, *100*; Armitage Mound in, 6; beech forests at, 17; as ceremonial center, 186–87, 188; circular earthworks in, 98–114 passim; construction of earthworks, 104–10; Courtney Circle at, 109–10; cross-dating at, *107*; described, 99–104; earthworks at, 3, *100*, *103*; funerary rites at, 111–14; Harris Matrix of 33AT441, 105, *108*; Hildreth's map of, 99, *100*; mounds at, 3–4, 68, *69*, 104–9, 186, 188; periodic aggregation at, *187*; and political complexity, 177; radiocarbon dating at, 102, 106, 109, 189; radiometric dating at, *107*; reexcavations at, 102; sacred circles at, 68; site density shift in, 33; as spiritual center, 112; as vacant ceremonial center, 102, 104

Plains Indians: cooking methods of, 76–77

plant domestication, 82, 95–96, 183

Pleasant Run, *169*, 172

Pleistocene epoch, 13, 164

plowed midden, 44. *See also* middens

plow zone: at Allen site, 131, 134, 142; at County Home site, 86

plow-zone subsoil interface: at Bremen site, 44, 46

point pattern analysis, 88

political units, 113–14, 177

Pollack, D., 134–35, 137, 148

pollen cores, 40

pollen profiles, 13, 22–24; from Late Archaic, *23*, 36–37, 79–80, 180

population density: at Allen site, 134–36; at County Home site, 84–90; in Late Archaic, 67, 84; at Swinehart Village site, 119–20

population growth: agricultures and, 177

population pressure: as factor in culture change, 184

postholes: at Allen site, 131, *132*, *133*, 134, *135*, 152; at Boudinot 4 site, 85, 94; at Swinehart Village site, 124

postmolds: at Bremen site, 48; at County Home site, 87–88, *88*; at The Plains, 106; at Walker site, absence of, 65

post oak, 18

postprocessualism, 178

posts: encircling, 117; as indicative of housing, 85, 87–88

potsherds. *See* pottery sherds

pottery, 16, 98; at Allen site, 131, 137–42, *141*; at Bremen site, 39, 46–48, 56, 57; for expanding use of nuts and seeds, 82, 182 pottery-firing areas: at Allen site, *141*, 141–42, *142*

pottery sherds: from Allen site, 130, 137–42; body, 137; from Bremen site, 47–48; cordmarked, 78, 138–40, *139*, 140; from County Home site, 78; described by Griffin, 4; fragments, 137–38; plain, *139*; at The Plains, 102; rim, 137–38; seriated, 4. *See also under specific names*

precipitation. *See* rainfall

pressure flake reduction, 50, *51*, 52

pressure-thinning flakes, 53

primary decortication flakes, 50

processual history of Hocking Valley, 81, 178–94

productivity: community aggregation for, 120–23

Professional Archaeological Services Team, 48

projectile points: at Allen site, 130–31, *139*, 143–49, *147*, *149*; at Bremen site, 41, 42, 46, 53–54, *55*; at County Home site, *74*; at The Plains, 102; at Scioto Trails site, 124; at Swinehart Village site, 117, *118*; at Walker site, 59, 62–64, *63*

Protohistoric period, *9*

Prufer, O., 6, 138, 140; settlement model of, 104

punctuated equilibria, 177, 193

Purdue, J., 77

quartzite cobbles: at County Home site, 72

Query Builder: in ArcMap, 28

rabbit, 75

raccoon, *18*

Raccoon Run, *169*

radiocarbon dating, 9, *10*, *11*; at Allen site, 129, 130, *130*, 151–52, 156, 157–58, *158*, 189; at Boudinot 4 site, 83–84, *84*; at Bremen site, 39, *47*, 47–56; at Chesser Cave, 140; at County Home site, *79*, 83–84, *84*, 189; and future research, 195; at The Plains, 102, 106, *107*, 109, 110–11, 189; of ridgetop mounds, 93

ragweed, 42

rainfall: average in Athens, 19–20; distribution, 20; in Late Archaic, 23, 36–37, 80, 180; spring trends in, *21*; variations in, 20–22; during Xerothermic interval, 23–24

Rais rockshelter, 48

raspberry seeds: from Allen site, 156, 160

raster GIS, 26, 37

reconstructions, 105, *108*, 108–9; at Allen site, 137; at Bremen site, 56–57; at County Home site, 76–78; and future research, 194; at Walker site, 64–65

rectilinear house form, 134, 137, 141

redbud, 17

red maple, 17

red oak: at Allen site, *155*, 157, *158*

reduction processes: described, 50–52

regional political units. *See* political units

regions, site distribution by, *31*

relative dating, 9; seriation, 8; stratigraphy, 8, 108

religious architecture: at The Plains, 98–114 passim

religious features: ridgetop mounds as, 93, 98–99

religious practices of Native Americans, 111–14

remnant detachment scars, 51; at Bremen site, 53

reptiles, 18

residential base camps, *168*; at Bremen site, 40–42, 56–57; at County Home site, 79, 82, 91; at Walker site, 64–65

residential core: at Allen site, 136, *142*

residential settlement patterns. *See* settlement patterns

retouched tools. *See* tools

ridges, 13; at Boudinot 4 site, 90; as setting of Bremen site, 39–40

ridgetop zones, 13, *168*; mounds, 35, 82, 92, 98, 111, 184, 185; settlement trends in, 171; vegetation in, *14*, 17–18; Walker site, 59, 61

ritual burning, 107; FCR and, 107–8; at The Plains, 112–13

ritualism and shared ceremonial behaviors, 185

riverine zones: fauna in, 18; food resources in, 37

roasting features. *See* cooking features

roasting pits, 71, 76

Robbins projectile points, 189; from Walker site, *63*, 64

Rock Mill earthworks, 3, 186

Rockmill site, *116*

Rock Riffle Run Mound, *5;* radiocarbon dating of, 93; subfloor in, 107

rockshelters, 35, 42, 190, 192; at Boudinot 4 site, 90; and future research, 194; sherds from, 138

Rodeffer, M., 42

Rolingson, M., 42

Romer's Rule, 193

Route 33 archaeological survey, 171

Rush Creek, 39, *169;* valley, 40

Rypma, R. B., 16; on upper-floodplain microenvironment, 17

sacred circles, 68. *See also* circles

Saginaw Valley, 77

Sahlins, Marshall, 175; on definition of tribe, 7–8, 175

Salinas community, 16

Salt Creek, 16; Walker site near, 61

salt licks, 16, 61, 79; in Sunday Creek, 92

sandstone: at Allen site, 141; at Bremen site, 54, *55;* at County Home site, 72; at Walker site, 62

sassafras, 17

satellite extraction sites, 180, 183

Saxe, A., 92

scarlet oak, 18

Schneider, A., 80

Schoenlaub, R., 49

Schultz site: cooking methods at, 77

Scioto River, 116, 173; drainage, 115, *116;* floodplain, 48; physiographic zone of, 15

Scioto River Valley, 23, 24, 114, 185, 189; Peters Cave, 138

Scioto Saline salt lick, 16

Scioto Trails site, 124

Taber Well site, *5;* excavation by OU field school, 6
taluses, 13
Taxman, S., 97
Teays River, 164; clay from, 140
Tehuacan Valley, Mexico: aggregations documented in, 68, 70
temperature: in Late Archaic, 23; spring trends in, *21;* during Xerothermic interval, 23–24
tempering materials, 138
Terminal Archaic: Cogswell phase in, 42
terrace domestication, 92
terrace zones, 13, 15, 164–65, *168;* Boudinot 4 site, 90; fauna in, 18–19; Fort Ancient communities in, *173;* habitation sites in, 57, 78, 79, 91, 94; importance in Late Archaic, 179; narrowness of, 185–86; as percent of Hocking Valley, 92; permanent settlement in, 19, 124; preference for, 120–24, 182; residential base camps in, 82; settlement patterns in, 170–73, 180; vegetation in, *14,* 17
territorial homesteads, 190
territoriality, 183, 184, 195; mounds and, 93, 184–85
thermally altered rock, *56*
33AT467/468 site, *5*
tick trefoil, 95–96
tools: at Allen site, 143–49, *146, 147;* at Bremen site, 39, 50–56, 57; chert, 41; finished, 52, 53; manufacturing processes, 50–52; at Walker site, 62–64
topography: for GIS database, 27; of Hocking River Valley, 164–65
trade: during communal gatherings, 80, 81; multiregional, 82
transitional zone. *See* upper-floodplain zone
trees: mast, 79; by physiographic zone, *19. See also under individual species*
trenching, 3–4; at The Plains, 99, 102, 104–5, *105, 106*
trends, settlement, 25–38
triangular projectile points: from Allen site, 144, 148, *149*
tribal community. *See* tribes
tribal societies, 7–8, 174–95; conservatism of, 192–93; decoupling of traits, 176; identity, 183, 186
tribes: contrasted with bands, 175–77; defined, 7–8; and development of horticulture, 79; and development of mound construction, 79; and evolutionary process, 81, 187; formation of, 2–3, 192; in Ohio Valley, 2; and organization flexibility, 192; redefined, 175–78
Trimble side-notched projectile points: at Bremen site, 41; at County Home site, 78
tulip tree, 17; at Allen site, 159
turkey, *18*
Turnbow, C., 136, 137, 148
turtles, 18
twigs, 72
typologies: ceramic, 4; and ethnographic data, 175–77; projectile point, 189

ubiquity, index of, 153, *154*
unidirectional cores, 50
University of Michigan: archaeologists from, 68
unnotched pentagonal cluster projectile points, 148
uplands, 13, 17–18; Bremen site in, 39–58; fauna in, 18–19; Fort Ancient communities in, *173;* habitation sites in, 57. *See also* ridgetop zones
upper-floodplain zone: vegetation, 17
Upper Grenshaw formation: clay from, 140
Upper Mercer chert: at Allen site, 143; at Bremen site, 40, *41,* 44, 49, 53–54; at County Home site, 72; at The Plains, 105; at Walker site, 62–63, *63*
U.S. Environmental Protection Agency, 27

Vanport chert: at Allen site, *143;* at Bremen site, 40, *41,* 44, 49, 53–54, *55;* at County Home site, 72; at The Plains, 105; at Walker site, 62–63, *63*
variability within categories, 177
vector GIS, 26, 37
vegetation, *14*
vertical linkages: and local communities, 184
Vickery, Kent, 41–42
village: in segmentary system, 7–8
violence, intercommunity, 80

Wabash River, 67
Wakeman, Joe, 104, 190
Walker site, *5,* 59–66, 183; artifact analysis from, 62–64; artifact density at, 65; artifacts from, *63;* chronological reconstruction, 64; excavation by OU field school, 6, 59–66; excavation units at, *60;* physical description, 61; reconstruction of, 64–65; settlement patterns, 170
walnut, 17; at Allen site, *154, 155, 157, 158;* during Late Archaic, 23; near Bremen site, 40. *See also* black walnut
Walnut Creek, 117
Water Plant site, 119; sherds from, 138
watersheds, 13, *14,* 26–28, *27;* site distribution by, *31. See also under names of specific rivers*
Watson, Patty Jo, 11
Wayne National Forest, 172
Westmoreland-Guernsey silt loam, 61
white ash, *14, 16,* 17
white oak, 17, 18, *19, 155, 157;* at Allen site, *155, 157, 158,* 159
white-tailed deer. *See* deer, white-tailed
wild grape, 17
willow, *14, 16,* 17; at Allen site, 159
Willow Creek, *169*
Wilson, Nancy, 99, 102; excavations at The Plains, 99, 102
Wisconsin glacier, 2, 13, 164
Wisconsin terrace, 110
Wise site, *5;* excavation by OU field school, 6
witch hazel, 17

wolf: remains found at mounds, 112
woodchuck, *18*
wooden artifacts, 12
Woodland period. *See* Early Woodland period; Middle
Woodland period
Woods site (West Virginia), 161–62
wood taxa: from Allen site, 154–55, *155*
Wymer, D., 16

Xerothermic interval, 23

x-ray diffraction, 140
x-ray fluorescence, 140

Yanomamö population, 119
Yerkes, R., 94
York, H., 29
Yucatec Mayas: cooking methods, 77

Zaleski chert: at Allen site, 143; at County Home site,
72; at Walker site, 62